IMAGES
of America

TUOLUMNE CITY

I0806264

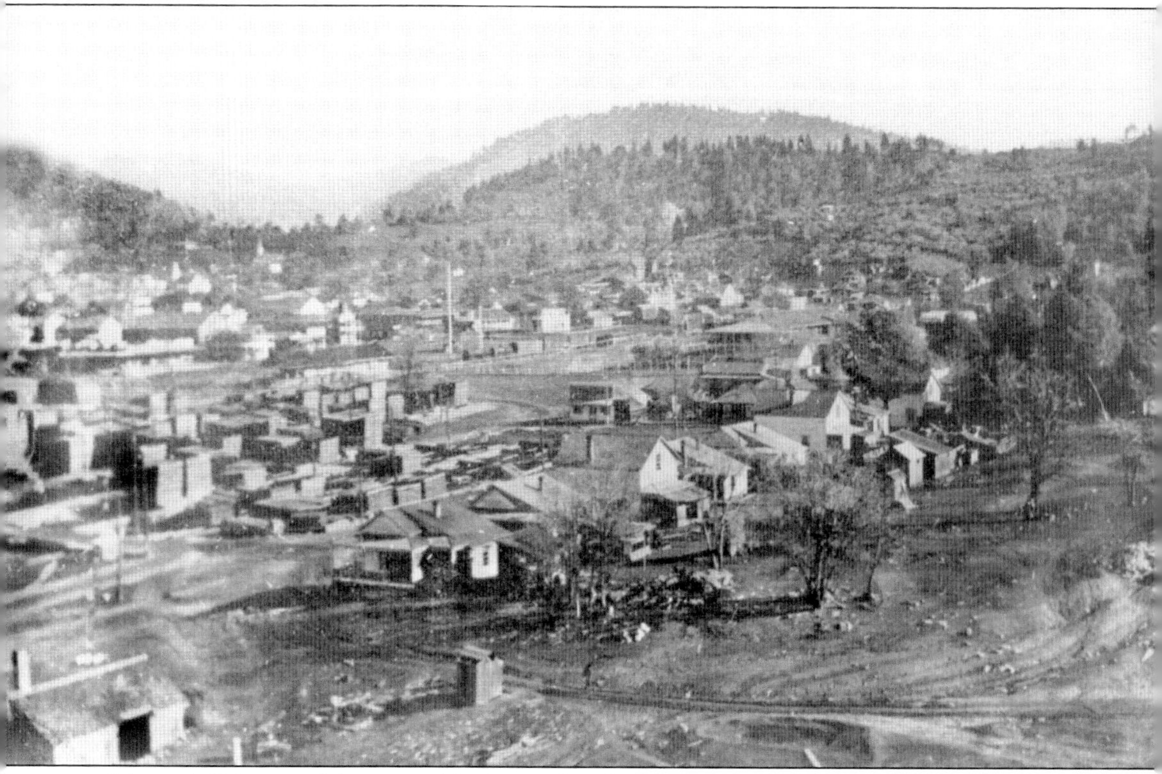

This c. 19303 view of downtown Tuolumne City looks northeast and shows the former site of the Westside Lumber Mill, located adjacent to what is now the town square. The timber industry dominated the economy of Tuolumne throughout much of its history and continues to shape its character to this day.

On the Cover: For the vast majority of able-bodied men, lumberjacking was the most reliable (though not the safest) way to make a living in Tuolumne City from 1900 to 1961. In this c. 1920 photograph, several lumberjacks pose on and around a train carrying a load of timber harvested from the enormous stands of fir and pine that surround Tuolumne.

IMAGES
of America

TUOLUMNE CITY

Jerry Whitehead III

ARCADIA
PUBLISHING

Copyright © 2012 by Jerry Whitehead III
ISBN 978-0-7385-8918-3

Published by Arcadia Publishing
Charleston, South Carolina

Printed in the United States of America

Library of Congress Control Number: 2011934018

For all general information, please contact Arcadia Publishing:
Telephone 843-853-2070
Fax 843-853-0044
E-mail sales@arcadiapublishing.com
For customer service and orders:
Toll-Free 1-888-313-2665

Visit us on the Internet at www.arcadiapublishing.com

To Lynne and Rick Jerome, whose help, guidance, knowledge, and support made this book entirely possible

Contents

Acknowledgments

Not only have the Tuolumne City Memorial Museum and its contingent of volunteer members been a great resource to Tuolumne citizens and visitors alike for years, they have been instrumental in helping me compile this book intended to share and preserve our town's history. While all members throughout the years have been key in amassing the varied, detailed, and whimsical collection of photographs, Rick and Lynne Jerome in particular have opened their doors and donated their time to help. This is as much their project as it is mine, and it would not have been possible without them. All of the images in this book were provided by the Tuolumne City Memorial Museum.

I would also like to thank the fine folks at Arcadia Publishing who helped guide me along during this process, in particular John Poultney, Amy Perryman, and Kristie Kelly. They were not only able to answer any questions I had but were also constantly sending friendly reminder e-mails as I approached my deadlines (which, even though I might not have immediately responded, were definitely appreciated!).

As a fifth-generation Tuolumne City resident, one can imagine how important my family is to me. I would like to acknowledge the role they played in getting this book off the ground. As the former editor of the local weekly newspaper, I had reviewed several of Arcadia's Images of America books and always thought Tuolumne would make a good fit but perpetually put it off because of being too busy. My sister Annie; brother-in-law Kenny; parents, Mary and Jerry Jr.; and wife, Norah, however, were the ones who inspired me over dinner one Sunday night to actually go ahead and send in a proposal. Their reassurance and encouragement were much appreciated and hugely important to this book's existence.

Finally, I would like to thank my wife, Norah, who was patient and endured me putting off some yard work and weekend chores in order to devote the time needed to complete this book. I am glad to be done with it for a variety of reasons, but I know how glad she is for me to be done so I can get back to my required husbandly duties. Thank you for your constant love and patience.

INTRODUCTION

One of the first things people notice about Tuolumne, California, is its unique name and spelling. The name derives from the dialect of the area's first inhabitants, the Me-Wuk Indians, whose various bands and tribes extended from the southern half of Amador County all the way down to parts of Mariposa County in the south and from the summit of the Sierra Nevada mountains in the east to the present-day western border of Tuolumne County in the west. Estimates put the Me-Wuk's numbers at over 100,000 before the arrival of the first white settlers.

The name itself has almost as many meanings as it does spelling variations, with some theories maintaining it means "lion's den," "cave people," or "cave dwellers," or even a group of stone-based wigwams. Regardless, the Tuolumne Band of Me-Wuk Indians consisted of hunter-gatherers who used the excellent locations provided by the interior foothills for settlements. They were also somewhat nomadic in nature, migrating west to what is now San Joaquin County during the colder, snowy winter months and trading with other Me-Wuk bands in the lower-lying valley areas. As with many Native American tribes in the Western United States, the era of imperialistic expansion by the Spaniards from the 1500s and 1700s saw the Tuolumne Band's numbers decrease because of conquest, conversion, conflict, and disease. By the mid-1800s, following the Mexican-American War, Mexico ceded California and other territories to the United States, and less than a year after the war's completion, gold was discovered in the Sierra, and the Gold Rush of 1849 began.

Tuolumne County was not immune to the Gold Rush, of course, and in 1854, the first white settlers moved into what is now Tuolumne City. In 1851, Franklin and Elizabeth Summers, along with their daughter Lee Ann, started the long trek westward from Missouri and arrived three years later to build the first nonnative dwelling in Tuolumne City. Frank Summers built a simple log house with a fireplace and dirt floor, located near where the West Side Lumber Company (WSLC) would eventually place their mill.

By 1856, the area was home to a wild gold rush with strikes all along Turnback Creek, which runs through the town, and soon, many more families arrived with hopes of striking it rich. However, some shady characters also called Tuolumne home, and in 1856, a dispute over land turned deadly for Frank Summers when he was shot and killed just outside the Fifth District Courthouse near present-day La Grange. Elizabeth Summers was left a 24-year-old widow with two children (newborn John joined the family in 1855) in a rough-and-tumble mining camp. To protect young Elizabeth, local miners began camping near the Summers' log home in the area briefly known as Quartzville (because of the high number of quartz lodes found nearby). Summers soon turned her home into a boardinghouse and, with her Missouri home cooking, swiftly had a successful business on her hands (even hosting Samuel Clemens, also known as Mark Twain, in later years). The miners wished to rename the town from Quartzville to Elizabethville in her honor; she politely declined but told them she would be honored if the settlement could be named after her husband, and the town received its first official name of Summersville in 1857.

In 1859, several of the town's women, including Sara Jane Crossett (who would later marry Charles Harvey Carter, a successful merchant who ran a popular general store that provided the miners with supplies), established the first school in Summersville; however, because of a typographical error, the second "s" was left off the legal documents, and it ended up being spelled "Summerville School." To this day, the school district is known as Summerville, and Tuolumne's elementary (Summerville Elementary) and high schools (Summerville High) both bear the name.

The Carters' large white house, located near the current intersection of Carter Street and Buchanan Mine Road (next to their general store), was a popular gathering place for townsfolk. Most of the gold from Turnback Creek and its surrounding tributaries had dried up by the 1860s, and almost all subsequent mining was for quartz. Since the quartz miners could often be found near Carter's store, all incoming mail was delivered there. When the town applied for an official post office, the US Postal Service refused to establish one under the current town name of Summersville due to the Somersville Post Office in Contra Costa County. Since the mail was already received at Carter's store and the area was the de facto town center, the post office was set up under the town name of Carters, and Tuolumne's name changed yet again. The influence of the Carters is still seen to this day—Carter Street is one of the main arteries through town, and the cemetery still is called Carters Cemetery.

The area's deep quartz deposits sustained the mining industry through the end of the 19th century. Over the years, the little town grew into a well-established community with stores, bars, hotels, drugstores, churches, barbershops, and much more. But the railroad industry was booming and stretching ever westward, and the Carters would not be immune.

In 1897, the Sierra Railway Company of California was established. Businessman Thomas S. Bullock (from New York City), banker William Crocker (from Sierra Pacific Railroad), and Polish prince Andre Poniatowski (representing French investors) orchestrated the laying of the initial 41 miles of track from Oakdale to Jamestown, a scant 12 miles from Carters. The line was completed by November 10 that same year.

In March 1899, Bullock, Crocker, and Poniatowski purchased approximately 600 acres near the outskirts of Carters from Frank and Delia Baker, Canadian immigrants who had set up a ranch on Turnback Creek in 1882. It was the group's intent to build a lumber mill on the site, as well as incorporate a logging railroad into the Jamestown line to create a new town where this industry and those who worked in it could thrive. The company was to be called the West Side Flume and Lumber Company.

The scope of the project was massive, but the group and its first employees did not lack determination. The first step for the new town centered entirely on how quickly it could add 12 miles of track to connect the current edge of Carters to nearby Jamestown to ship in supplies for construction. The tracks were followed by a brand-new lumber mill, a rail station, grand corporate offices, and a three-story sanitarium operated by Dr. Eugene H. Reid that housed the company doctor who delivered most of the area's babies for years, as well as an opulent hotel known as the Turnback Inn. The owners of West Side hoped to eventually create a line that led directly into the nearby Yosemite Valley and market themselves as a direct stopover for the many tourists who funneled into Yosemite National Park each year.

In stark contrast to the business of most other mill towns, West Side owners gave many of their workers a stake in the new town site by selling them lots on which to construct homes and businesses instead of creating company-owned houses and stores. In less than a decade, this "New Town," as it was known, was booming. As more and more people established themselves in New Town (present-day Tuolumne), Carters began to wane. Catastrophic fires all but destroyed Carters in 1905 and again in 1906. Today, the old Carters town square remains at the very north end of Carter Street; it is surrounded by several homes and is marked by a large, open green area (known as "the Common") and a historical marker, as well as an old fire hose cart and house.

The new town of Tuolumne, as it officially became known in 1906, continued to grow. A new elementary school (which kept the Summerville moniker) was built on land donated by the Bakers, and in 1912, the wives of the mill owners talked their husbands into building a high school in Tuolumne's city limits so children could avoid the train ride into neighboring Sonora (approximately 10 miles west of Tuolumne). The old high school is at the corner of Pine Street and Gardner Avenue and is currently home to the Mother Lode Christian School.

For the next 60 years, life in Tuolumne was directly tied to and dominated by the logging industry and West Side. The mill, the railroad system, and the timber harvest were the backbones and heartbeats of the town; when the mill whistle blew at 7:00 a.m., schoolchildren knew it was time to get up and prepare for the day ahead. Conversely, when the closing whistle blew at 4:30 p.m., signaling the end of the workers' shifts, it was time to head home.

The life of a logger was not easy. Trains typically headed into the surrounding forests at 4:00 a.m. to begin harvesting sugar pine, incense cedar, ponderosa pine, and white fir. During the cold, snowy winters typical of the western slope of the Sierra Nevada, the railroad tracks were often covered in snow. By spring, once the tracks were cleared, lumber camps began to open alongside the tracks. Mill workers and their families often packed their belongings and hitched a ride on the trains to spend summer in the woods, living in small sheds or cabins and moving along by train, camp to camp, as the trees were harvested. The trees were felled, trimmed into logs, packed on the trains, and shipped back to the West Side mill, where they were dumped into the millpond and stored to provide year-round work at the mill. Much of the wood harvested from the timber swaths surrounding Tuolumne and manufactured into lumber at the West Side mill was key in building many of California's early towns.

As with any town composed almost entirely of wooden buildings, fire was a consistent hazard (as Carters saw in the early 1900s). In 1918, a colossal fire raged through downtown Tuolumne, and many of the town's businesses and dozens of homes were destroyed in as little as two hours. The town eventually rebuilt, replacing many buildings with more modern structures that were more flame-retardant. As a symbol of the citizens' resolve and determination to persevere, hundreds of sycamore trees were planted on the streets that lined the path of the 1918 fire. These sycamores are now large and well established, shading many of Tuolumne's streets and homes. They serve as a reminder of the necessary resolve of Tuolumne citizens, which they were forced to tap again soon after the 1918 fire.

During the Great Depression, the West Side Lumber Mill was forced to close down for five years, from 1930 to 1935. Since the timber industry was the lion's share of Tuolumne's economy, few thought the town could survive. It more than likely would not have if not for two public works projects: the addition of a gymnasium and classroom building at the high school and a veteran's hall, now known as the Tuolumne Memorial Hall, which still serves as the town center and meeting hall.

When the mill reopened in 1935, it was a lifesaver for the community, and the town was overjoyed. To celebrate, Tuolumne hosted a Lumber Jubilee that included a parade through the town and contests in which area lumberjacks could show off their skills with axes and saws. The tradition continues to this day and is commemorated each summer.

On October 28, 1960, the last logging train made its way into the Tuolumne Yard with engineer Shorty Maddox at the helm. This commemorated the last narrow-gauge logging operation in the Western United States, although there were brief periods in the 1970s when West Side trains ran for tourist operations begun by businessmen (including Glen Bell, founder of Taco Bell) who sought to turn West Side's considerable tract of land into a new venture. By the 1980s, a large section of the West Side track was removed for salvage, which sealed the fate of these unique narrow-gauge lines.

Although Tuolumne has yet to fully recover from the disappearance of the West Side Lumber Company and the timber industry, the town is on a slow but measurable rebound, thanks in no small part to the Tuolumne Band of Me-Wuk Indians, which, after the passing of California Proposition 1A in 2000, was able to begin construction on Black Oak Casino. The casino opened on May 15, 2001, on a limited level and has since seen several major expansions and provided hundreds of jobs within the community (the casino is one of Tuolumne County's largest employers). The newly constructed Cherry Valley Boulevard even provided the town of Tuolumne with its first stoplight. With several large updates in the works (including a resort hotel and plans for an 18-hole golf course and residential and commercial retail units), Black Oak Casino and the Tuolumne Band of Me-Wuk Indians look to continue to work with the citizens of Tuolumne to keep the community thriving while still maintaining its history and roots as a charming and welcoming Gold Rush–era foothill settlement.

One

Early Days

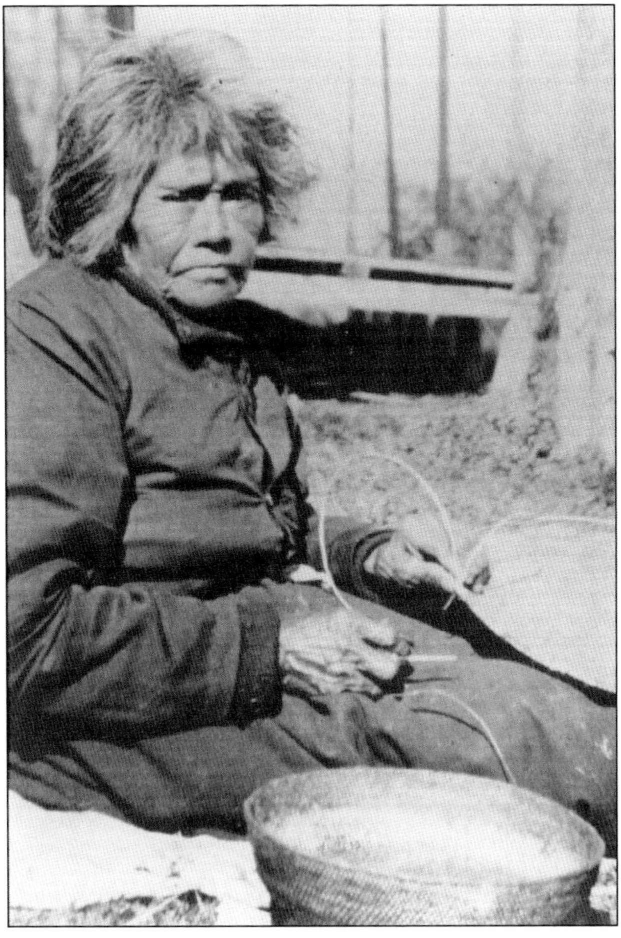

Tuolumne's first inhabitants were Native Americans. The Tuolumne Band of Me-Wuk Indians was a peaceful race of hunter-gatherers who flourished along the western slope of the Sierra Nevada. In this 1925 photograph, a Me-Wuk woman named Mathilda weaves baskets, for which the tribe was well known. A fine collection of Me-Wuk baskets is currently housed at the University of California, Davis.

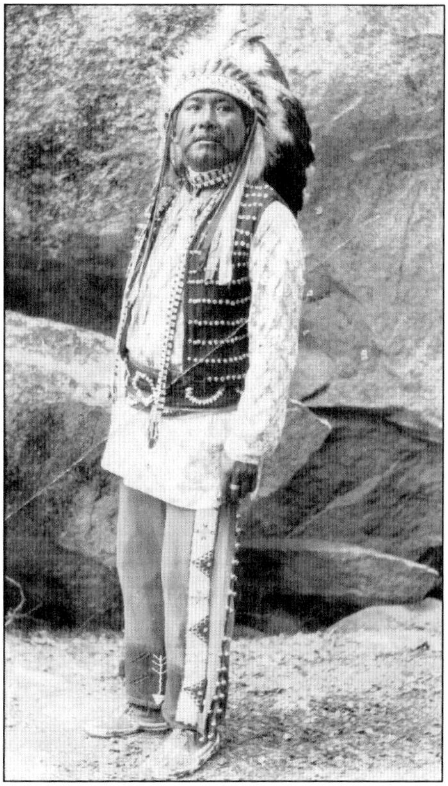

As gold fever (or, more appropriately for Tuolumne, "quartz fever") took hold among the California foothill settlements in the 1840s and 1850s, it marked the end of a once-flourishing tribe of native Me-Wuk peoples. As the miners wreaked havoc upon the environment by disrupting streambeds and blasting hillsides, large amounts of sediment entered Turnback Creek, Tuolumne River, and other streams, destroying the ecosystem of fish and other aquatic life that the Me-Wuk had fed upon for years. Game animals, which were also an integral part of the Me-Wuk diet, were shot to feed miners, and the influx of cattle grazed heavily upon oak acorns, a source of nutrition for the Indians.

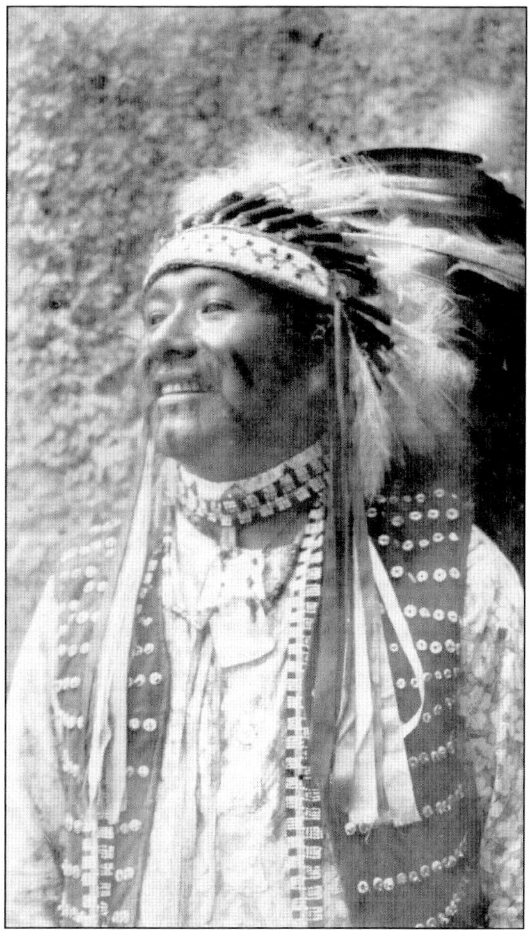

Diminished food supplies, newly imported diseases, and conflicts with white settlers diminished the Me-Wuk population by as much as 90 percent by the early 1900s. In these 1930s images, a Me-Wuk man displays some typical garb, including the flicker feather headband used in traditional dances.

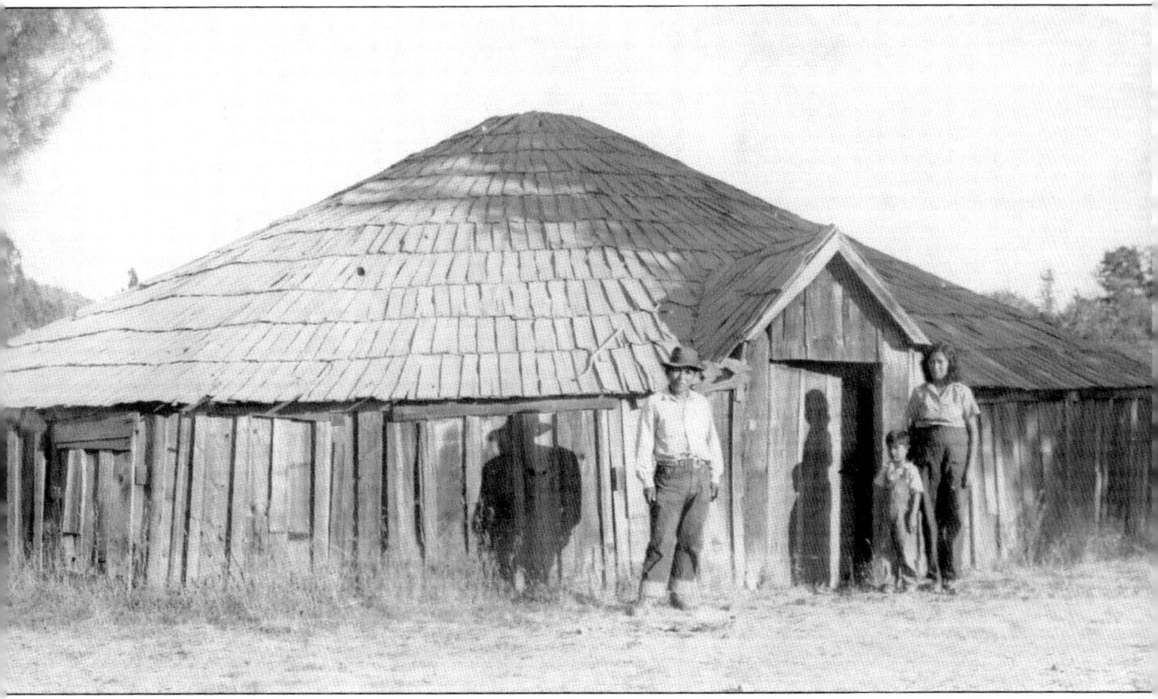

An important aspect of the Me-Wuk culture was the roundhouse, or *hangi* (in Me-Wuk dialect). The roundhouse was ceremonial in nature and was not only the heart of the village but also a place of worship. Ceremonial roundhouses typically ranged from 30 to 40 feet in diameter and were covered by an earthen mud mixture, tree bark, or shingles. Dances were routinely held in the roundhouse to pay homage and give thanks to Mother Earth for the bounty she provided the Me-Wuk tribe. In this photograph, a Me-Wuk family gathers outside a hangi on the Tuolumne Rancheria federal Indian reserve, which was created in 1910 to house the remaining landless Indian families. Pictured from left to right are Will Tado, son Ernest, and wife Minnie.

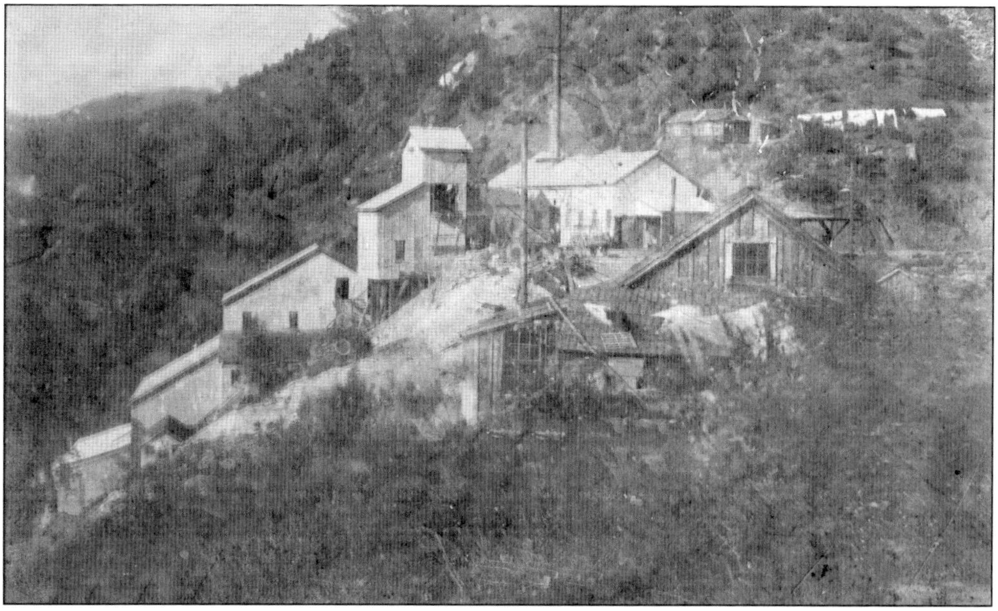

The Gold Rush fueled the growth of many California towns, including Tuolumne. This 1899 photograph shows the Providence Mine, located on the east side of the North Fork of the Tuolumne River (and still accessible by foot or horseback at the end of Providence Mine dirt road off Apple Colony Road). It was in operation until 1928 and produced a total yield of approximately $700,000 worth of gold. Because of its distance from town, the Providence Mine relied on pack trains to bring in supplies from Charles H. Carter's general store.

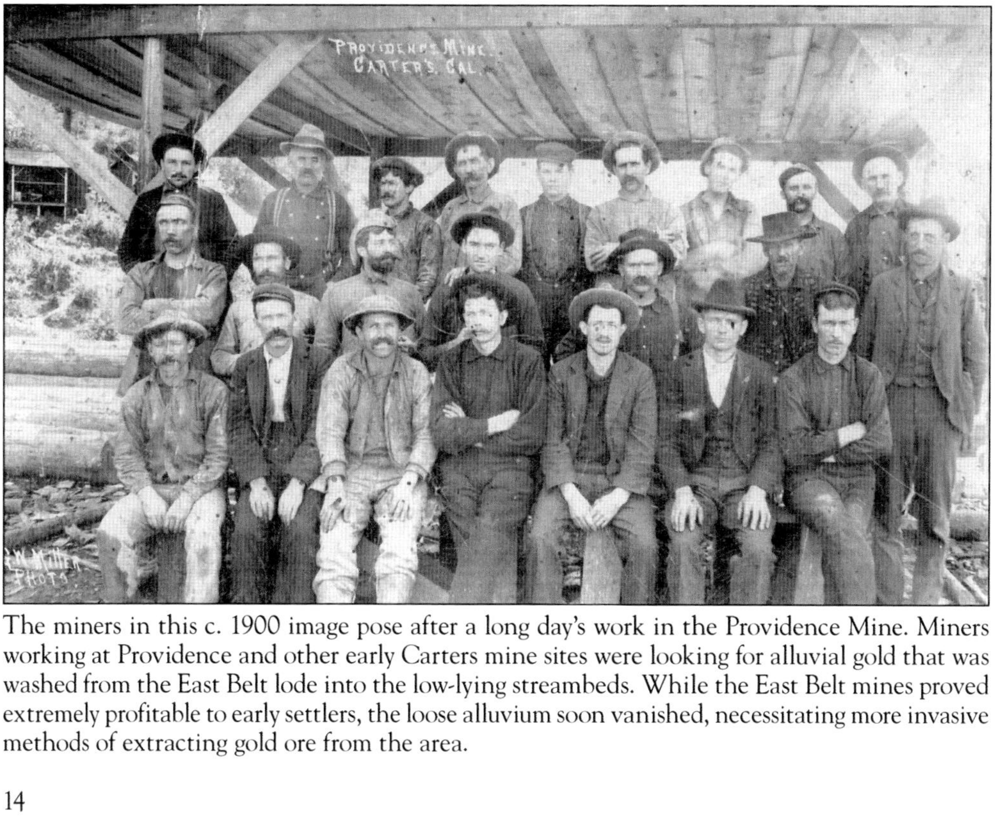

The miners in this c. 1900 image pose after a long day's work in the Providence Mine. Miners working at Providence and other early Carters mine sites were looking for alluvial gold that was washed from the East Belt lode into the low-lying streambeds. While the East Belt mines proved extremely profitable to early settlers, the loose alluvium soon vanished, necessitating more invasive methods of extracting gold ore from the area.

The early community of Summersville/Carters thrived on the gold and quartz mining trade. The settlement of the first few pioneer families quickly exploded into a busy and bustling town, with businesses springing up everywhere in order to offer services to miners seeking riches in the adjacent hills and streams. This 1890s photograph shows one of the main thoroughfares of Carters, with businesses offering everything from hot baths to groceries.

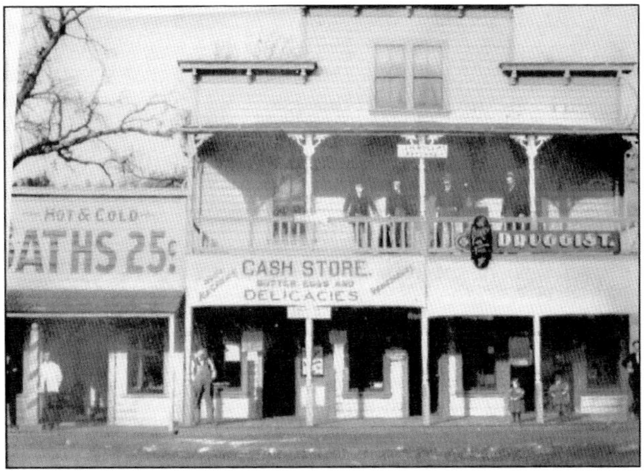

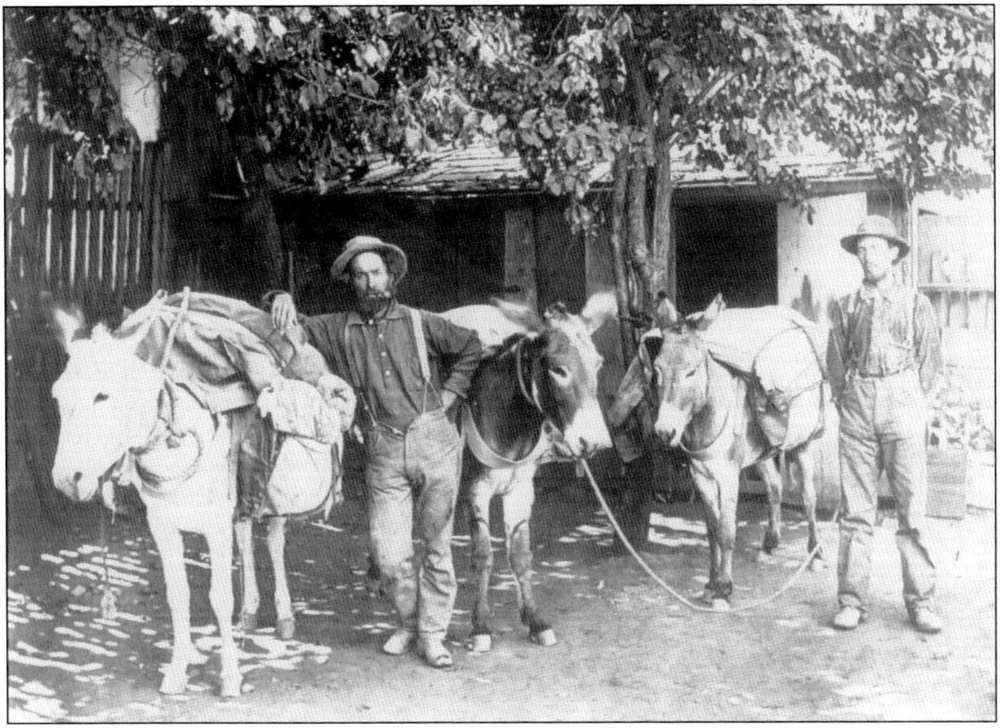

Miners in Summersville stock up on supplies to load on pack animals before trekking out to the surrounding gold mines. These small donkeys, also known as burros, were abandoned during the Gold Rush era (1856–1870s), scavenging for food where they could. Although beloved by children and used for transportation by many an inebriated citizen, their droppings (and the resulting flies) and pillaging of gardens proved too much for the town's women, who banded together to drive the burros from the city limits between 1922 and 1935.

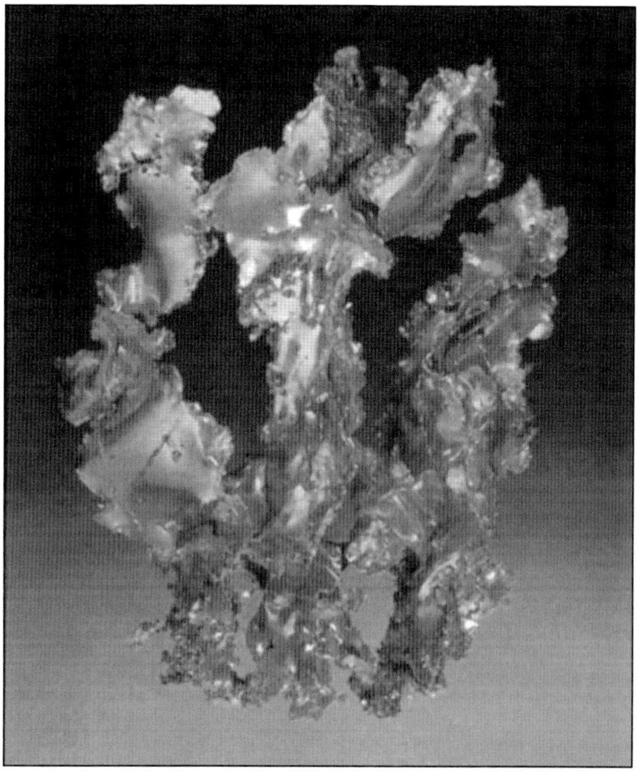

This particularly large and clean gold specimen was taken from the Eureka Mine and is currently on display in the gem and mineral collection at the Smithsonian in Washington, DC. The Eureka Mine was one of the most profitable mines in the Tuolumne area. Founded in 1856 by William and James Blakely, brothers and miners from Cornwall, England, the mine was active until the 1930s and produced several million dollars in ore. It was the Blakely brothers who, after becoming rich and influential thanks to the Eureka Mine, wanted to change the name of the early settlement known as Quartzville to Elizabethville. It was instead named Summersville in honor of Elizabeth Summers's late husband, Frank.

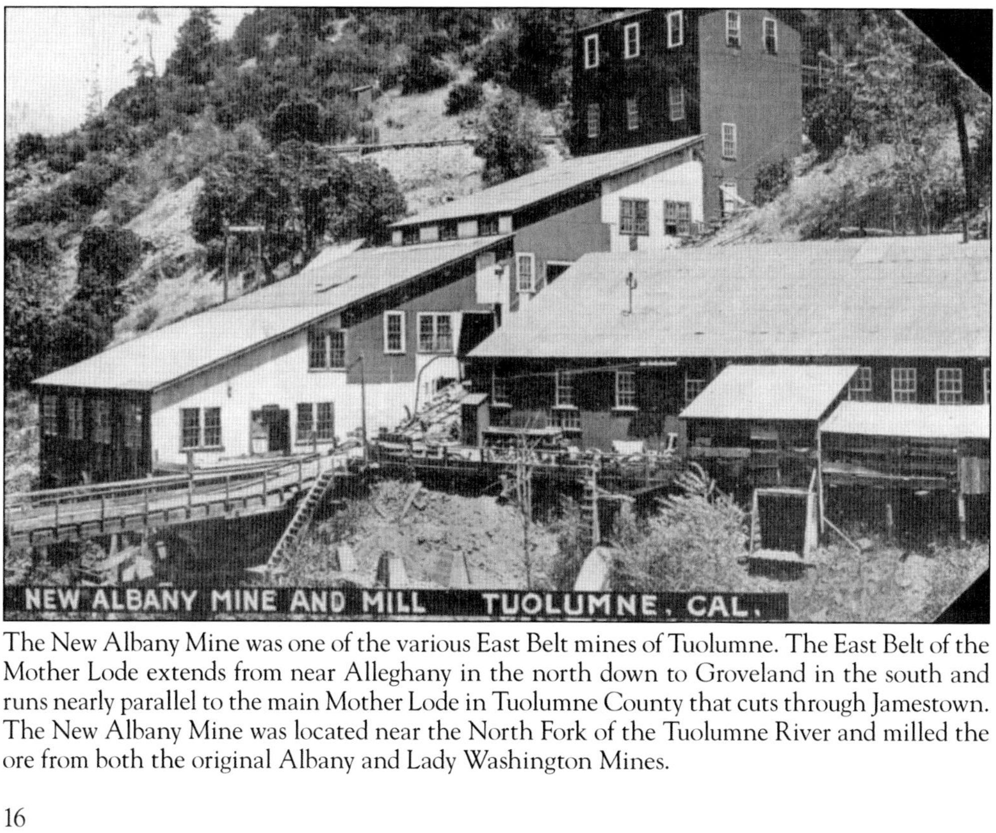

The New Albany Mine was one of the various East Belt mines of Tuolumne. The East Belt of the Mother Lode extends from near Alleghany in the north down to Groveland in the south and runs nearly parallel to the main Mother Lode in Tuolumne County that cuts through Jamestown. The New Albany Mine was located near the North Fork of the Tuolumne River and milled the ore from both the original Albany and Lady Washington Mines.

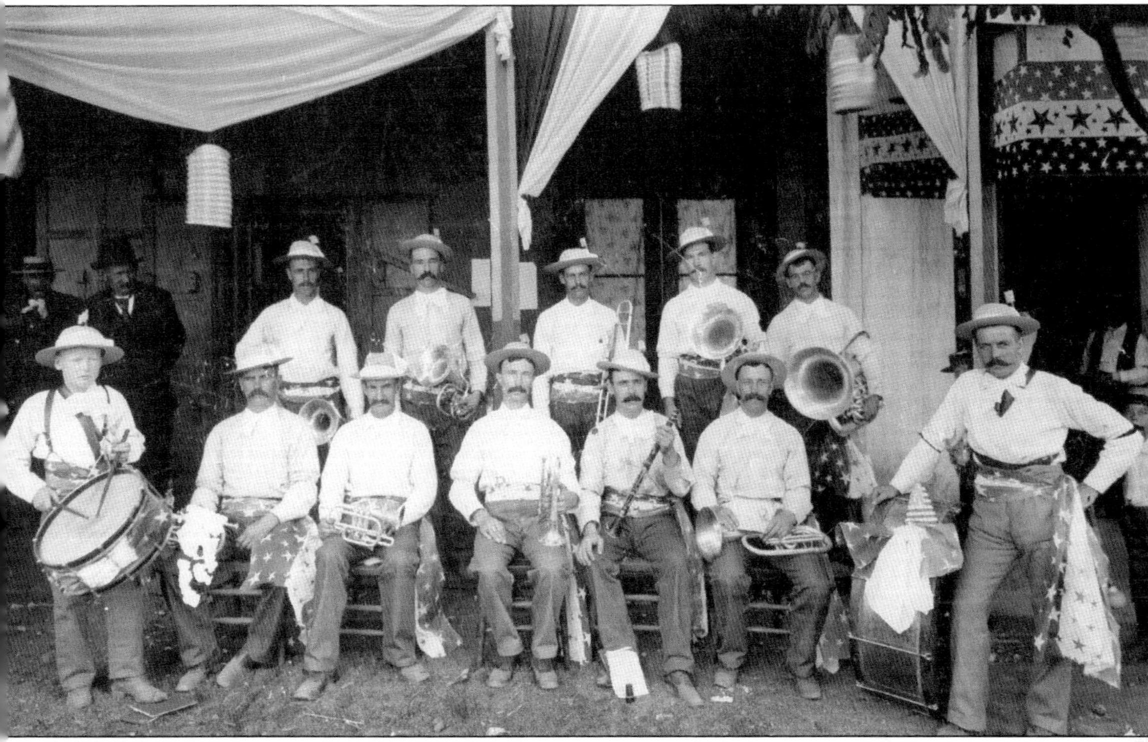

During the late 1800s, when an upstart mining community such as Summersville/Carters lacked refinement and entertainment, the Marshall family band could often be seen playing at celebrations held in and around Carters. As recounted by George A. Marshall in a 1964 edition of *Journal of the West*, "Our house became the center of the community's social activity, for we possessed the most accomplished musicians of the area. Most of the family could perform on some sort of musical instrument, acceptably and vociferously in the younger brackets. My father played the drums in our local band, my older brother [William] the E-flat tuba, another brother played the solo alto, and I took the lead part with a solo B-flat cornet." The Marshalls and their numerous relatives were instrumental in setting up and constructing the Arastraville Schoolhouse between the settlements of Cherokee and Arastraville, only a few miles north of Summersville.

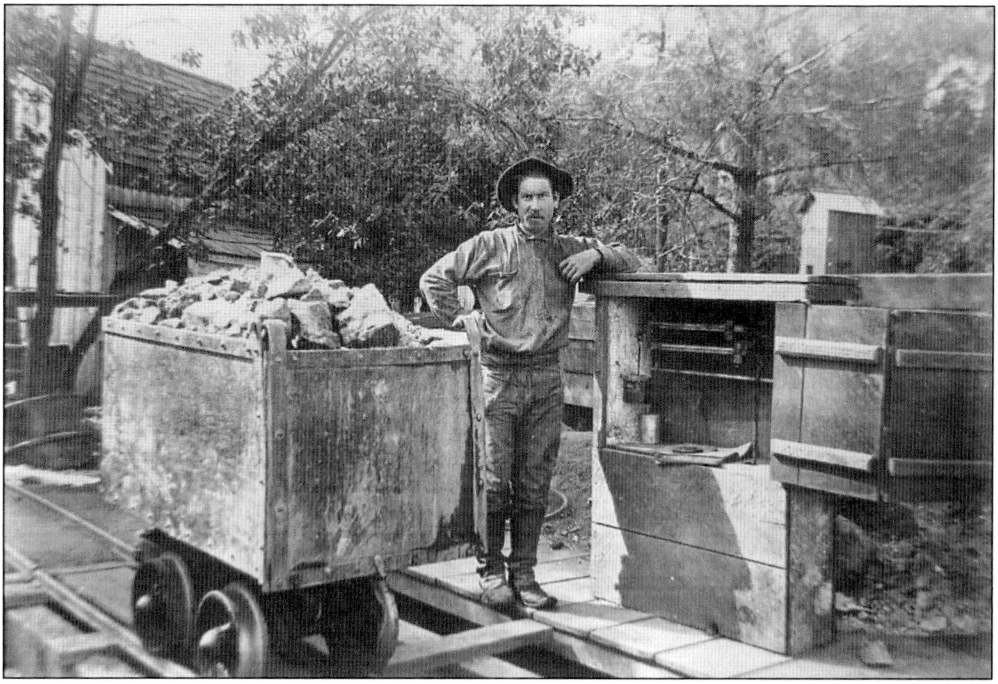

In this c. 1898 image, a miner poses next to a cart filled with rock taken from the Black Oak Mine, located about one mile north of current-day Soulsbyville. The Black Oak Claim was 1,500 feet in length and 600 feet wide and was worked through a 1,700-foot-deep shaft on a 70-degree incline. About 500 pounds of dynamite were used each month to break up the rock and transport the resulting chunks. At its peak, the Black Oak Mine employed 86 people and featured a water-powered stamp mill with twenty 700-pound stamps.

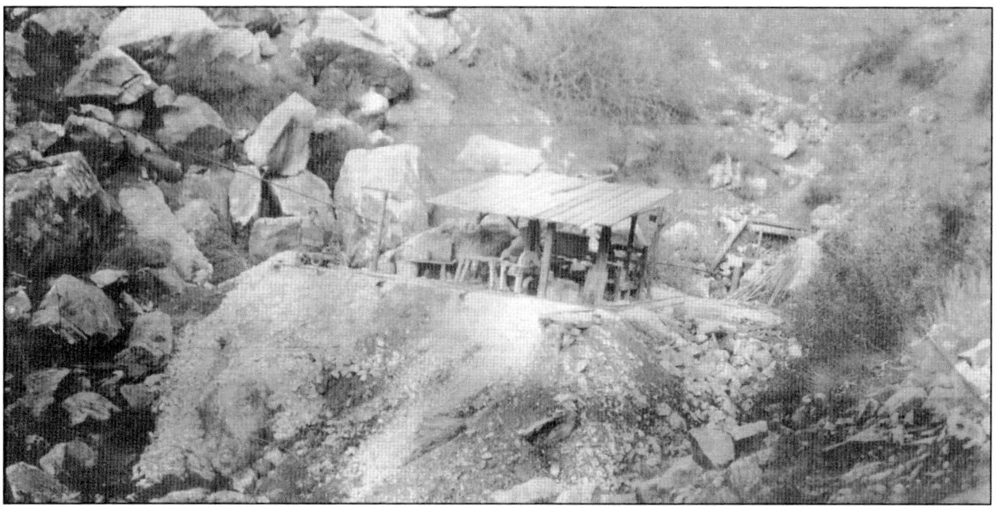

Seen here is one of the earliest mining camps that was located in Long Gulch, which flows from Turnback Creek into the Tuolumne River, located just east of Apple Colony Road. Charles H. Carter opened his first trading store from a tent at this location—a precursor to his general store that would give the town its second name. Long Gulch was worked by hydraulic mining; water for this process was delivered by the Eureka ditch that funneled water from the Stanislaus River. This ditch is still in use today and provides Tuolumne with much of its drinking water.

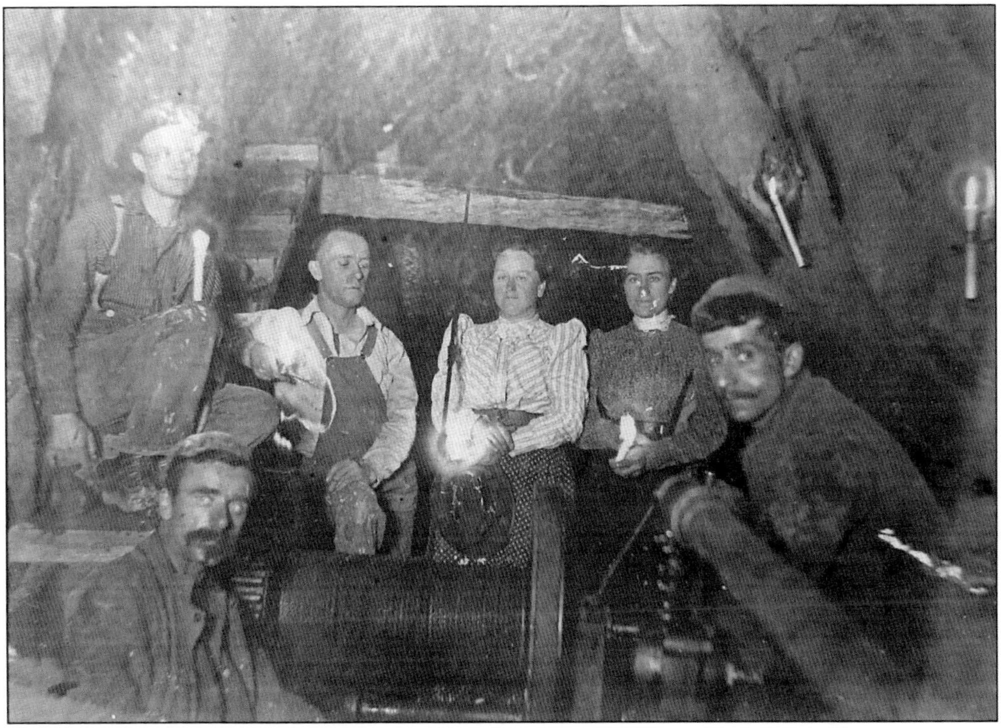

Women were relatively rare in the mines and surrounding camps during the late 19th century. "Respectable" women were often left to cook the meals for the miners, do their laundry, and nurse them back to health after the inevitable mining accident or gunshot wound—both of which created many widows, such as Elizabeth Summers. Like Summers, several widowed women opened boardinghouses or small hotels to earn an income. This photograph was taken in the Black Oak Mine; the seated gentleman in overalls is Guy Scott, and his daughter Caroline is seated on the far right. Caroline would later marry Guy Johnson, whose adoptive father was one of the owners of the West Side Lumber Company.

Miners in the Black Oak Mine haul off a load for processing. The only light in these early mines was supplied by candlelight, and all workers carried at least a few spares (along with copious amounts of matches). The majority of the mining was done via dynamite after miners chiseled eight-inch holes by hand with hand drills and sledgehammers.

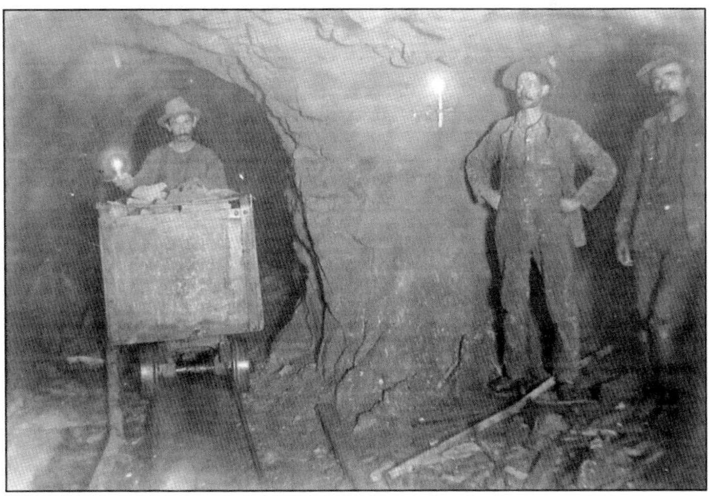

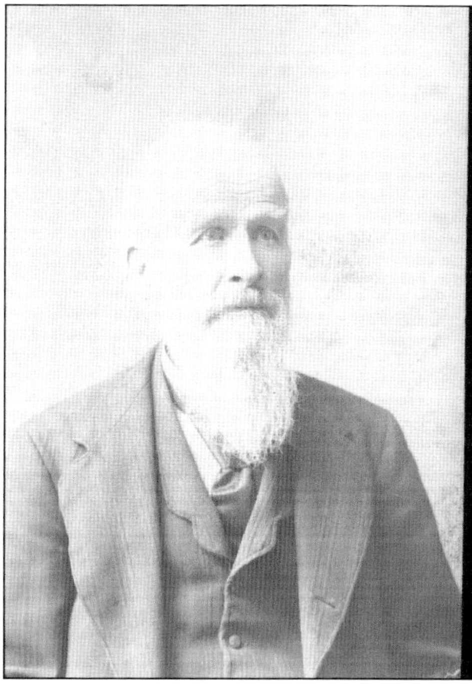

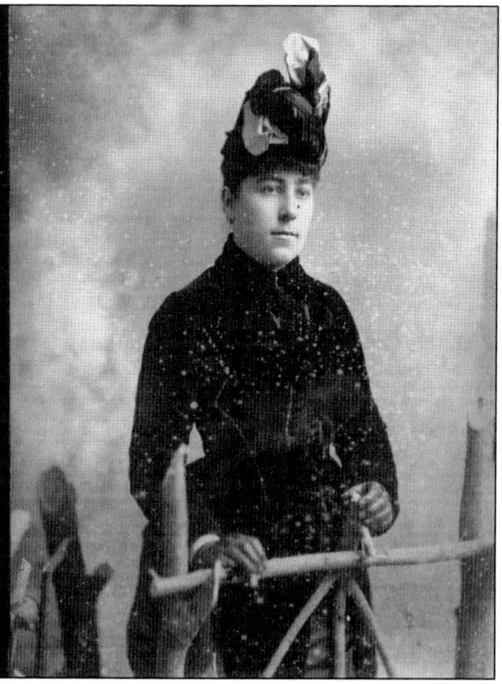

Along with Franklin and Elizabeth Summers, the Carters (Charles H. and his wife, Sara Jane [nee Crossett]) were undoubtedly one of the most prominent early families to settle in Summersville. C.H. Carter first operated a trading supply tent near the mines next to Long Gulch. By the time the Eureka Mine was founded by the Blakely brothers in 1858, Carter (and the rest of Long Gulch) packed up and moved closer to the Eureka claim, where he set up his popular general store that would serve as the town center. Summersville was renamed Carters in honor of the couple.

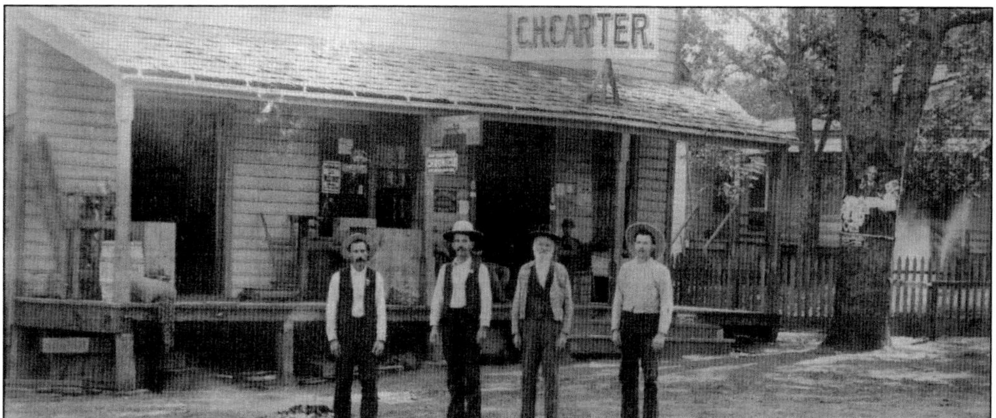

Charles H. Carter (second from the right) stands in front of his general store. The store's location in the middle of the new town, combined with the trees that provided cooling shade to the surrounding area, made Carter's general store one of the most popular gathering places in Summersville—so much so that mail was delivered there for all the town's citizens. As the town continued to grow and an official post office was needed, the US Postal Service denied the claim due to the name of Summersville being too similar to Somersville, located in nearby Contra Costa County. Since Carter's store was already the town center, renaming Summersville to Carters was a no-brainer; the town was known as Carters by 1890.

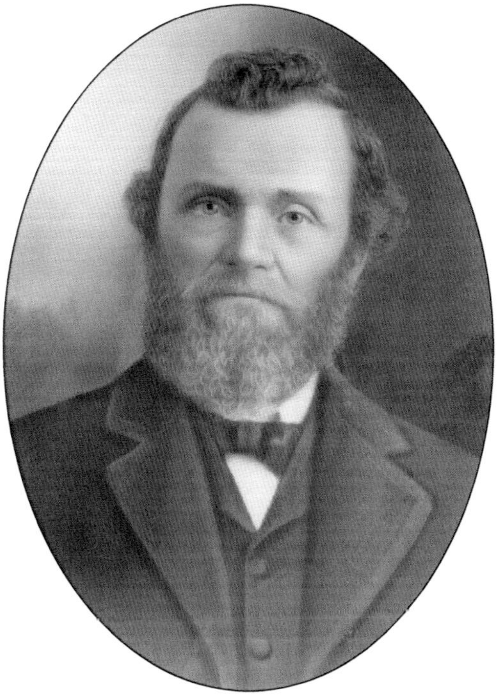

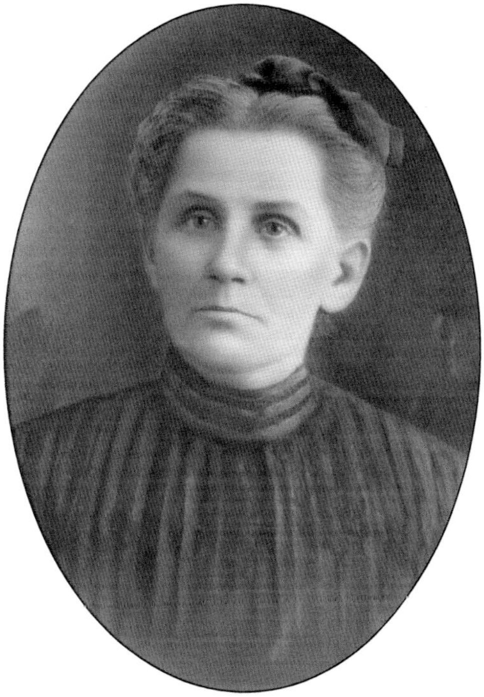

Frank and Delia Baker emigrated from Quebec, Canada, in the early 1870s and set up an enormous ranch that would encompass the entirety of present-day Tuolumne (a large portion of it still remains past the southern end of the city limits off Apple Colony Road, and Baker Avenue still bears the family name). Delia, who tragically lost her first husband, John, and all five of their children to a diphtheria epidemic in Canada, remarried Frank, and together they had seven children: Bert, Maudy, George, Oscar, Mark, Ada, and Theresa. Four of the children remained in Tuolumne and contributed to the community. When Frank and Delia sold 600 acres at the end of Carters to the West Side Lumber Company in 1899, they specifically stipulated in negotiations that a previous plot donated to house a school must remain intact and be used for scholastic purposes.

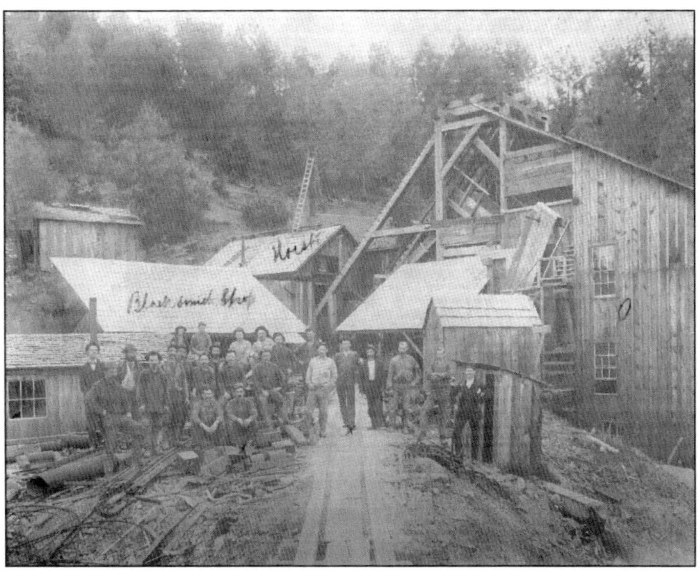

As might be gleaned from the size of the claim and the number of workers and buildings inhabiting it, the Eureka Mine (pictured here in the 1860s) was one of the most profitable and busiest claims in the entire East Belt of the Mother Lode. Discovered by William and James Blakely in 1858, it was only about a half mile east of the present-day town center (at the intersection of Tuolumne Road and Carter Street).

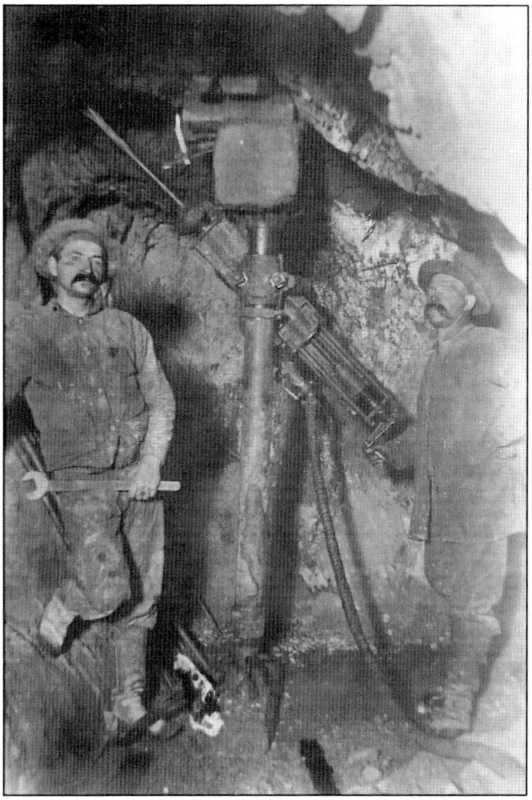

Workers in many of the mines surrounding Summersville (as it was known when this photograph was taken in the 1880s) began operating compressed-air drills, as seen here in the Eureka mine. These somewhat modern innovations, similar to today's jackhammers, sped up the process of stripping away the rock.

The Arastraville School was constructed in the early 1860s approximately halfway between the small settlements of Cherokee (located near the present-day intersection of Tuolumne and Cherokee Roads, appropriately enough) and Arastraville (about 1.5 miles north of the present-day town center) to serve the children of the miners in the Cherokee area and the Me-Wuk children. (The name Arastraville derives from the Mexican *arastra*, an antiquated device used to crush quartz and obtain gold.) Here, teacher Maria Kenny poses with her class in the late 1890s. There is now a preschool on the old Arastraville School site.

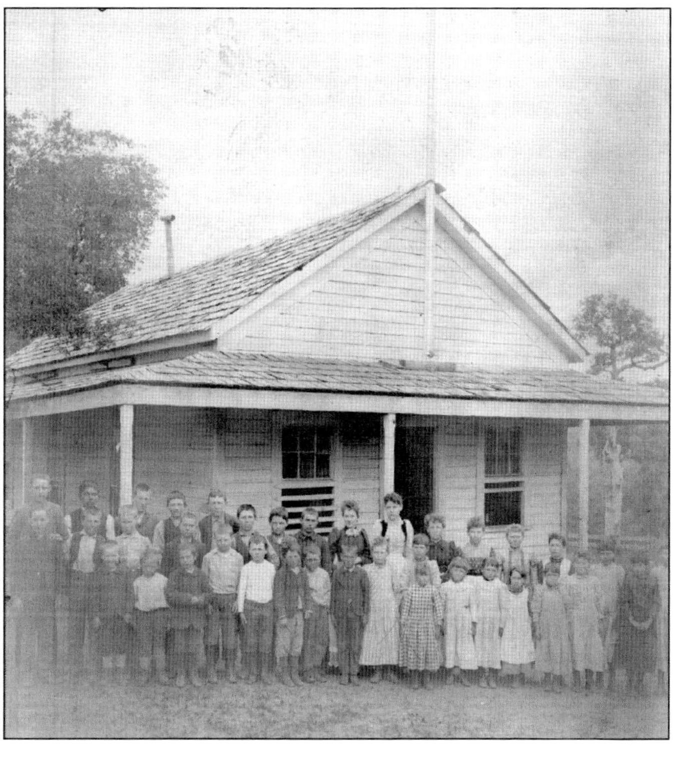

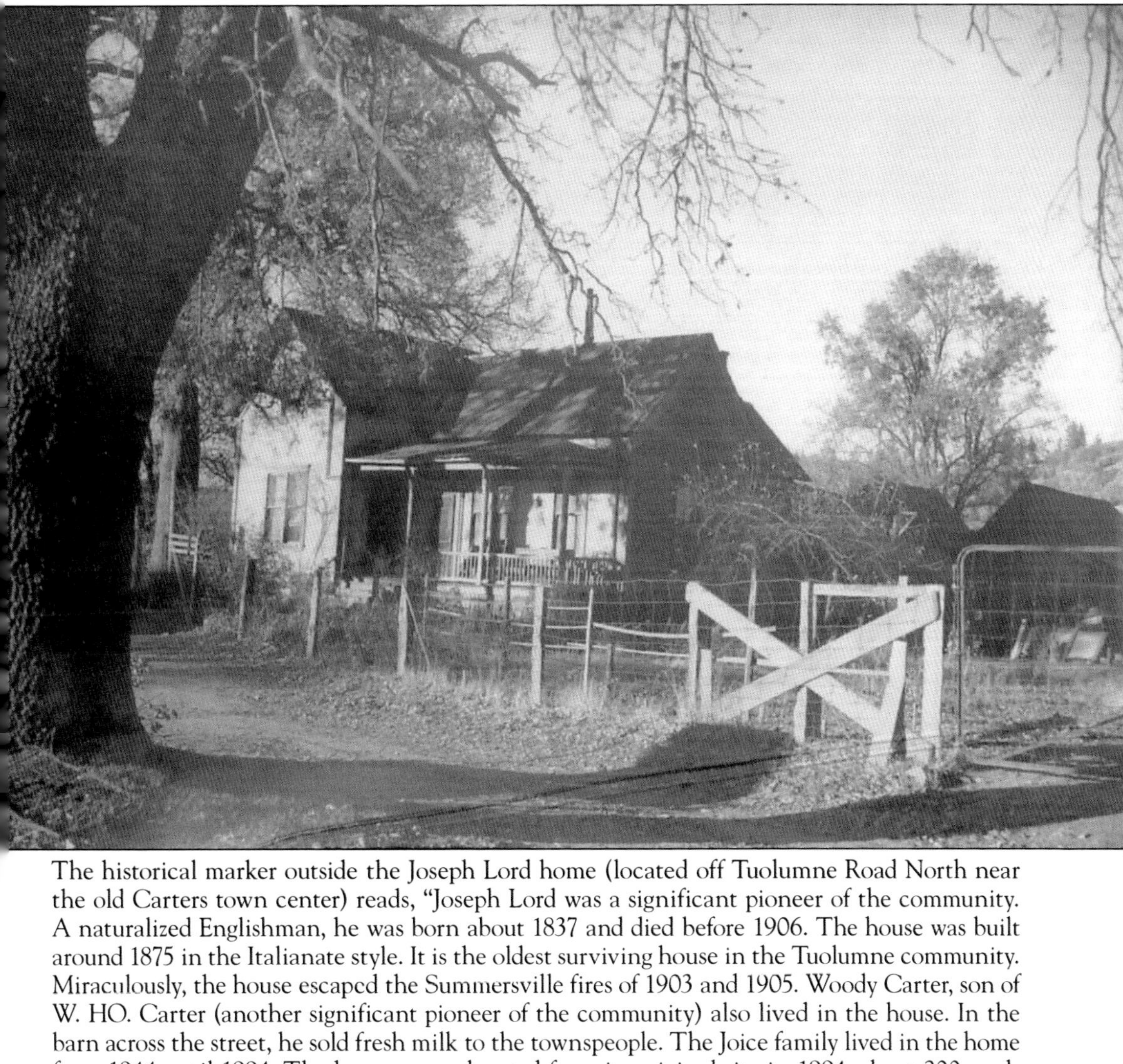

The historical marker outside the Joseph Lord home (located off Tuolumne Road North near the old Carters town center) reads, "Joseph Lord was a significant pioneer of the community. A naturalized Englishman, he was born about 1837 and died before 1906. The house was built around 1875 in the Italianate style. It is the oldest surviving house in the Tuolumne community. Miraculously, the house escaped the Summersville fires of 1903 and 1905. Woody Carter, son of W. HO. Carter (another significant pioneer of the community) also lived in the house. In the barn across the street, he sold fresh milk to the townspeople. The Joice family lived in the home from 1944 until 1994. The house was relocated from its original site in 1994, about 200 yards east of its present location. The Lord House and barn (located 150 yards east) were restored by John and Juliana Feriani."

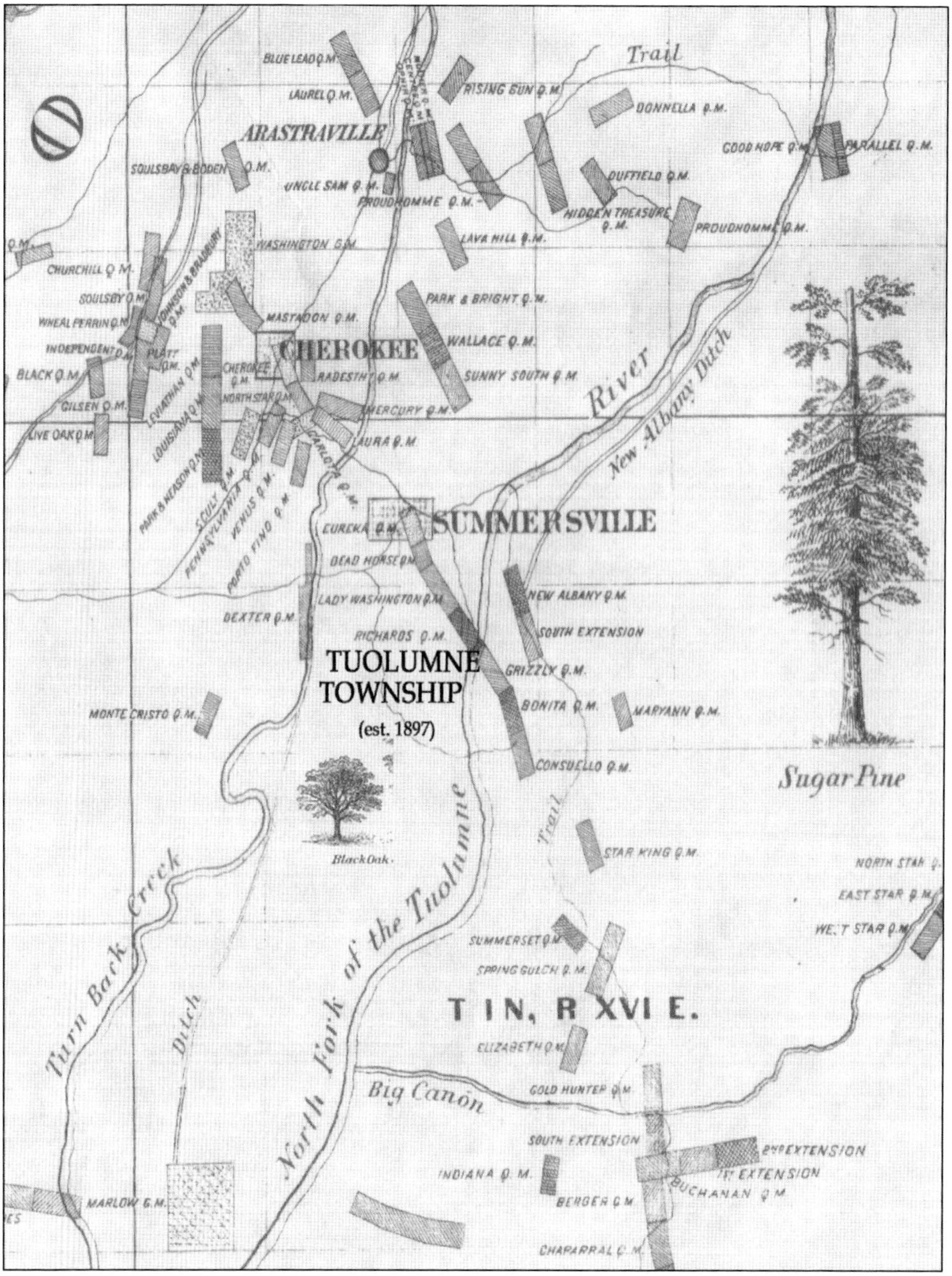

This map, taken from government surveys and mining records by mining engineer J.P. Dart in 1879, shows the principal quartz and gravel mines of what was to be called the East Belt region. The East Belt ran parallel and just east of the main Mother Lode in Tuolumne County. During the first few years of the Gold Rush, camps were established in this area as alluvial gold was discovered in various locations throughout the belt. Some of the shallower placer camps established during the Gold Rush heyday included Arastraville and Cherokee Diggins to the northwest of Summersville/Carters, as well as Roach's Camp, Long Gulch, Rough and Ready, and Marlow Diggins to the south and southwest. The deeper quartz mines (highlighted on the map) operated until approximately 1915.

Like so many of Tuolumne's first major families, the Roziers have a street in town that bears their surname (or in this case, an avenue, which runs east-west between Gardner and Chestnut Avenues). William Milton Rozier, son of Wiley and Mary, was born in North Carolina and fought in the Mexican-American War before moving to Columbia in Tuolumne County during the early 1850s after hearing about the gold boom there.

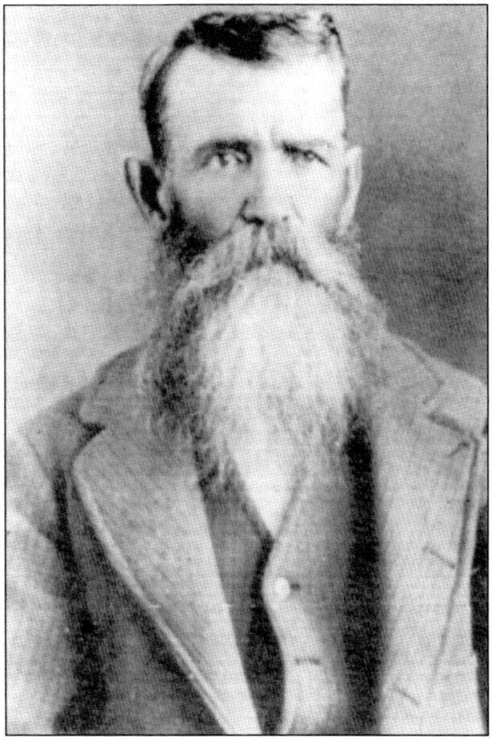

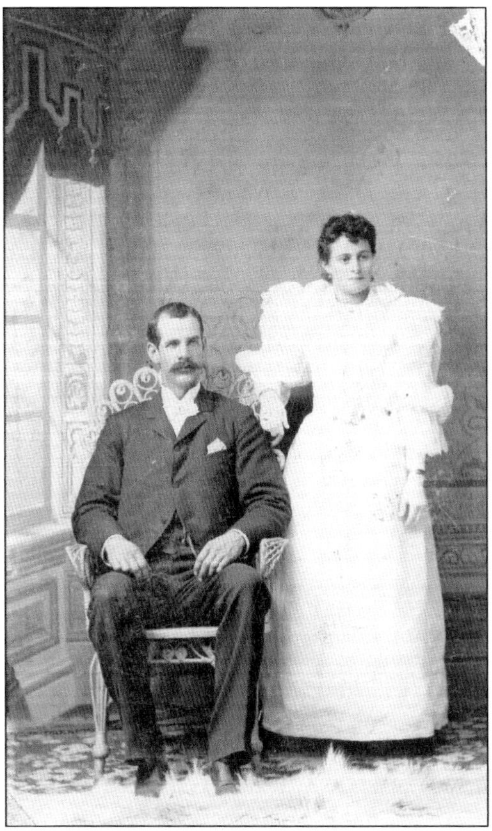

Alfred William Rozier (middle child of William Milton and Margaret Doyle) and Mary Elizabeth Hartman pose for a wedding-day portrait on June 27, 1899. Rozier was a regular partner of his father's on several of his placer mine claims but was also a noted theatrical performer. While he made his living as a stamp mill man, his first notable job, at age 19, was harvesting and hauling grain on the famous naturalist John Muir's ranch in Martinez. Their daughter Marie Rozier, born July 8, 1904, taught at Summerville Elementary until 1963 and was a cofounder of the Tuolumne City Memorial Museum. She passed away in 1997

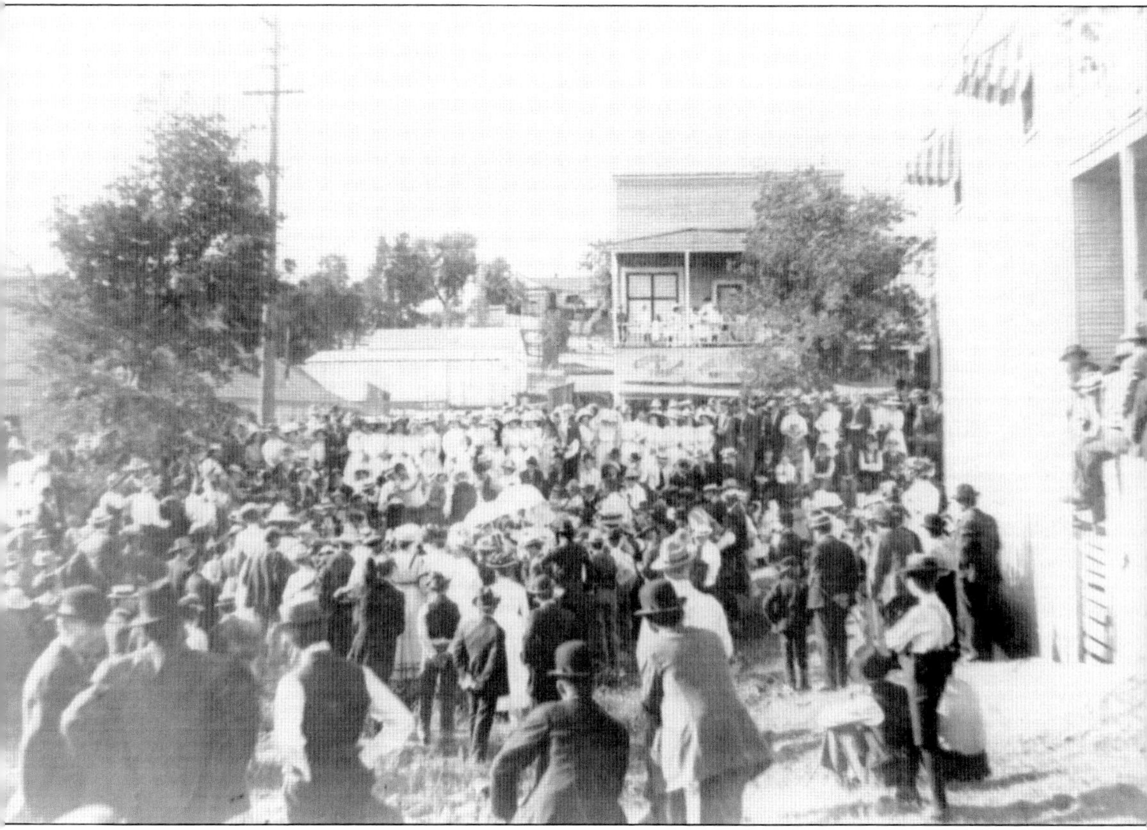

This July 4, 1906, celebration in Carters shows a crowd gathering around Elmer McDow as he displays his prowess in a drilling contest. Feats of mining skills were common during festivals and celebrations in early Tuolumne, a tradition that eventually resurfaced in the annual Lumber Jubilee, which is still held annually each summer. According to George A. Marshall's recollection in the 1964 *Journal of the West*, "The principal event of these affairs was the drilling contest. Two large blocks of granite rock were placed at the center of the square and the competing teams of two men each, one to hold the drill while the other smote it with a large hammer, engaged in furious competition. I do not remember the depth attained by the winners but the rocks are still there in the square and could be measured for depth." Indeed, the granite blocks are still visible on Buchanan Road near the old Carters town square.

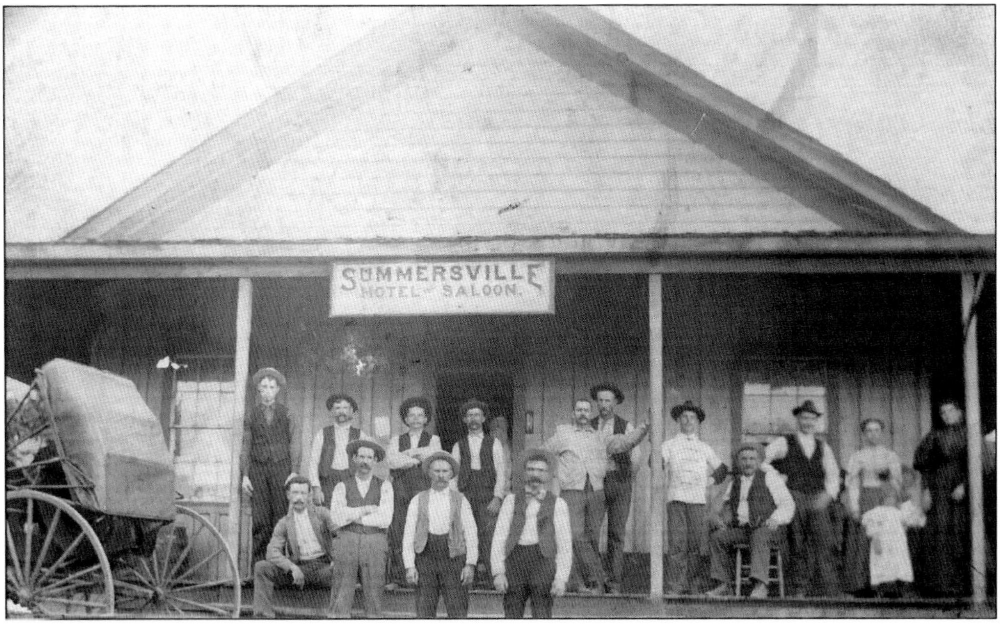

One of the earliest boardinghouses on record, the Summersville Hotel and Saloon was one of several hotels and lodging facilities that were built in early Summersville to house the numerous gold and quartz miners that travelled into the area with nowhere to stay while working claims. This 1880s photograph is one of the few extant pieces of documentation of the hotel before it was lost to fire in 1905. It was located on Center Street between Buchanan Road and Woolworth Avenue.

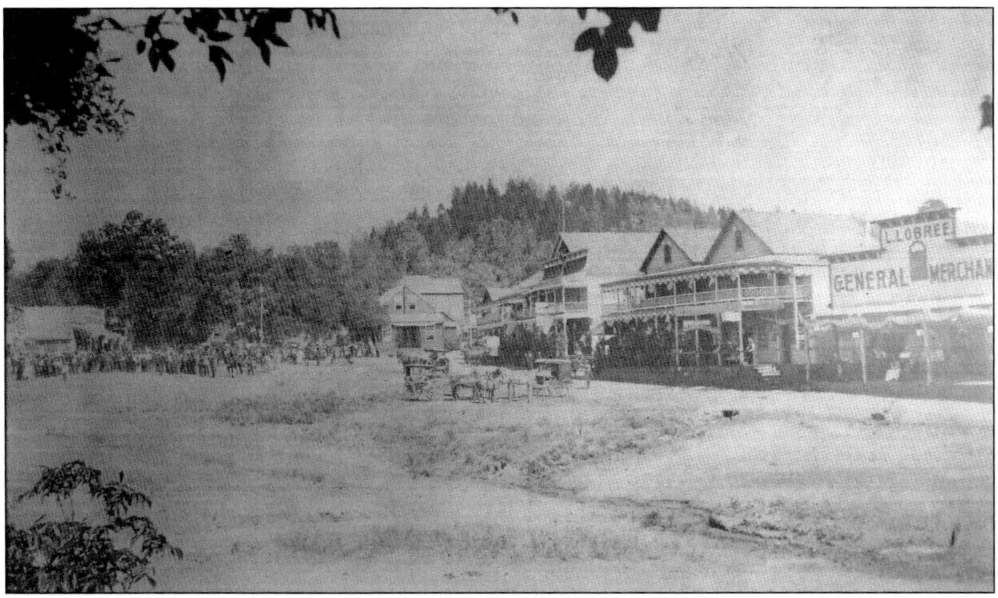

The old town business district of Carters/Summersville was a bustling place and home to many celebrations and festivals. Work was hard, the days were long, and life was rough in early mining towns around Tuolumne, so citizens would take any chance they could to kick up their heels and party. This unknown gathering (from around 1895) was held before this entire center was also lost to the fire of 1905. The photograph looks northeast and was taken near where Buchanan Road and Carter Street intersect.

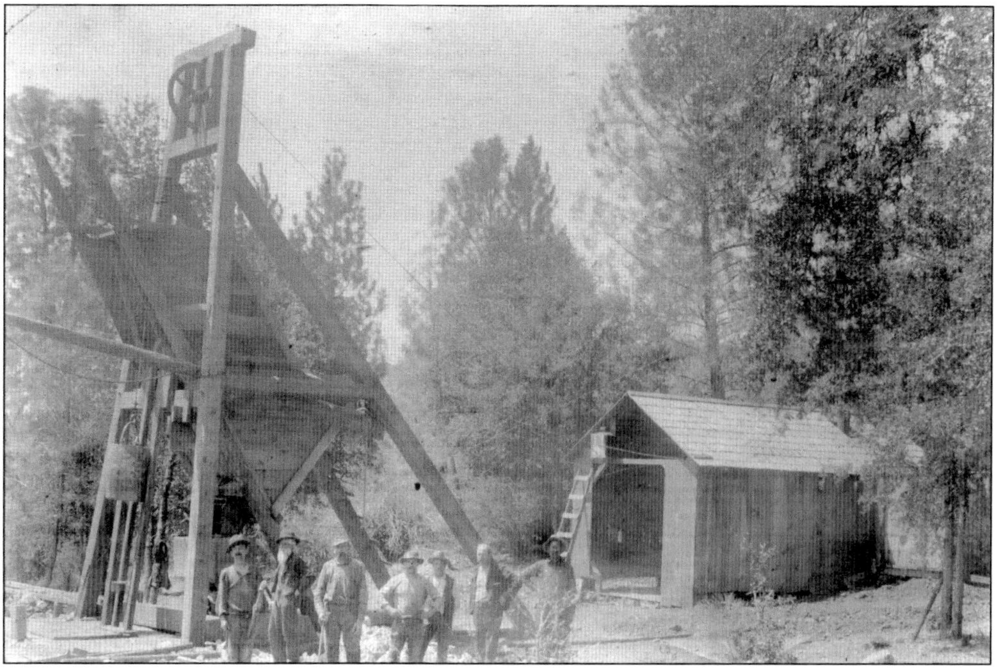

Miners gather for a photograph near the hoist at the Laura Mine, located two miles north of Tuolumne along the Soulsbyville ridge. Tapping into the same vein as the much larger Eureka mine, the hoists were typically steam powered and carried raw ore from the shafts to the surface and, in this case, a nearby 10-stamp mill. Development of the Laura Mine consisted of an incline shaft 436 feet deep.

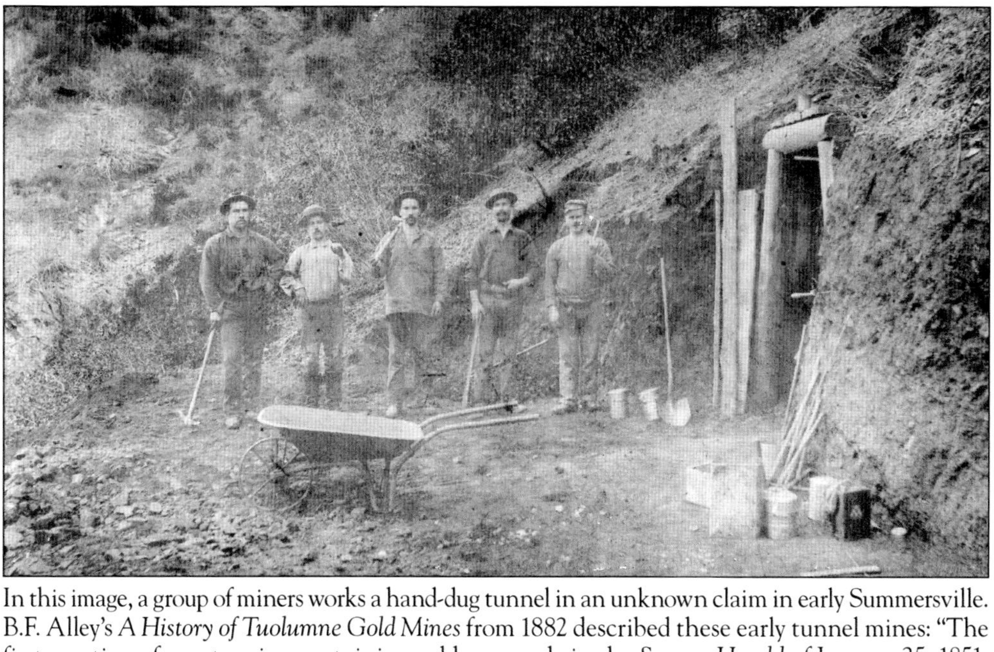

In this image, a group of miners works a hand-dug tunnel in an unknown claim in early Summersville. B.F. Alley's *A History of Tuolumne Gold Mines* from 1882 described these early tunnel mines: "The first mention of quartz veins containing gold was made in the *Sonora Herald* of January 25, 1851. . . . Quartz mining, as an industry, was soon after thoroughly established in Tuolumne, and the interest that attached to it has continued unabated to the present day."

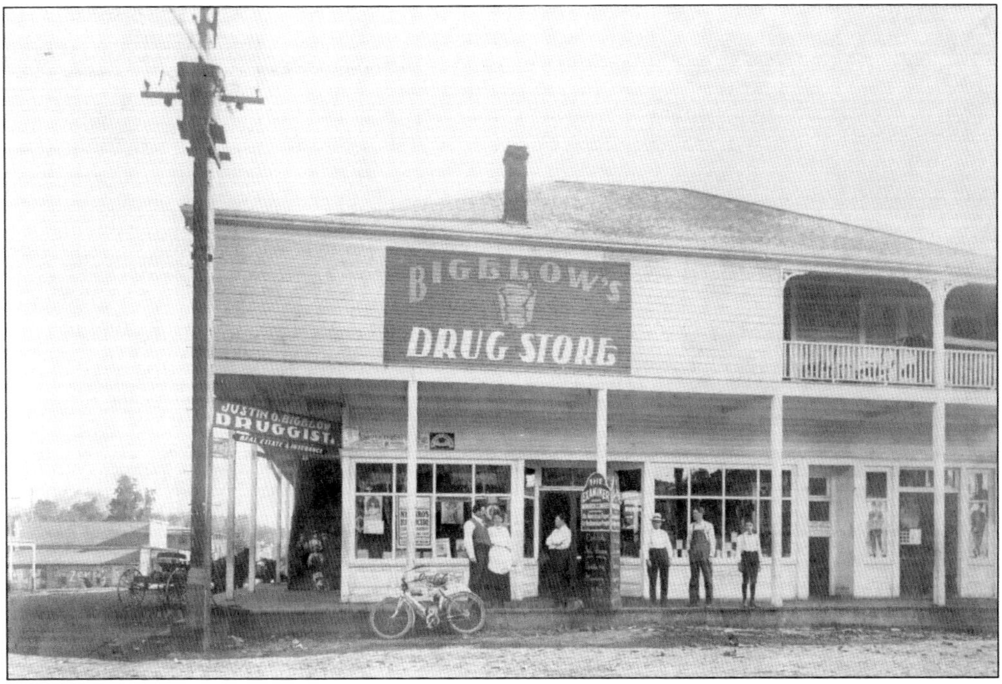

Justin O. Bigelow opened up Bigelow's Drug Store in 1901 on the corner of Chestnut Avenue and Pine Street, becoming Tuolumne's first pharmacist. In 1900, Bigelow moved from Arizona, where he was born and raised, after completing his PhD in pharmacology. Business was booming with injured miners (and eventually West Side mill workers), who went to see the town doctor, Dr. Eugene Reid, who would then write prescriptions for Bigelow to fill.

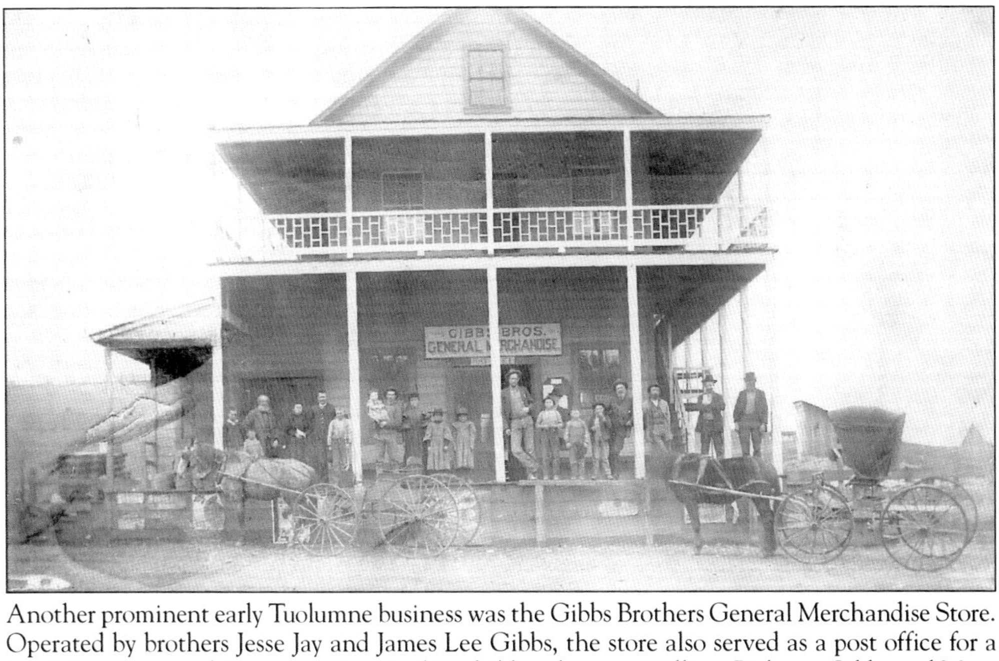

Another prominent early Tuolumne business was the Gibbs Brothers General Merchandise Store. Operated by brothers Jesse Jay and James Lee Gibbs, the store also served as a post office for a brief time. Jesse and James were just 2 of 16 children born to William Dulaney Gibbs and Mary Francis Summers, sister of Tuolumne's first resident, Franklin Summers.

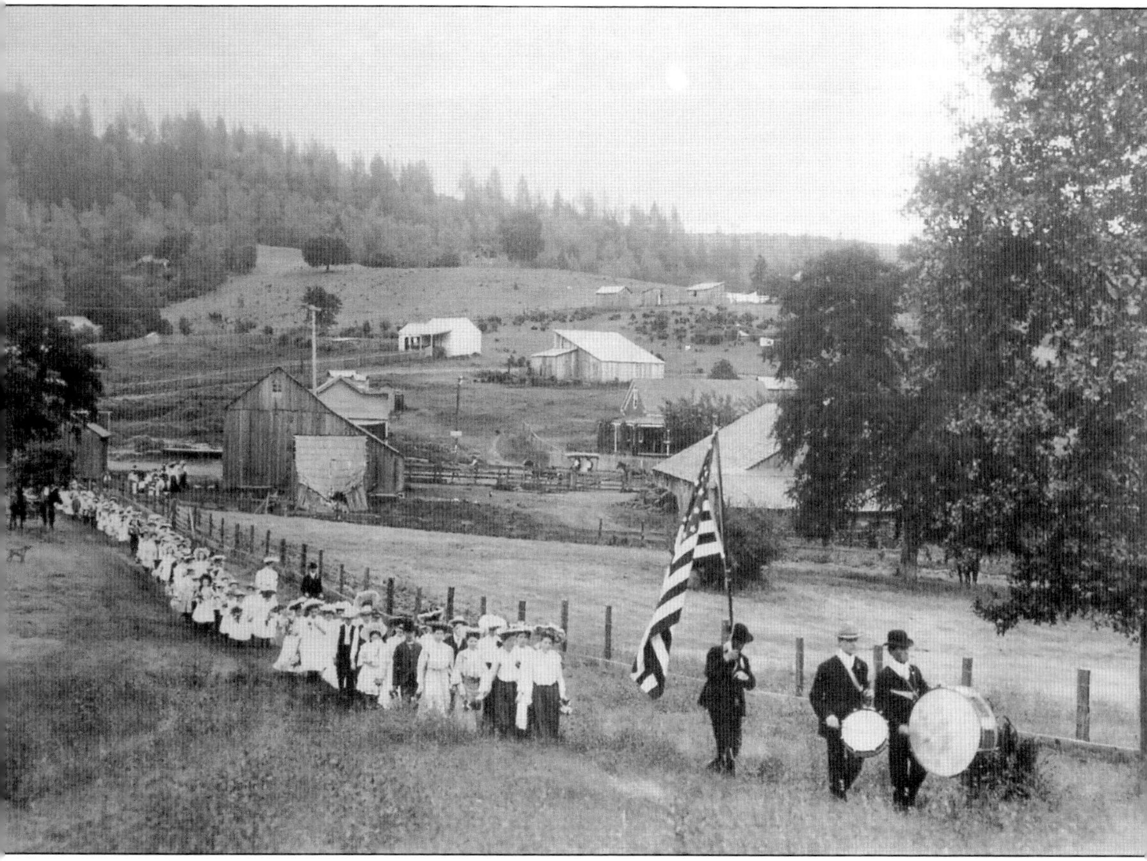

Even before the two world wars devastated cities and towns across America with unprecedented loss of life, Carters/Summersville/Tuolumne has always had (and continues to have) a deep and abiding respect for members of its country's armed forces. In this photograph from May 30, 1905, the majority of the township makes the trek up the hill at the north end of town to Carters Cemetery on Memorial Day to honor veterans of recent wars—most notably the Civil War and Mexican-American War. The first burial described in local history is that of a young James Ham, a murder victim in 1856. The first documented burial is that of Silas Gibbs, only eight days old and the fourth child of William and Mary Gibbs, who died on January 2, 1860. The cemetery has considerably expanded and serves as the final resting place for over 3,000 people from all walks of life; it is widely considered to be the most attractive cemetery in Tuolumne County.

Two

West Side and the Timber Trade

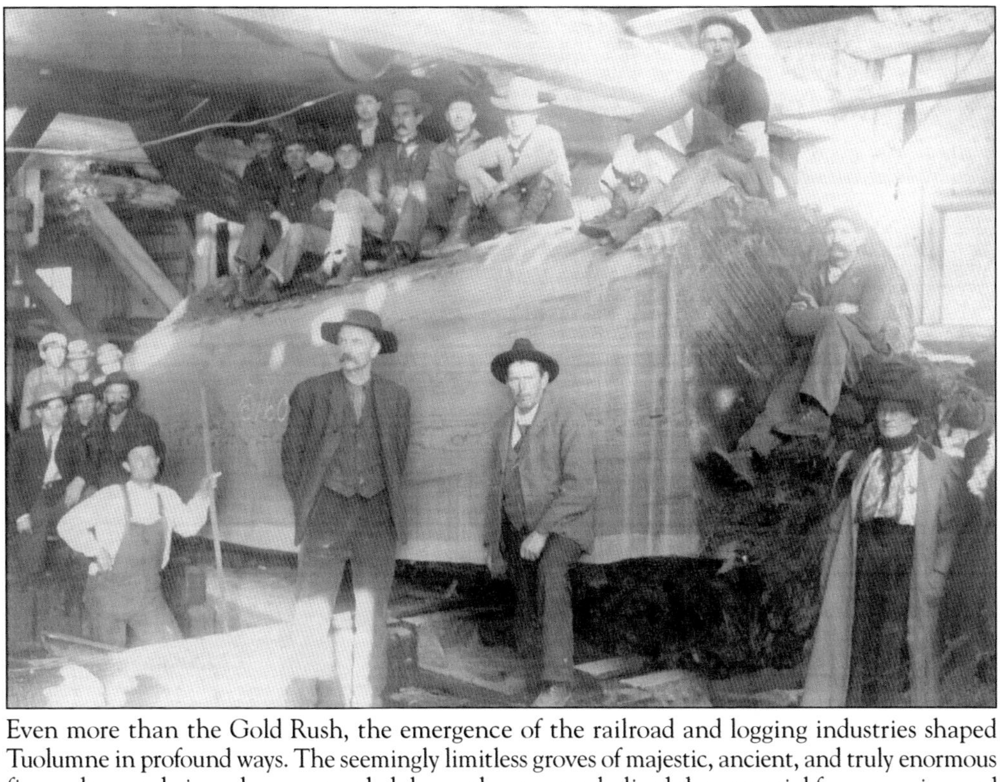

Even more than the Gold Rush, the emergence of the railroad and logging industries shaped Tuolumne in profound ways. The seemingly limitless groves of majestic, ancient, and truly enormous firs, cedars, and pines that surrounded the settlement symbolized the potential for expansion and economic growth. The town took pride in knowing that timber harvested from their area was being used to build cities and towns across the new state of California.

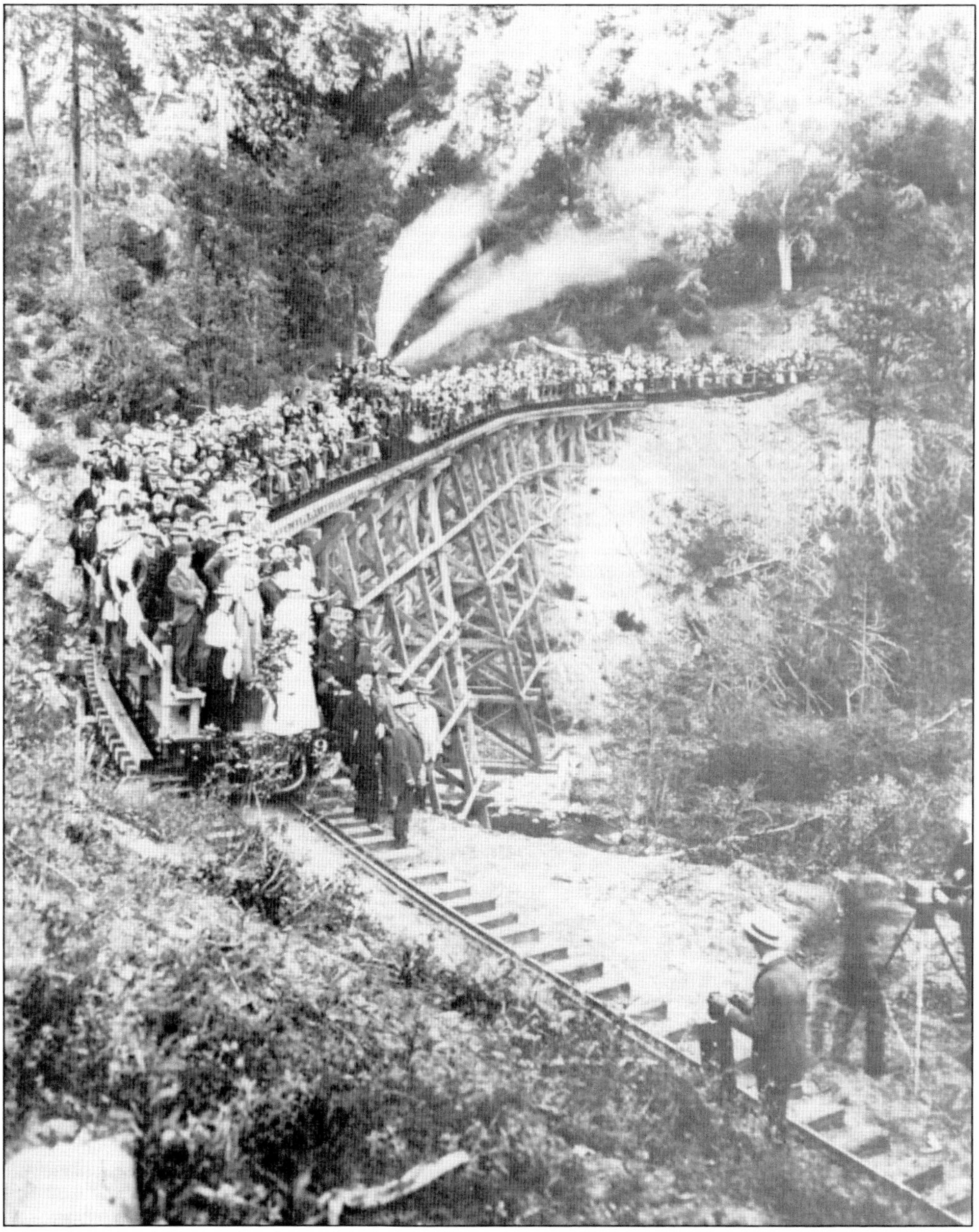

This photograph from May 25, 1900, depicts the grand-opening ceremony of the West Side Lumber and Flume Company. Nearly the entire town (then Carters, but soon to be Tuolumne) joined in by standing along the Railroad River Bridge and trestle. Businessman Thomas S. Bullock from New York City, banker William Crocker from Sierra Pacific Railroad, and nobleman, investor, and Polish prince Andre Poniatowski purchased approximately 66 square miles (over 55,000 acres) of forested land earlier in 1900 with plans for a huge mill and lumber-processing plant that would, in essence, create a new town. The West Side Flume and Lumber Company would soon lose the "Flume and" from its name, as the group's initial plan to build log flumes from the deep forest all the way into the town's mill center proved impossible after surveying the area's numerous steep canyons.

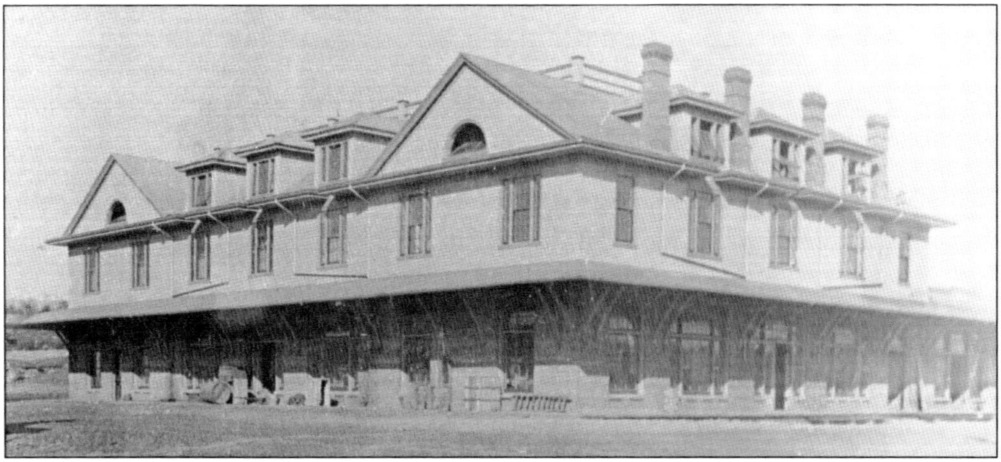

This 1900 photograph, taken facing southwest from the present-day intersection of Chestnut and Main Streets in downtown Tuolumne, shows the original main office building of the West Side Lumber Company, completed on May 26, 1900. All corporate offices were housed here, and the day-to-day operations for the massive company, such as payroll and insurance, were all performed under this roof. Notice the four chimneys on the right, along the building's north wall; these contributed to its eventual demise by fire on October 2, 1902. It was reconstructed as a one-story brick building at the corner of Main and Bay Streets.

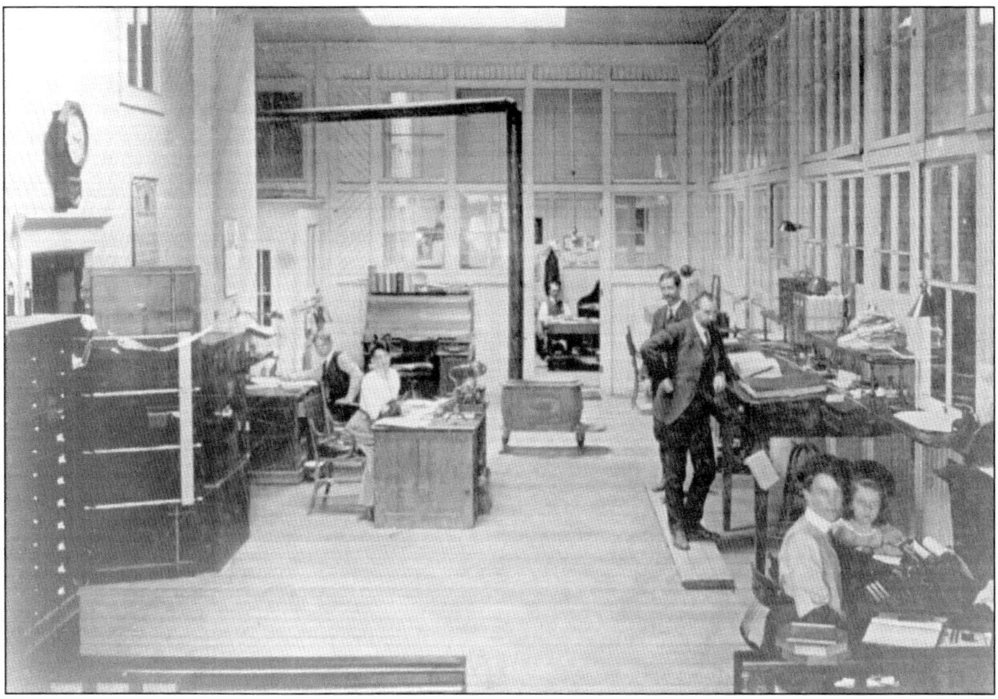

Many employees—other than the obvious lumberjacks, locomotive engineers, and mill workers—were needed to run the West Side Lumber and Flume Company, as evidenced by this c. 1905 photograph of the office's interior. Ledgers needed to be kept; letters and memos needed to be created, received, and sent out; checks needed to be cashed; and payroll needed to go out in an orderly and timely manner. West Side provided Tuolumne with hundreds of jobs for decades to come.

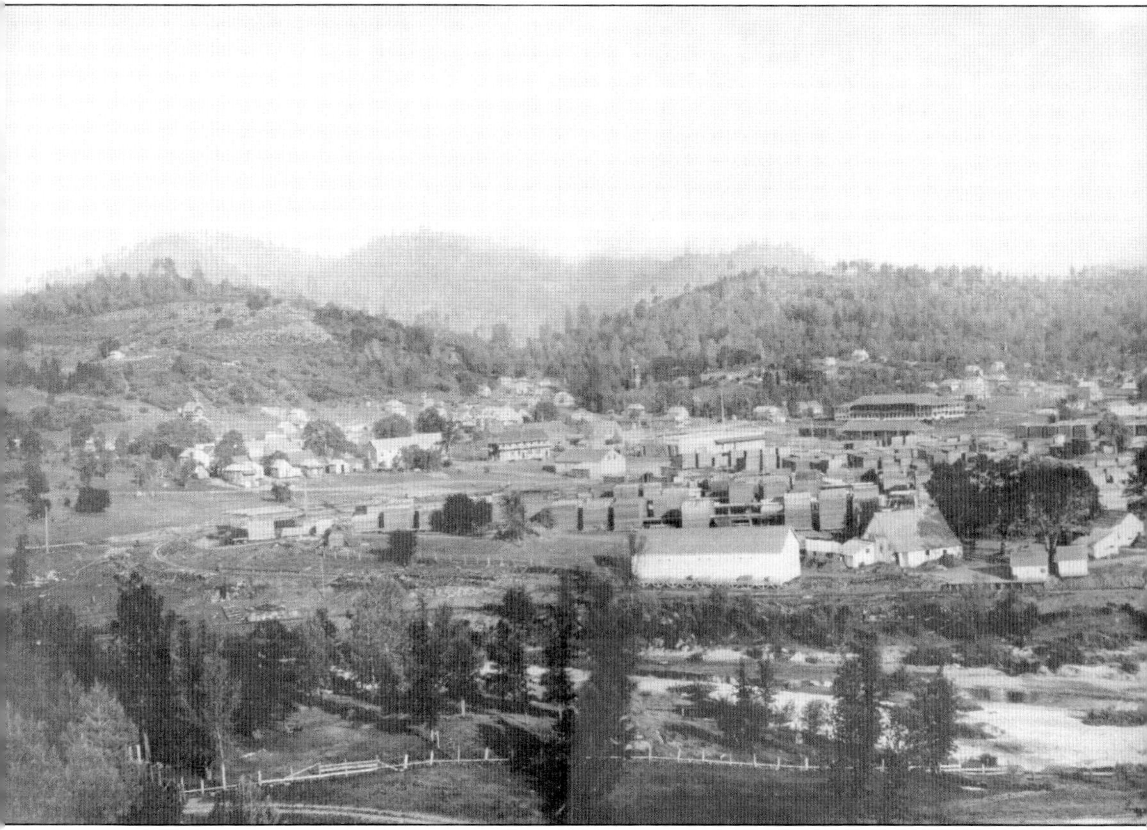

This bird's-eye view of the mill and surrounding land and buildings shows the scope and (now realized) grand vision of the founding members of the West Side Flume and Lumber Company. In this 1906 photograph, taken while facing east near the present-day Tuolumne Road, the

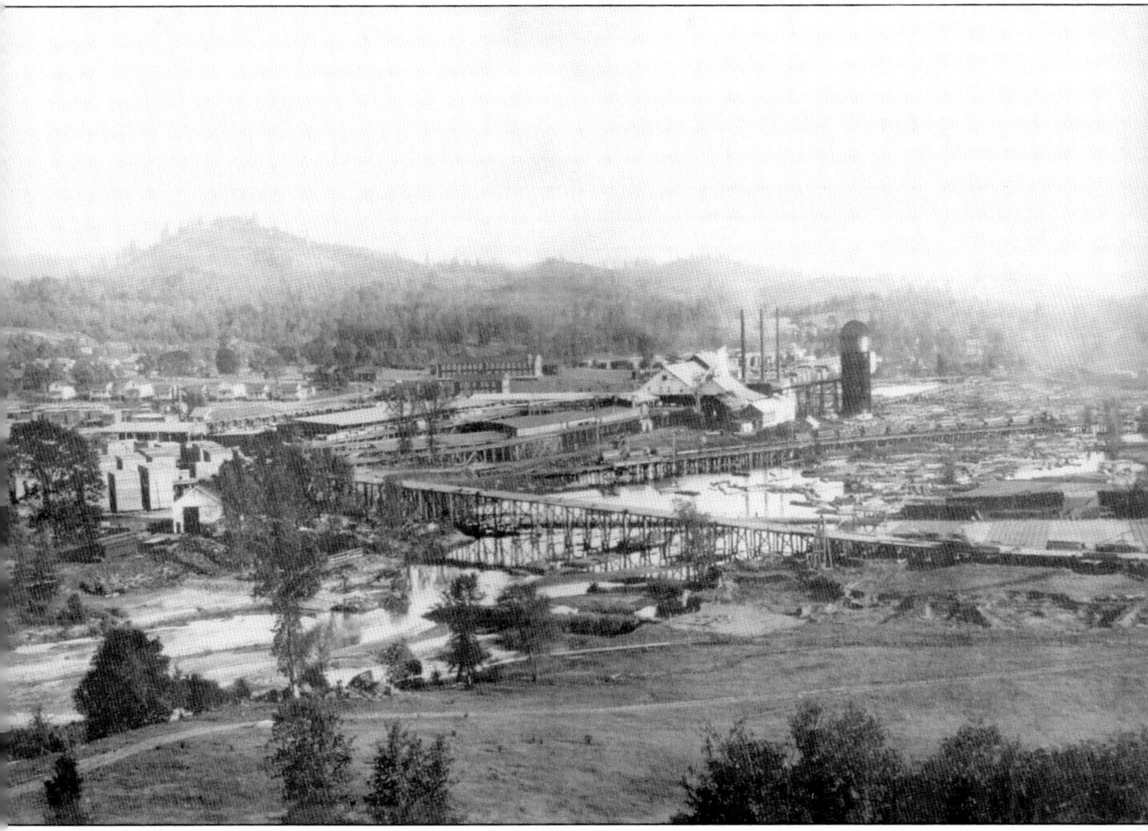

millpond and main mill are visible to the right, and the numerous drying stacks are visible from the approximate center of the photograph to almost the far left of the frame. The original buildings of Summersville/Carters are visible in the distance.

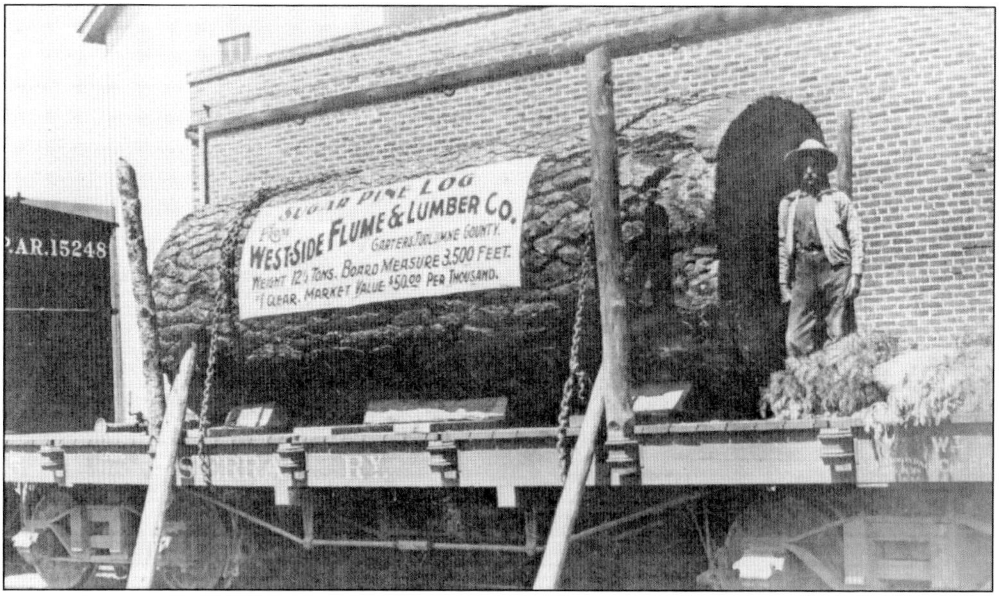

This massive section of a sugar pine tree harvested by the early West Side Lumber and Flume Company around 1910 was put on display on a flatbed railroad car for the Stockton Exposition. The timber logs harvested from the surrounding area were among the largest in the state after being allowed to grow untouched for hundreds of years before the arrival of white settlers in the mid-19th century.

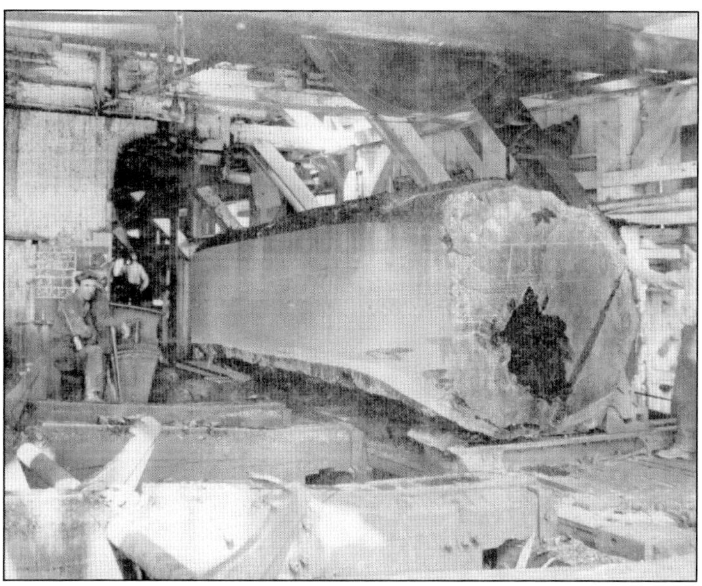

West Side mill workers at the planing mill stand next to another gigantic log as it is sliced on the vertical to make large sheets. These sheets were approximately one inch thick, four feet wide, and eight feet long. They were then typically stacked in the drying yard to remove excess moisture before shipment or further processing. These sawyers manually determined how to maximize each log in terms of lumber board feet.

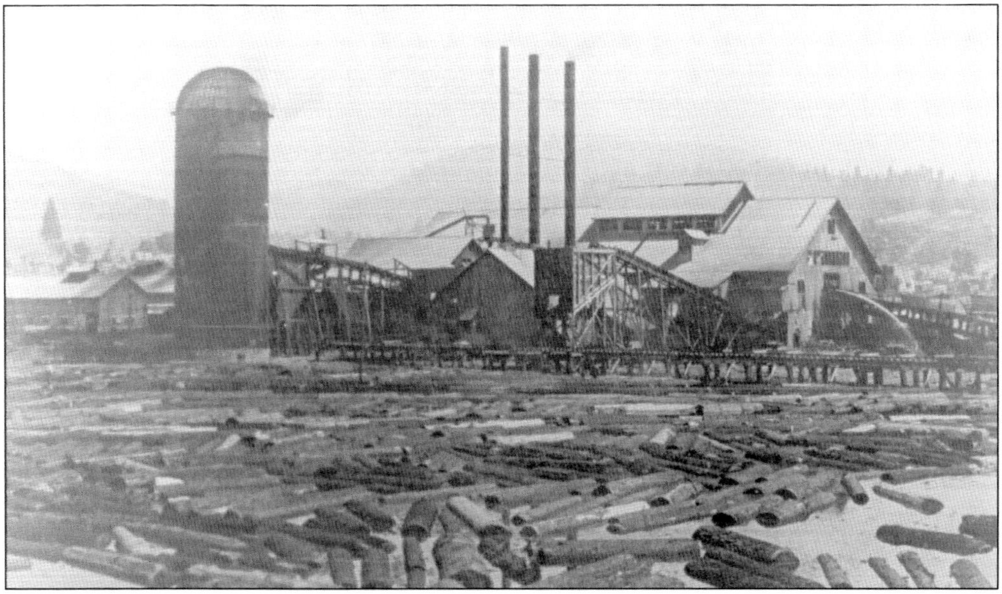

This view looking east toward the West Side millpond offers a good glimpse of the main lumber facility. The elevated tracks (coming into the frame from the right side of the photograph) constituted the main narrow-gauge railroad line into the mill, where a majority of the harvested logs would be deposited in the pond directly from the tracks.

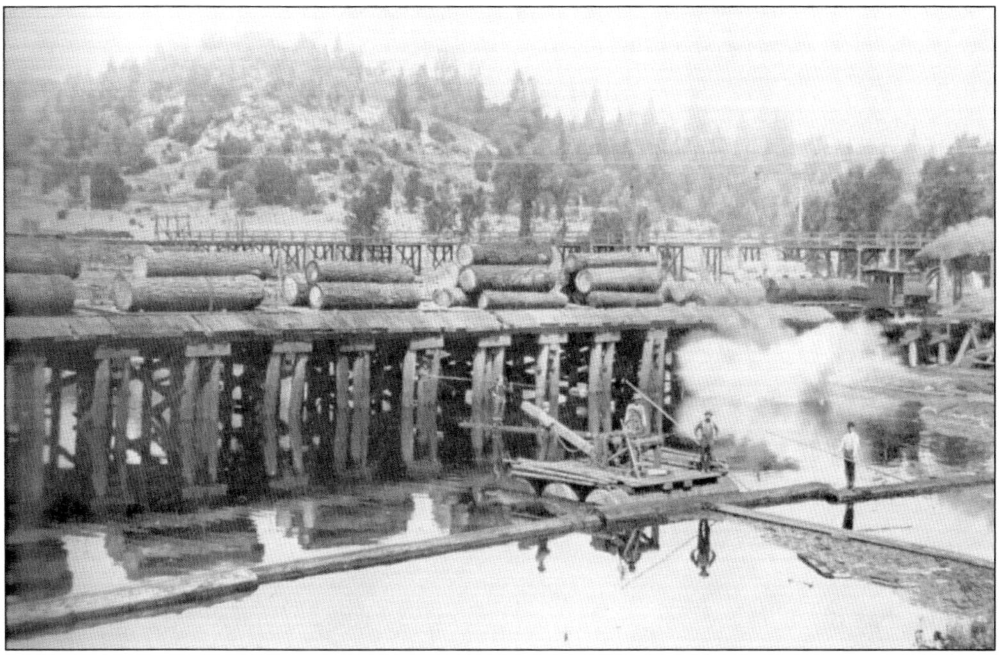

This c. 1900 photograph shows the harvested logs traveling up the elevated tracks mentioned above, as well as the steam-driven winch house on pontoons in the foreground. The millpond served as a storage facility of sorts, as logs came in from the forest faster than they could be processed. Logs were stored in the huge man-made millpond during the busy seasons (spring and summer) and could then be processed during the winter, when the tracks were covered by deep snow. This ensured year-round operation and work for the mill and many of its employees.

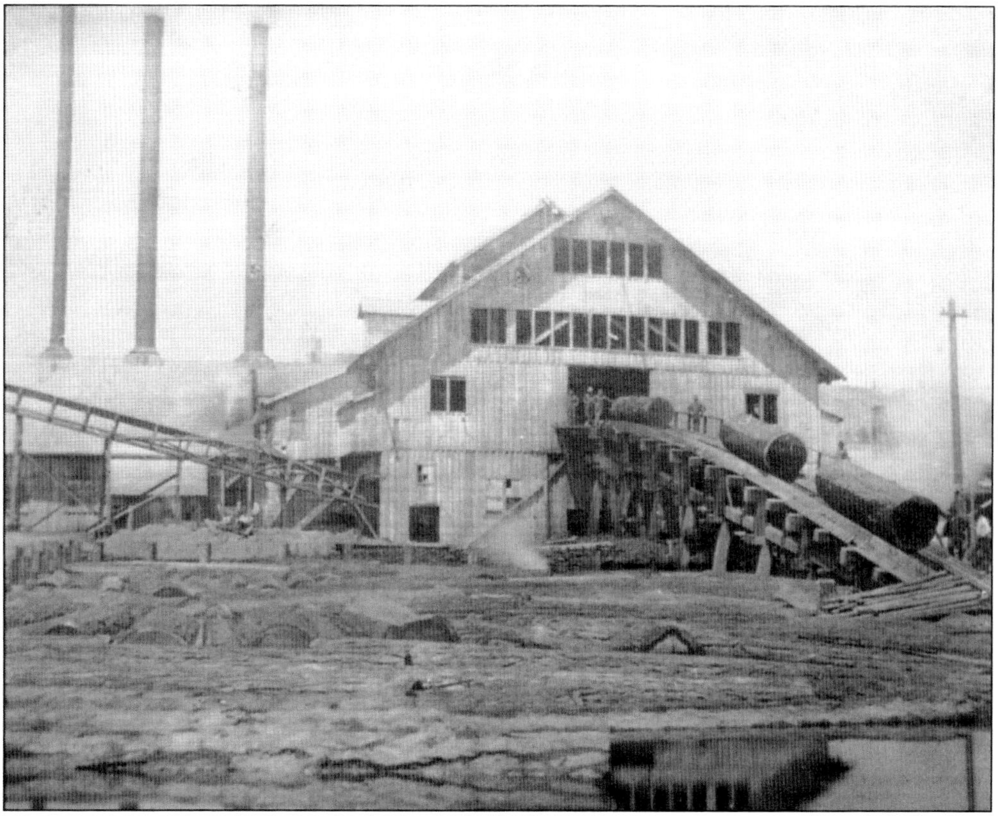

The gradually inclining lumber ramp that led into the saw log facility from the main track fed the mill a near constant supply of trees from 7:00 a.m. to 4:30 p.m. five days a week, making it one of the busiest sections of West Side. The workers at the top of the ramp took an assuredly much-appreciated pause to pose for this photograph in 1906.

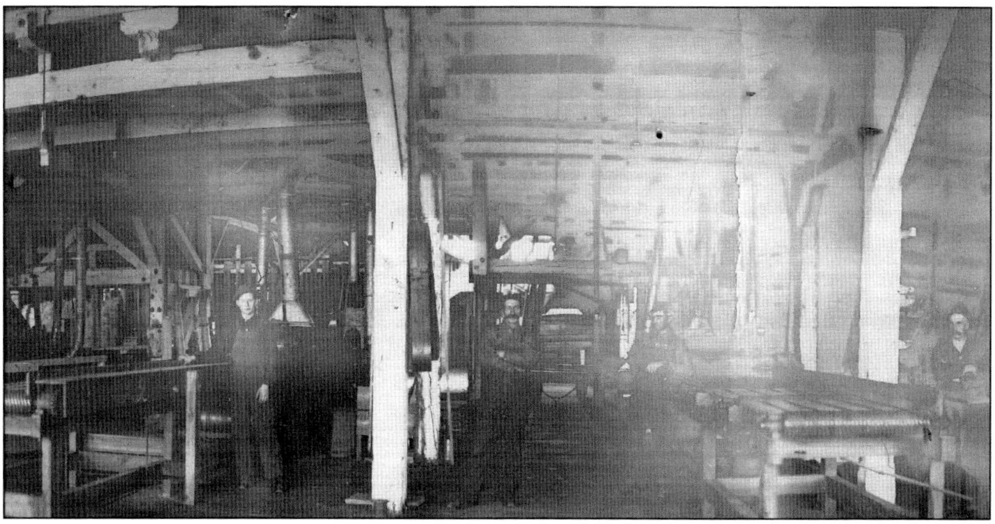

This c. 1905 photograph again shows the planing section inside the Westside Lumber Mill. Raw planks moved across these tables via conveyor belts for finishing details to ensure the final planks and boards were made to exact specifications.

Two lumberjacks watch as this massive sugar pine falls. Trees like this—taller than 200 feet—were not uncommon sights to early West Side lumberjacks and would provide thousands of board feet in raw lumber to be processed and shipped.

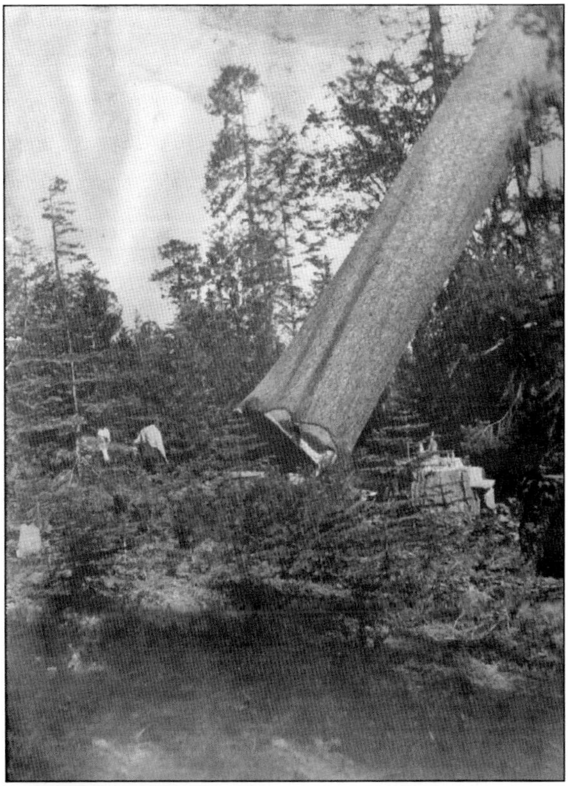

The use of handsaws and axes by West Side lumberjacks was still fairly common until after World War II, when hand-held chainsaws were mass produced, as shown by this pair standing next to an approximately eight-foot-wide and freshly harvested sugar pine, which was felled by a misery whip saw. Note the copious amounts of sap dripping from the edge of the bark.

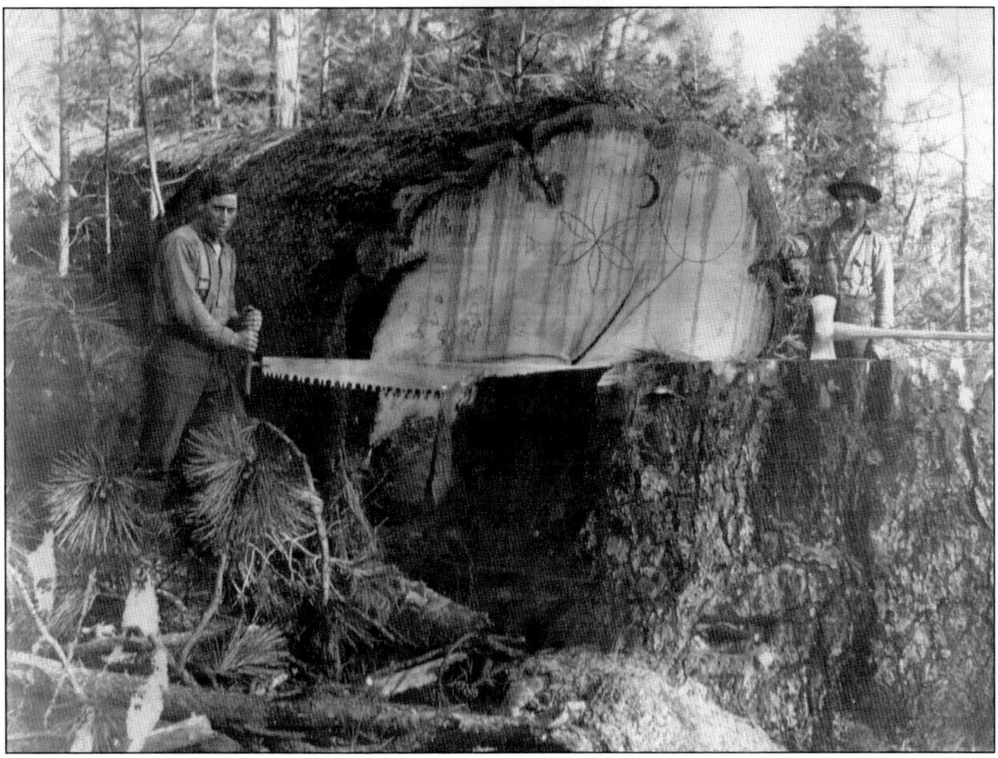

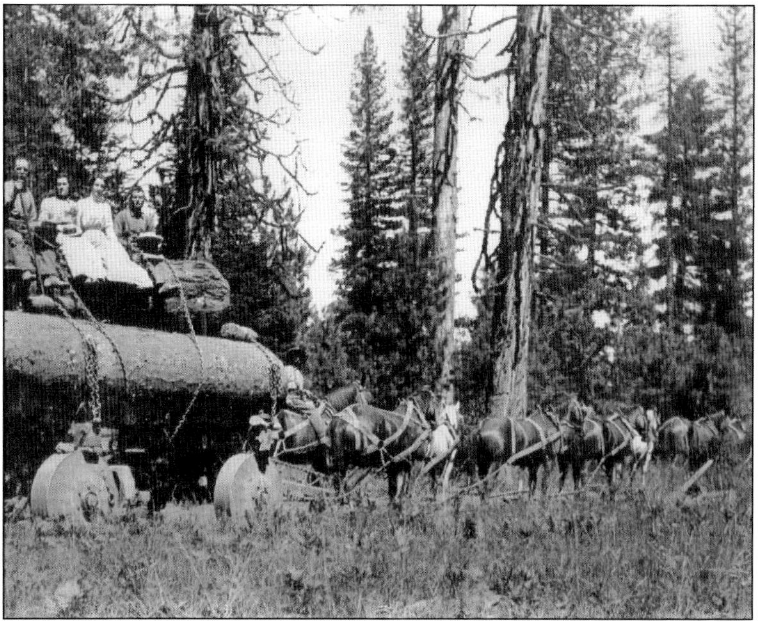

The Brown family rests atop an impressive load of logs on Empire Road leading into Pinecrest. When harvested trees were in remote areas either too far away or in too treacherous an area to bring a hoist or crane in, teams of horses and mules commonly pulled the logs closer to the tracks to be loaded on waiting railcars.

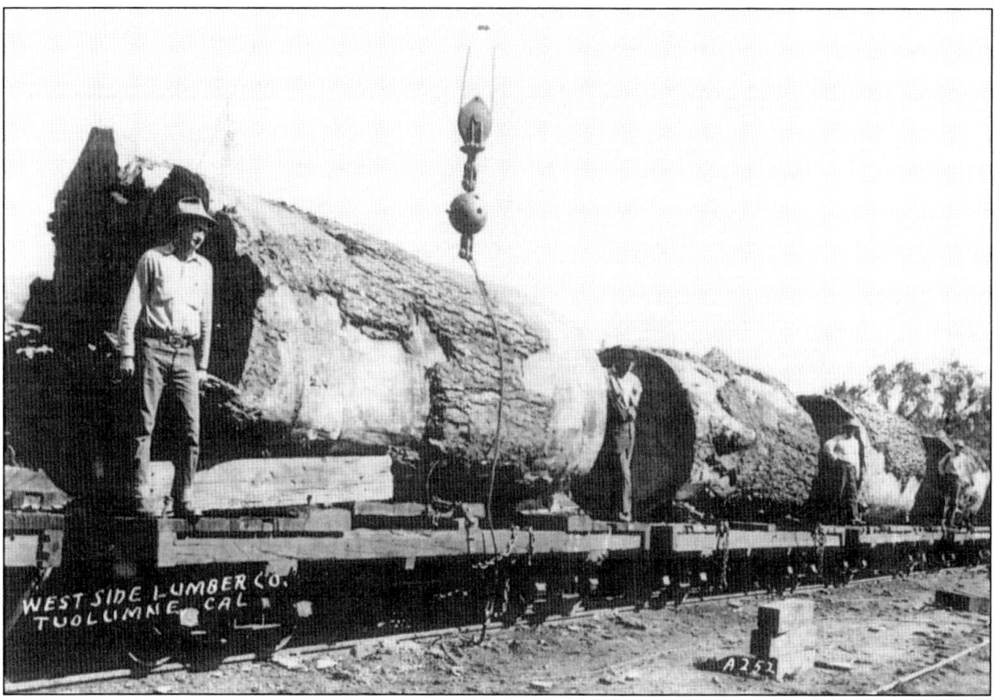

This photograph displays a prime example of the railcars mentioned above. The clearly visible hoist, operated by steam power, lifted the logs to be stacked on the cars for delivery to the mill. What made the railway system employed by West Side unique was that it was a narrow-gauge railroad with only 36 inches between the rails.

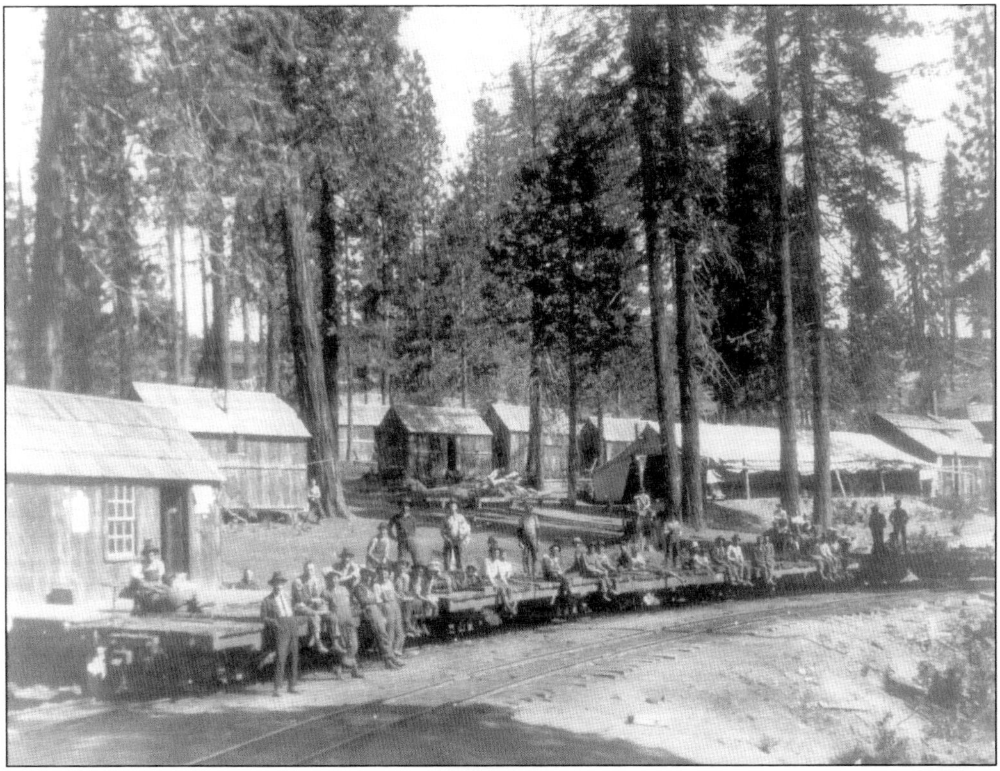

A large contingent of West Side workers poses with an empty train of flatbed railcars. The surrounding encampment was one of many logging camps that started up in the spring once the weather warmed up and the snow cleared. The camps were often set up in a particularly thick grove so the family members of the workers could be nearby for the long logging season, since the majority of workers stayed out in the forest during prime harvesting time.

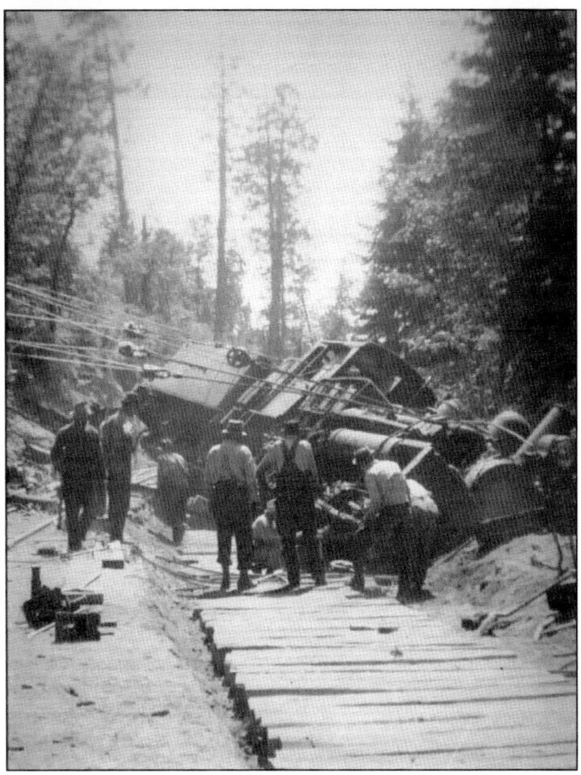

Trouble on the tracks! One of West Side's engines has spilled off the rails—thankfully, not while encumbered by a full load of logs. Several of the hoists normally used to help stack logs onto the railcars (known as steam donkeys) were put toward lifting the heavy locomotive back onto the tracks.

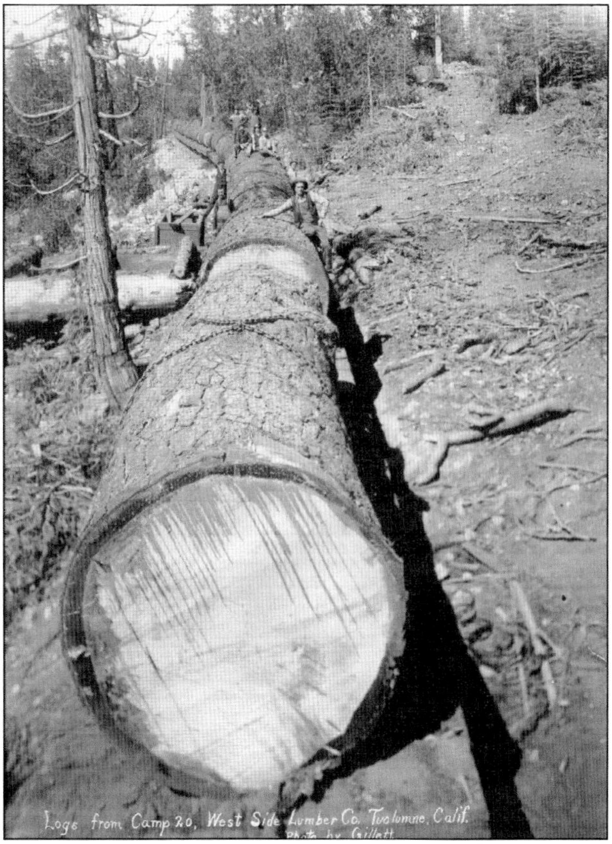

Several lumberjacks pose with logs harvested from the outskirts of Tuolumne. This c. 1910 picture was taken near Baker's Siding, one of the numerous camps that sprung up along the tracks during the warmer months. This train's load is comprised of logs from one gigantic sugar pine tree. Baker's Siding is located between the current-day Mira Monte subdivision and Tuolumne Road North; the tracks are still visible today.

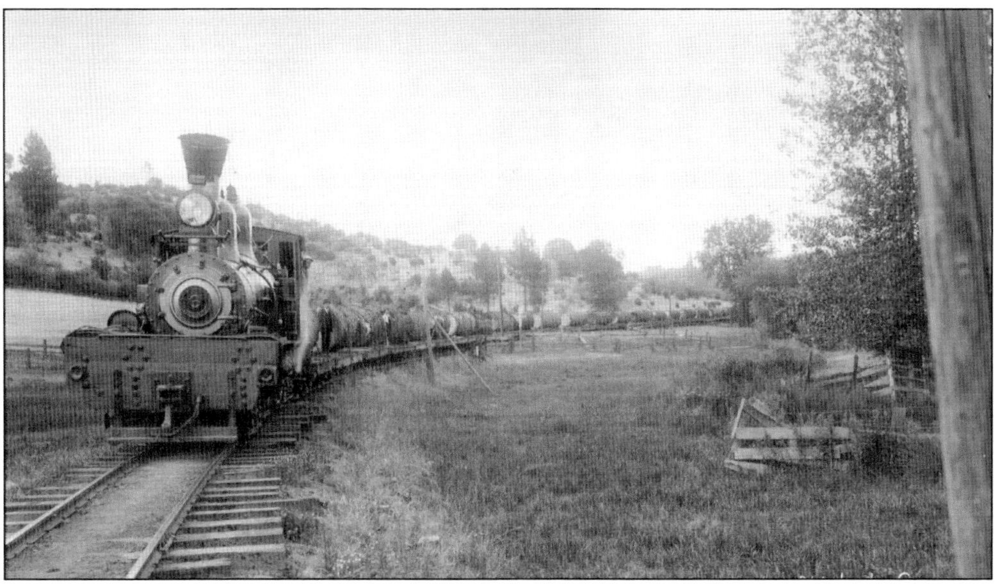

West Side Engine No. 6 chugs along the track with 30 cars' worth of both logs and passengers on its way back to the mill. Taken near Camp 20, this photograph shows the distinctiveness of the narrow-gauge track, which has only 36 inches between the rails (compared to 56.5 inches for standard-gauge tracks, which make up over 60 percent of the world's existing railways today).

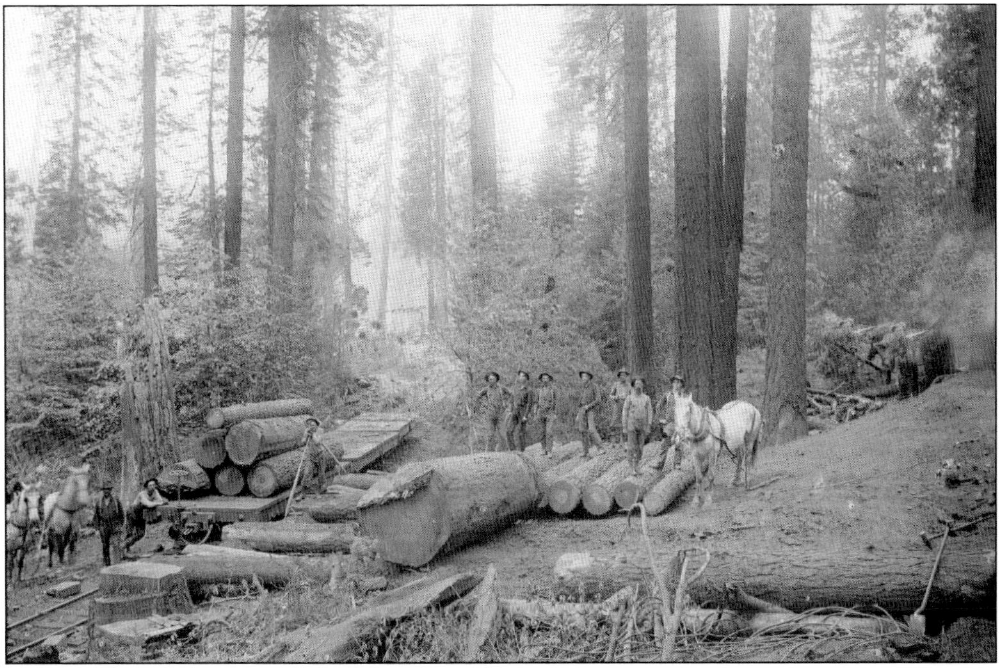

Narrow-gauge tracks were an absolute necessity to extend West Side's rail line into the far reaches of the surrounding Stanislaus forest, as standard-gauge lines would not have been able to navigate the tight turns and sudden changes in elevation. Often, flatbed cars would be dropped off, and smaller horse-and-hand teams would manually chop, stack, and deliver the logs.

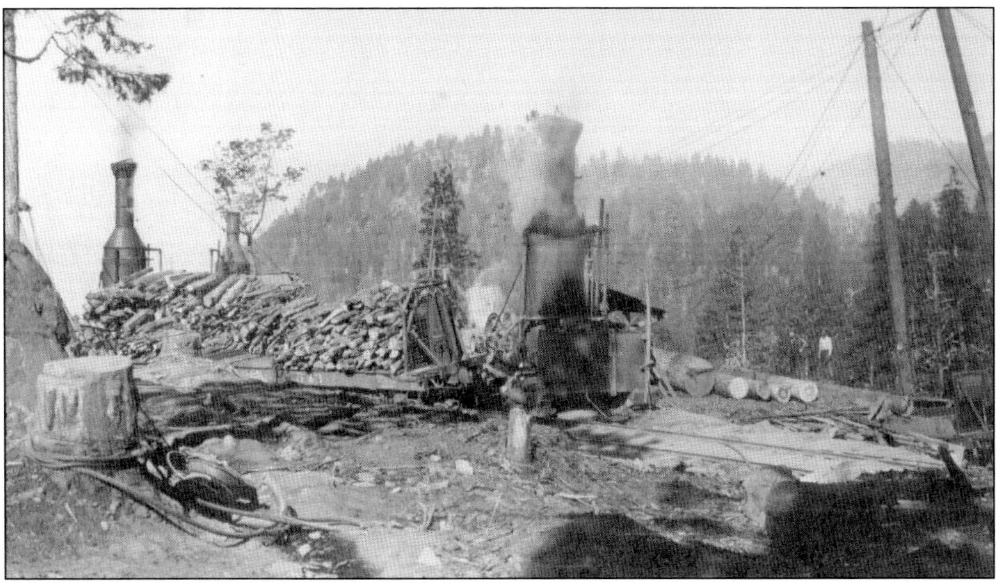

Three steam-powered hoists resting on a ridge near the tracks were used to haul up small- and medium-sized logs for placement on the car. These hoists, known as steam donkeys, were a vital part of the logging operation in Tuolumne because their power was an absolute must to drag the logs up the steep sides of the river canyons. Steam donkeys came in a variety of sizes, depending on the job at hand. Smaller Dolbeer machines eventually gave way to larger Willamette donkeys. The flatcar seen here is holding wood fuel for the donkeys

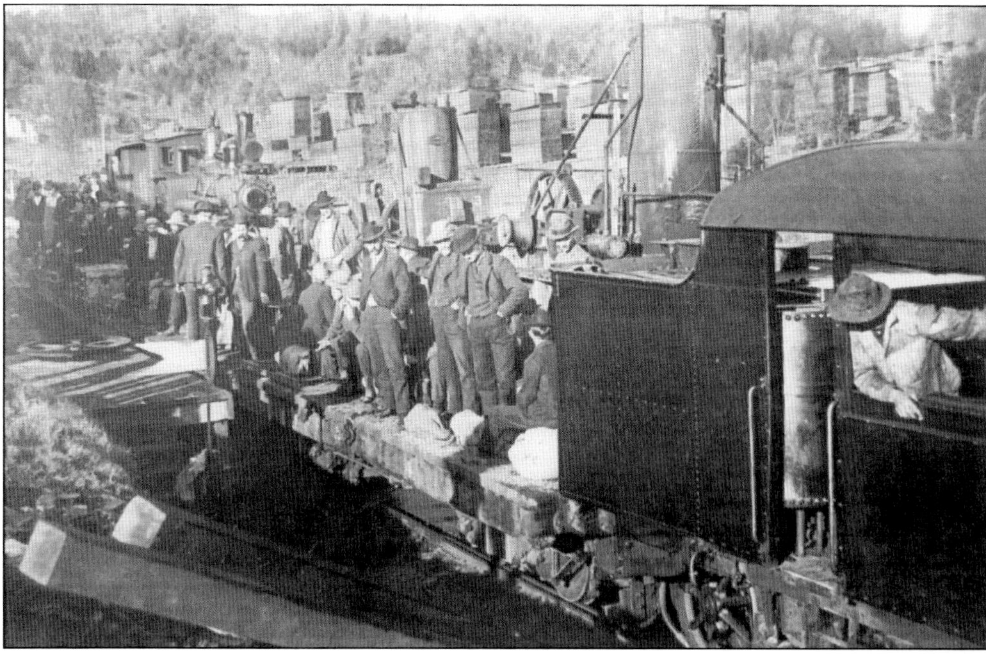

A rail train devoid of logs but full of lumberjacks makes its way out of the West Side station and toward the logging camps. The amount of luggage shows that these fellows were not just heading off for the day, but for the season, and would make their summer homes in sheds and shanties along the tracks.

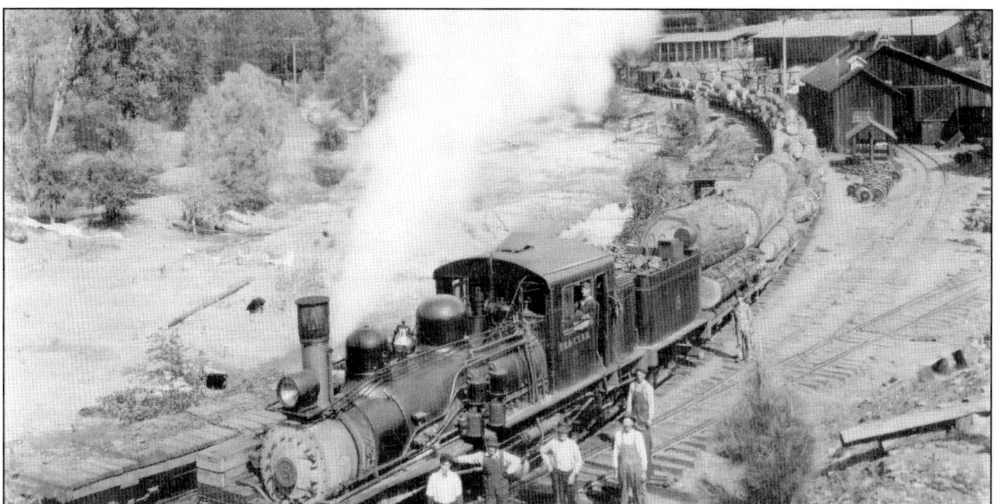

Engine No. 8, built by Lima Locomotive Works in Lima, Ohio, hauls in another full load from the Hetch Hetchy & Yosemite Valley Railroad (HH&YV), as designated by the initials on the lead car, in the early 1900s. Engine No. 8 was retired from service in 1922 and is now displayed at the Santa Fe Depot in Cañon City, Colorado, after service on the Georgetown Loop in Clear Creek County, Colorado. Pictured left to right in the foreground are Jack Tenney, dispatcher; La Vern Shorts, brakeman; "Hot Box" Smith, River Bridge watchman; Olaf Dahl, section one boss; George Weaver, conductor; and Bill Symonds, car shop foreman. Fireman Carl Whylidko is in the engine cab window.

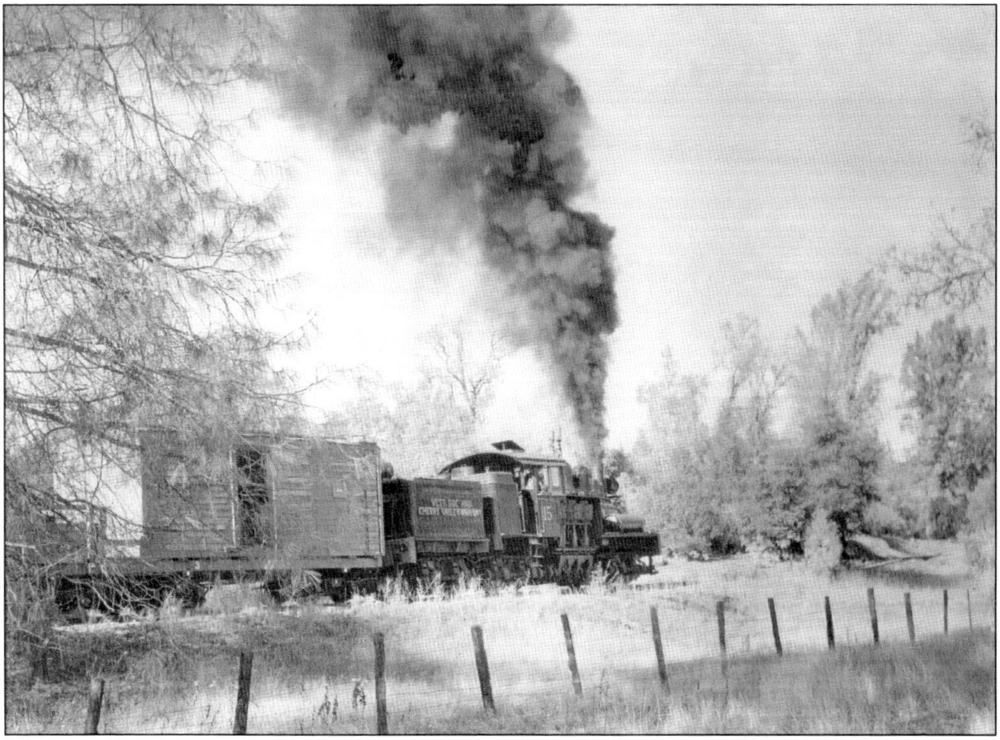

Engine No. 15, another Lima Locomotive Works train and a three-truck Shay variety, pulls out along the West Side and Cherry Valley Railway in this c. 1939 photograph. Engine No. 15 was retired from West Side duties when the plant shut down in 1960 and was on static display in Tuolumne until it was, thankfully, bought by the Yosemite Mountain Sugar Pine Railroad in 1986. It is one of only two steam locomotives operated on the historic line in Fish Camp, California, that begins near the southern entrance to Yosemite National Park.

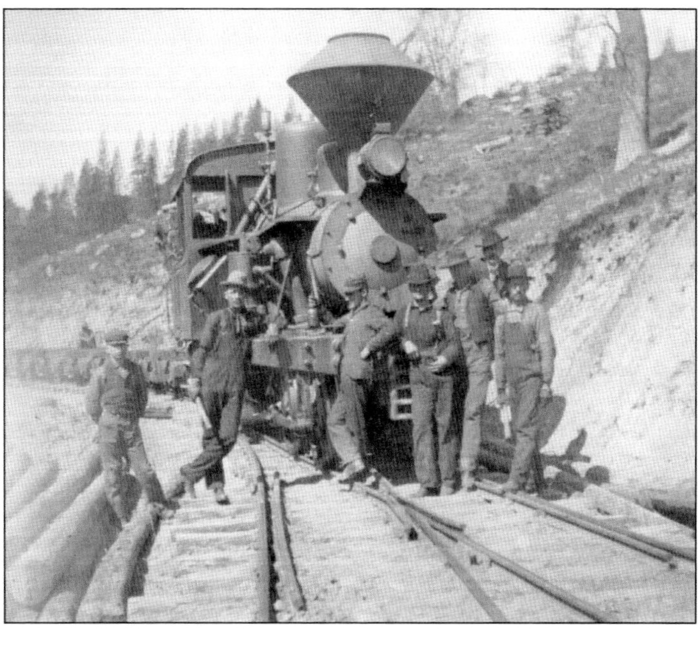

This 1900 photograph shows the crew of the Heisler-built Engine No. 1 pausing for a photograph. The Heisler was the last major variant of all geared steam locomotive designs and also the fastest. Built in 1899, Engine No. 1 was eventually sold to the Swayne Lumber Company in Oroville, California, before finally being scrapped in 1940.

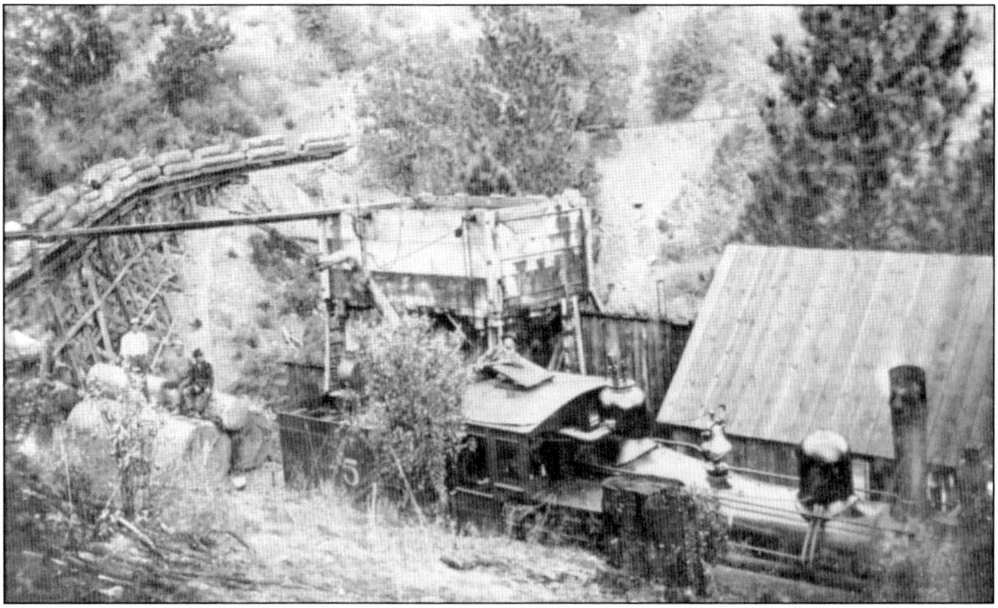

West Side Engine No. 5, a two-truck Lima train, takes on water for its steam engine in this c. 1915 photograph. This train, built in 1902, unfortunately did not make it to the end of the West Side mill's days and was scrapped in 1950. Filling stations, or water tanks, were common sights along the narrow-gauge track, as refills were a frequent necessity.

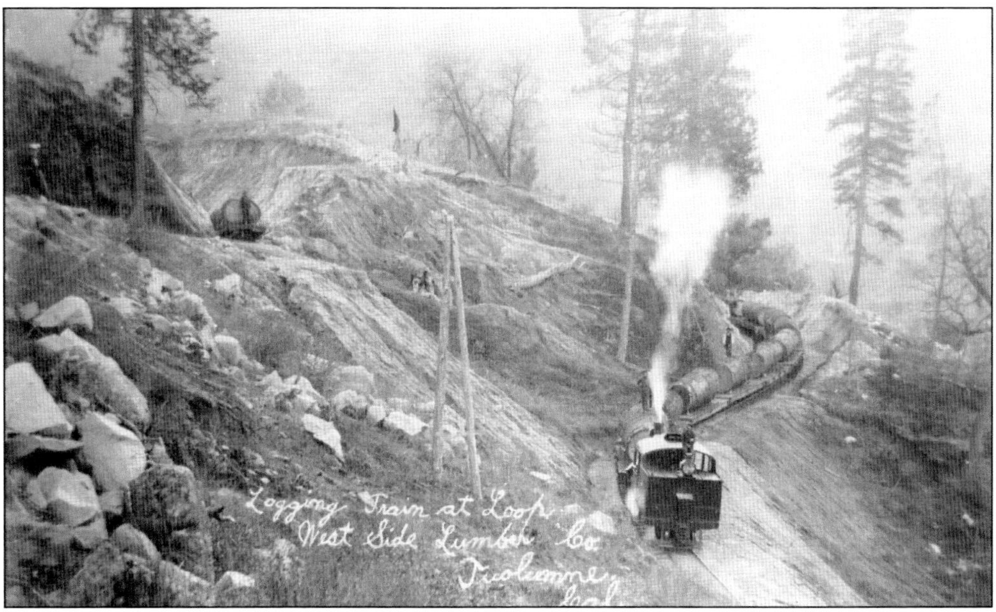

Perhaps no other picture can better illustrate the need for the West Side Lumber Company to use a narrow-gauge track than this one, taken around 1900. Known colloquially as "the loop," this menacing section of track not only features a sharp, 60-degree turn (for an eventual 180) but also a significant drop in elevation. Lumberjacks tested fate by hitching rides atop the logs.

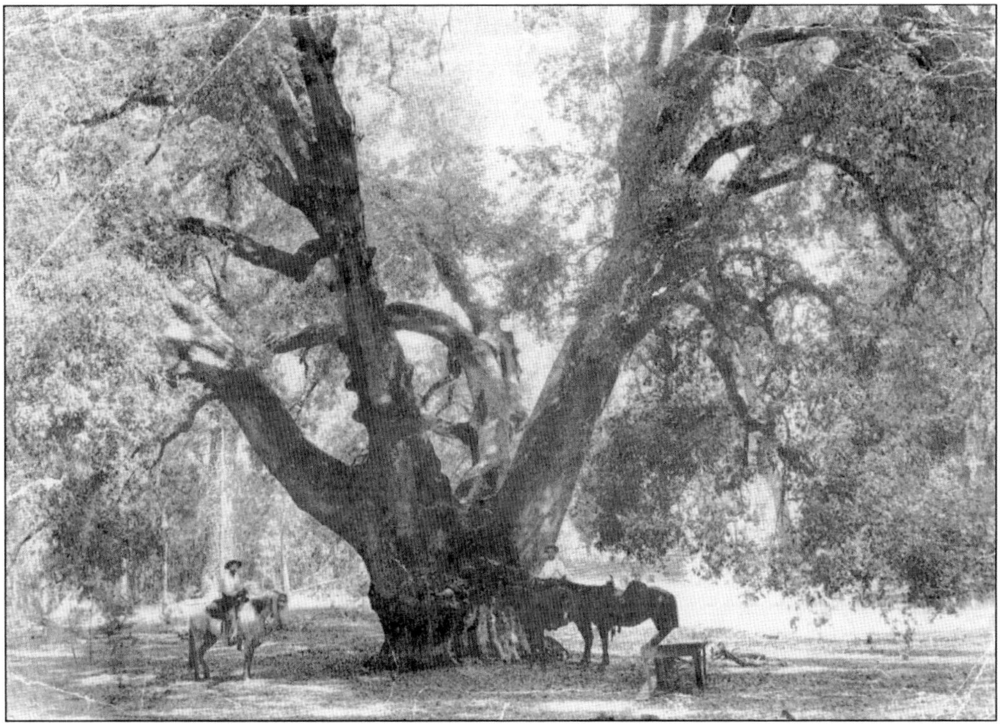

Touted in the early 1900s as "the World's Oldest Oak Tree," this gigantic and ancient spreading oak was later downgraded to "the State's Oldest Oak Tree," and by the 1920s "Tuolumne County's Oldest Oak Tree." Whatever its age, the tree near the edge of the main railway by Buchanan Mine was considered old when the line was built in 1900 and is still alive today.

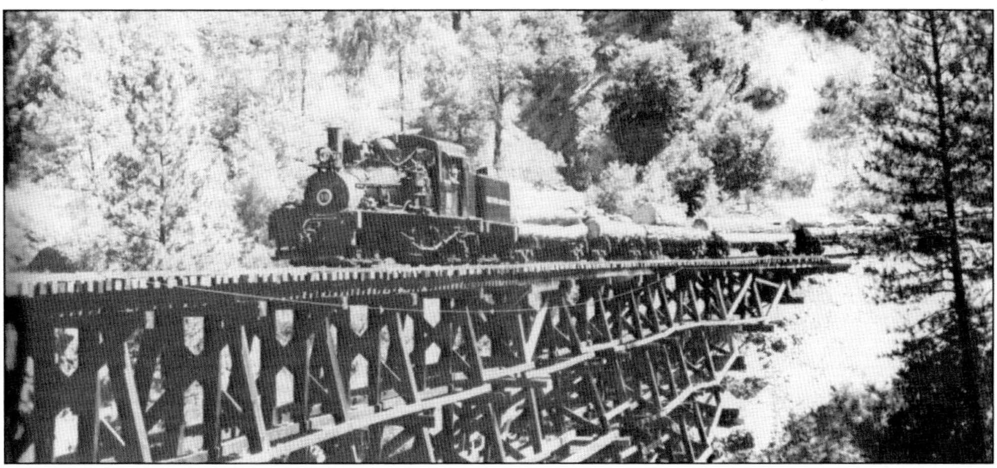

Engine No. 10 of the West Side Lumber Company, completed in 1928, was yet another Lima Locomotive Works–produced, three-truck Shay-style locomotive. Here, it lumbers across the River Bridge, the first wooden trestle on the West Side roadbed. This curved bridge was 62 feet tall and 300 feet long and provided access to the timber-rich areas east of the North Fork of the Tuolumne River. While the water-refilling tank and a watchmen's cabin near the bridge are no longer in existence, the cement foundation in the streambed remains in place. Engine No. 10 was later bought by the Yosemite Mountain Sugar Pine Railroad and, along with Engine No. 15, is one of two operating locomotives along the tourist line.

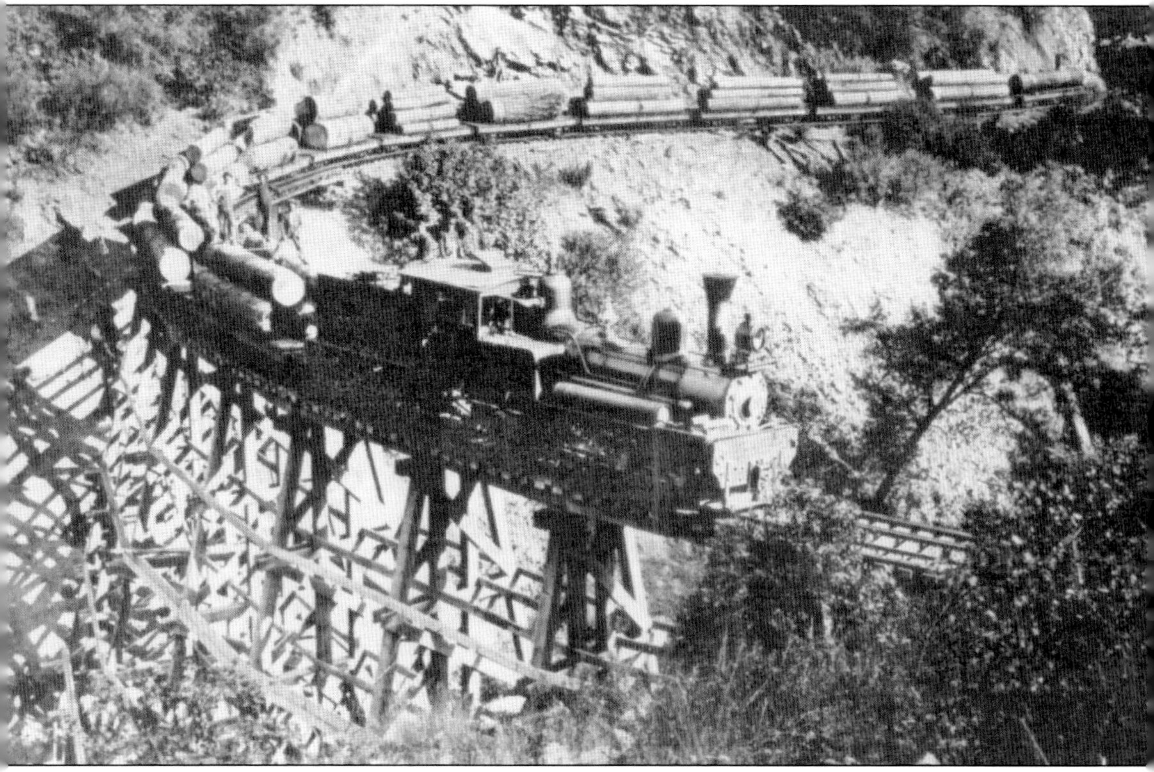

As West Side continued to grow, the demand for Tuolumne's timber products grew with it, as did the rail lines. By 1922, West Side's main line had expanded northeast to Bourland Creek, approximately five miles south of Pinecrest Lake and nine miles east-northeast from Tuolumne. At approximately 5,400 feet in elevation, the terrain in this region was exceptionally diverse, and trestles were built to cross the major bodies of water (three other notable trestles include the River Bridge on the North Fork of the Tuolumne, a trestle across the Clavey River, and one over Niagara Creek). The Bourland Trestle was one of the largest, soaring 76 feet above the creek bed and reaching 315 feet in length. Watchmen cabins were built at each trestle and manned by full-time West Side employees to ensure that no embers from the locomotives would set the wooden structures ablaze. The Bourland Trestle has shown remarkable resiliency; although severely damaged by a flood in 1997, it is one of only two surviving trestles in Northern California. Curious railroad enthusiasts should visit soon, though, as heavy high-elevation snows and water erosion are taking their toll on this wooden giant.

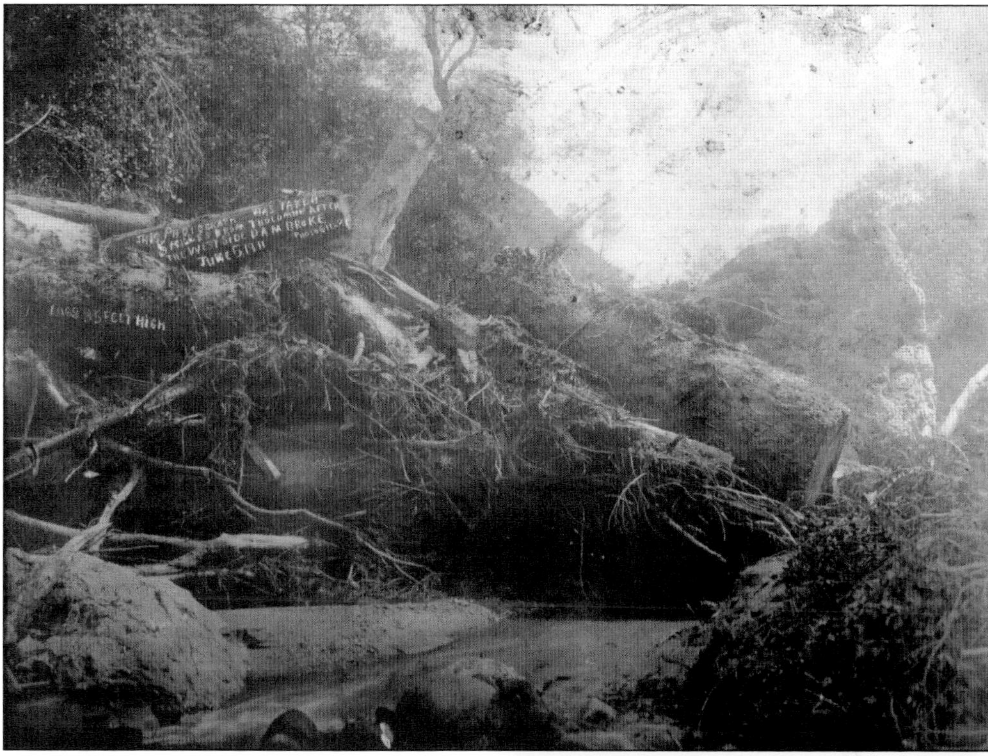

An integral part of the West Side Lumber Flume and Lumber Company was the millpond, which stored excess logs for processing during the snowy months, helping to keep the mill going year-round. The pond was not a natural creation; it was created by damming up Turnback Creek. On June 5, 1911, that dam broke and made quite a mess; this picture shows some of the carnage. These logs were strewn as far as five miles downstream and jammed 35 feet high in some places.

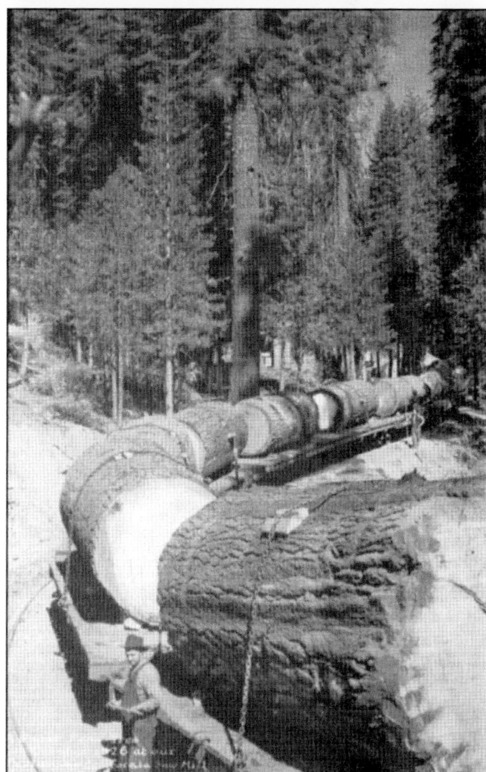

Another particularly large specimen of the forest meets its end and is shipped back to the mill for processing. This tree was a sugar pine, one of the most popular trees in the forests surrounding Tuolumne, and measured 226 feet high and over 50 inches in diameter, making it one of the larger trees harvested in 1926.

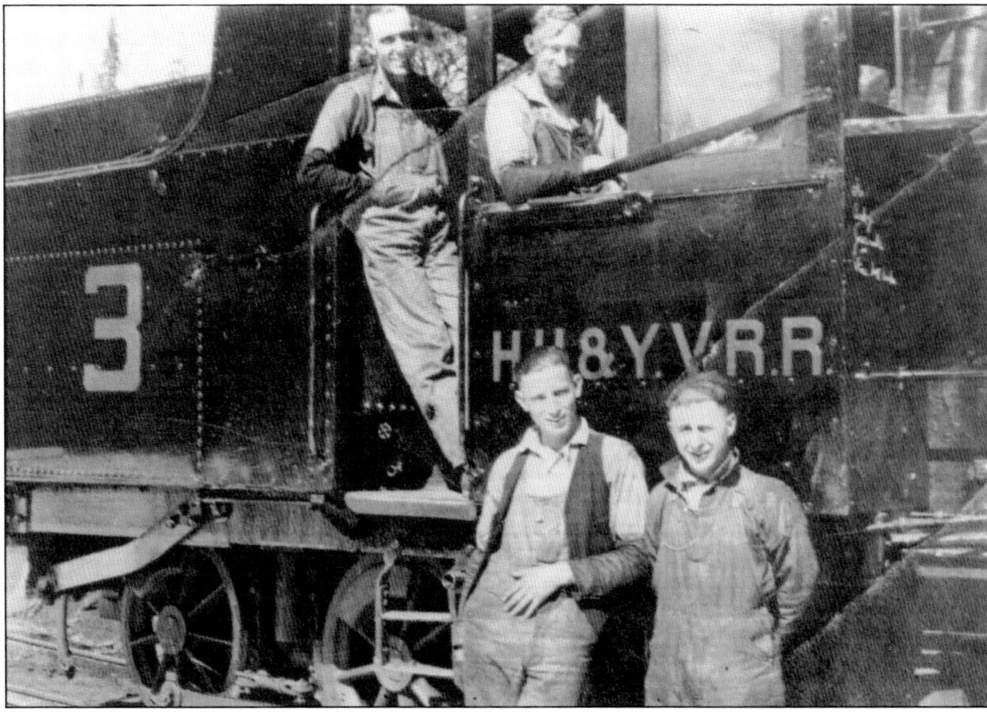

The crew of the Hetch Hetchy & Yosemite Valley Railroad Engine No. 3, a Heisler-built, two-truck locomotive, take a picture before heading off for a haul along the HH&YV line in about 1910. Built in 1900, Engine No. 3 saw a colorful life: it was converted from narrow gauge to standard gauge in 1947, only to be converted back to narrow gauge in 1962. It is currently operational at the Roaring Camp and Big Trees narrow-gauge tourist railroad that runs up steep terrain from Felton, California, to the top of nearby Bear Mountain.

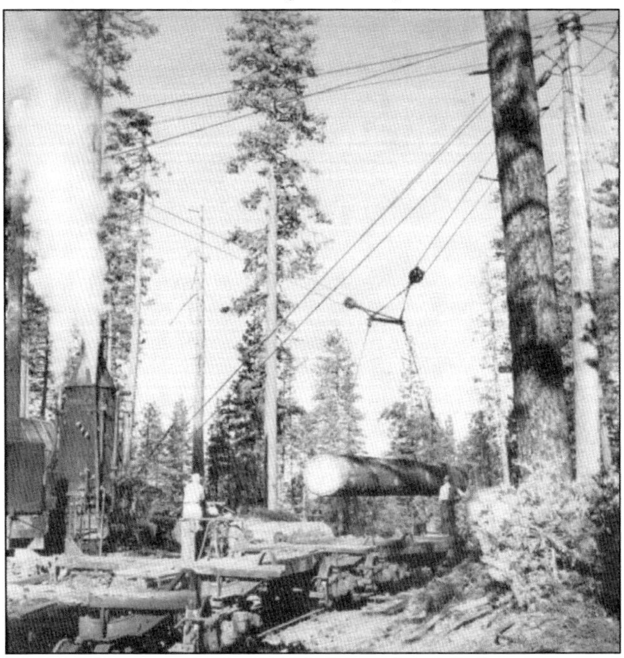

A West Side crew works a steam donkey hoist to load harvested logs onto a waiting railcar. The force of steam power and an elaborate system of pulleys allowed lumberjacks to not only haul fallen trees up the hillsides to the track, but also delicately place them on the cars for stacking and eventual shipment.

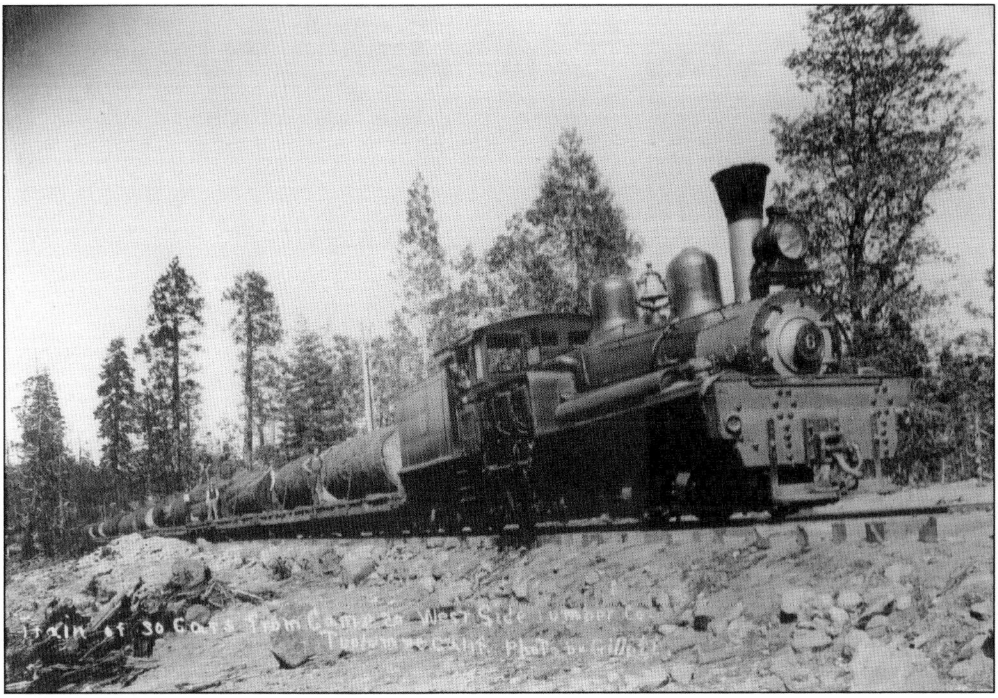

With its long line of 30 cars filled with logs and lumberjacks, West Side Engine No. 6 rolls in from logging camp 20 on its way back to Tuolumne. Engine No. 6 was a Lima-built, two-truck Shay that was completed in 1903.

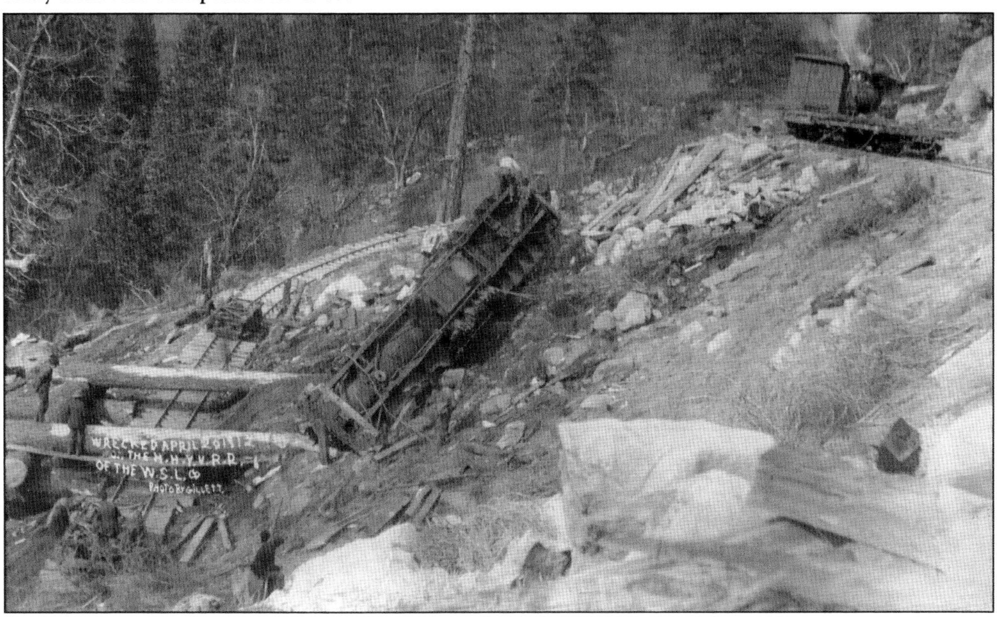

An engine on the treacherous Hetch Hetchy & Yosemite Valley Railroad took a spill down an embankment on April 20, 1912. Not only did the rough terrain play a factor in many of the HH&YV locomotive accidents, but a train's load was often over capacity, which inhibited maneuverability and increased the train's momentum. The need for quick expansion of the lines also often led to subpar rail work.

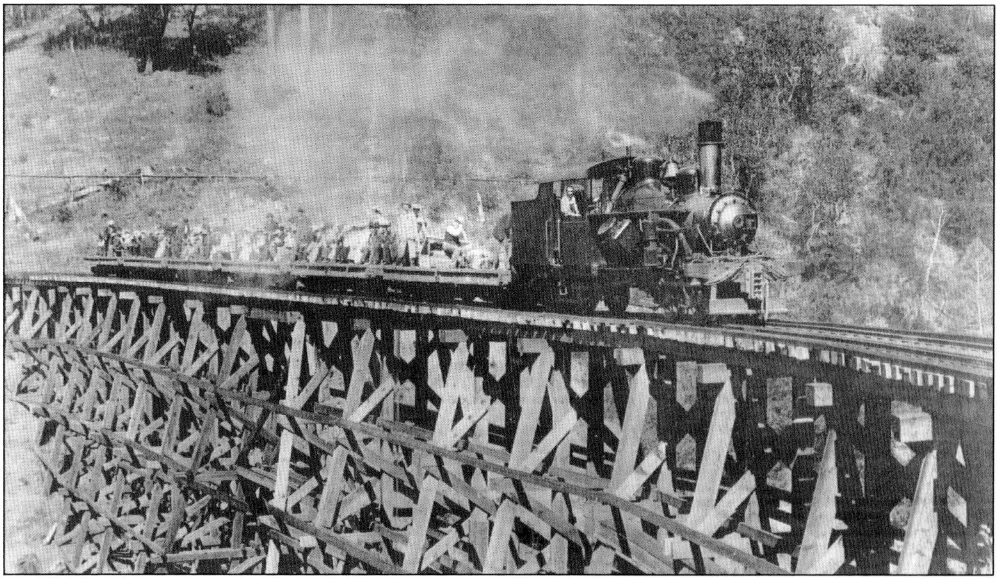

A group of passengers (including some of the original West Side Lumber Company owners) hitches a ride on this West Side Lumber Company engine to enjoy the breathtaking views afforded by the North Fork Trestle. At an elevation of over 5,400 feet, this line only operated from late spring (once the snows melted) to early fall (before the winter weather kicked in).

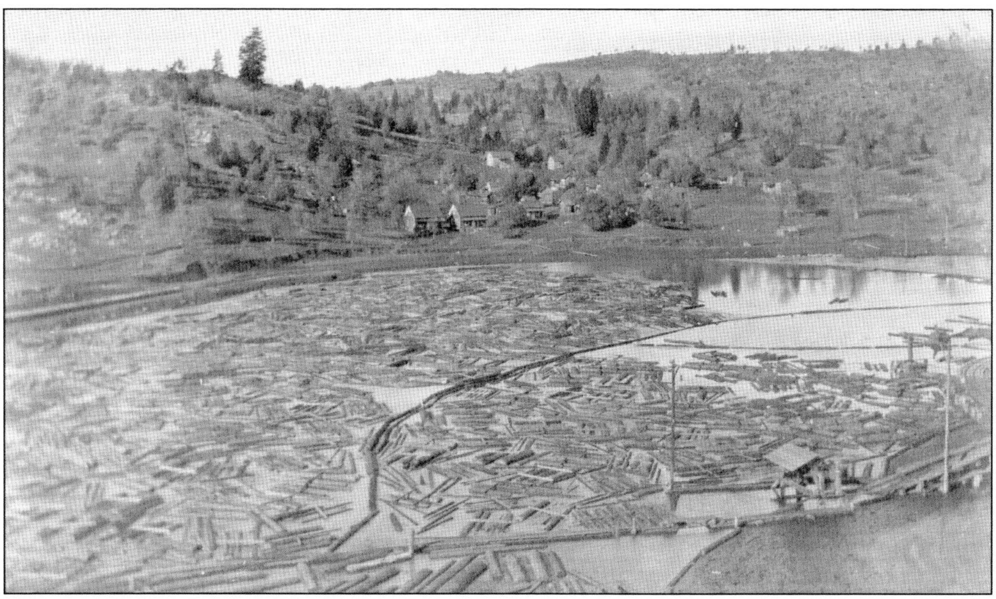

This bird's-eye view of the millpond (presumably taken from the top of the West Side office building looking west) offers a much better idea of the large size of the millpond. Created by damming Turnback Creek, it could hold hundreds of fully grown spruce, fir, cedar, and pine trees until they were ready to be processed.

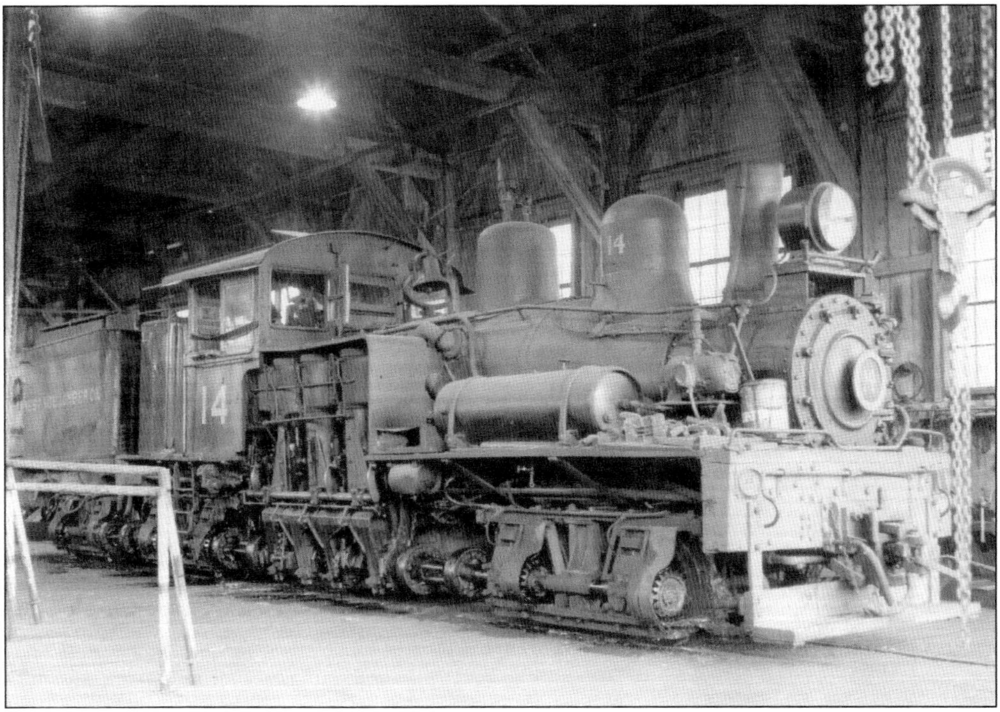

Pictured here docked in the Sierra Depot Railway Station in Tuolumne for regularly scheduled maintenance and repairs, West Side Lumber Company Engine No. 14 was built in 1916. A Lima-manufactured, three-truck Shay, it, like Engine No. 9, remained active on the Georgetown Loop after West Side shut down. It is currently on display at the Colorado Railroad Museum in Golden, Colorado.

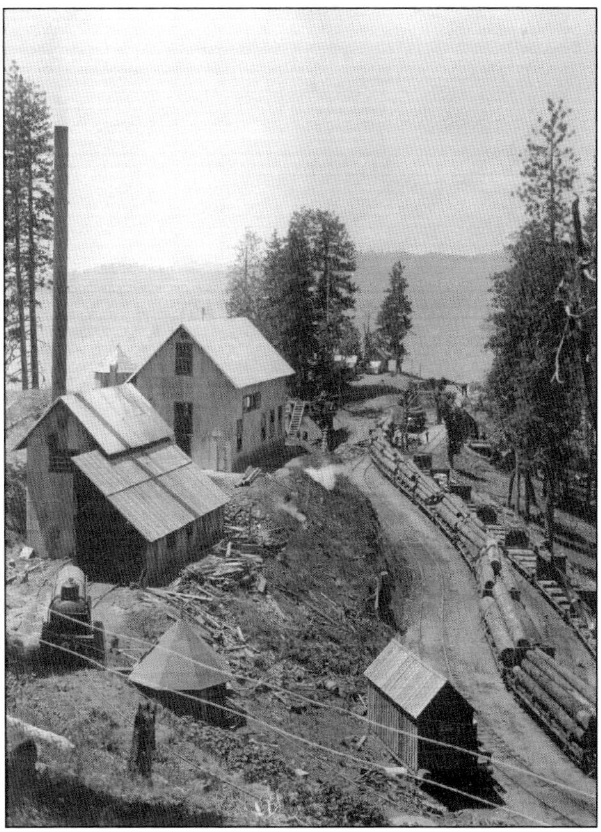

Camp 20, one of the busier logging camps along the West Side tracks, contained several buildings, many of which housed the West Side employees who lived deeper in the forest during the warmer months. Rusted steam donkeys and the remnants of these camps can still be found along hiking trails.

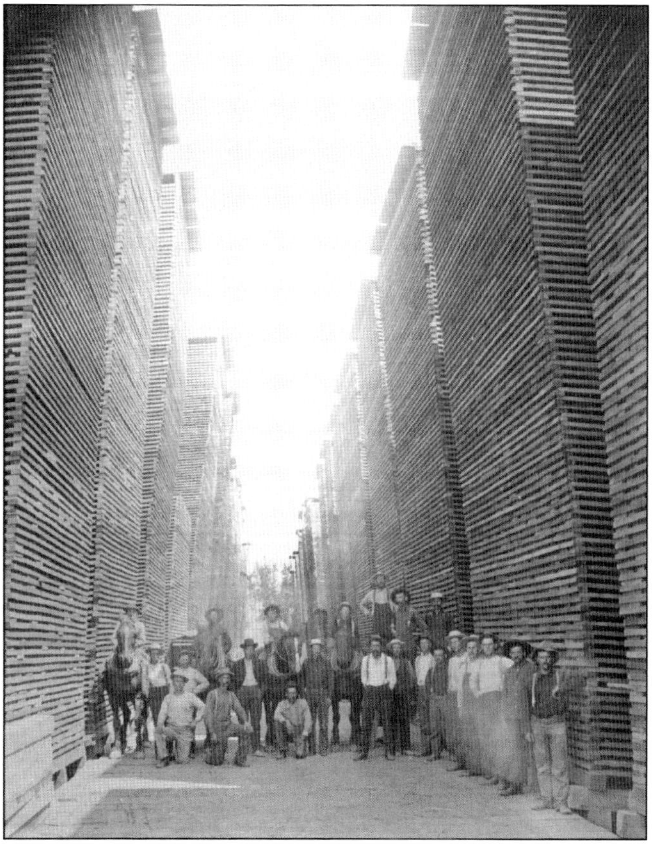

In this c. 1910 photograph, West Side employees stand amidst the massive Sonora Drying Yard, located northwest of the mill. The sheets and boards of raw timber were stacked as high as 50 feet to air dry before being shipped off to hardware stores across the country. Each stack pictured here is comprised of 25,000 board feet of lumber.

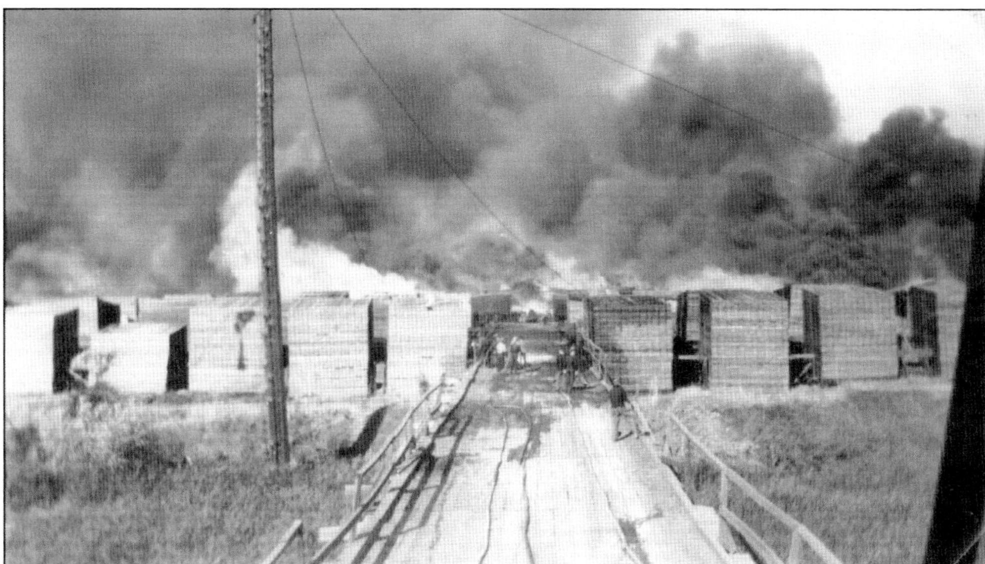

Fire was always a danger with so much timber, as evidenced in this photograph from the drying yard. Thankfully, these stacks of timber were not as high as 50 feet, but these flare-ups were all too common and wreaked havoc on the lumber mill. This photograph shows the Sonora Drying Yard fire of 1936, which was spread by the Mono Winds all the way through neighboring Standard.

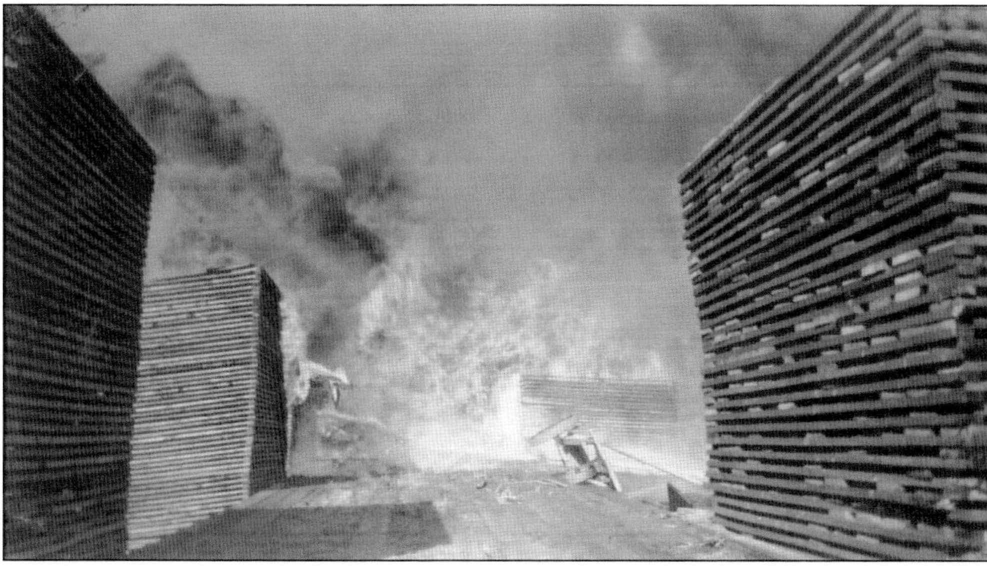

Because of the way that the boards and sheets were stacked, with just enough air between each layer to allow for evaporation, spark-ups quickly ate through the drying yard, costing West Side thousands of dollars in lost inventory. This image is also of the 1936 Sonora Yard fire, which was finally stopped at Sullivan Creek.

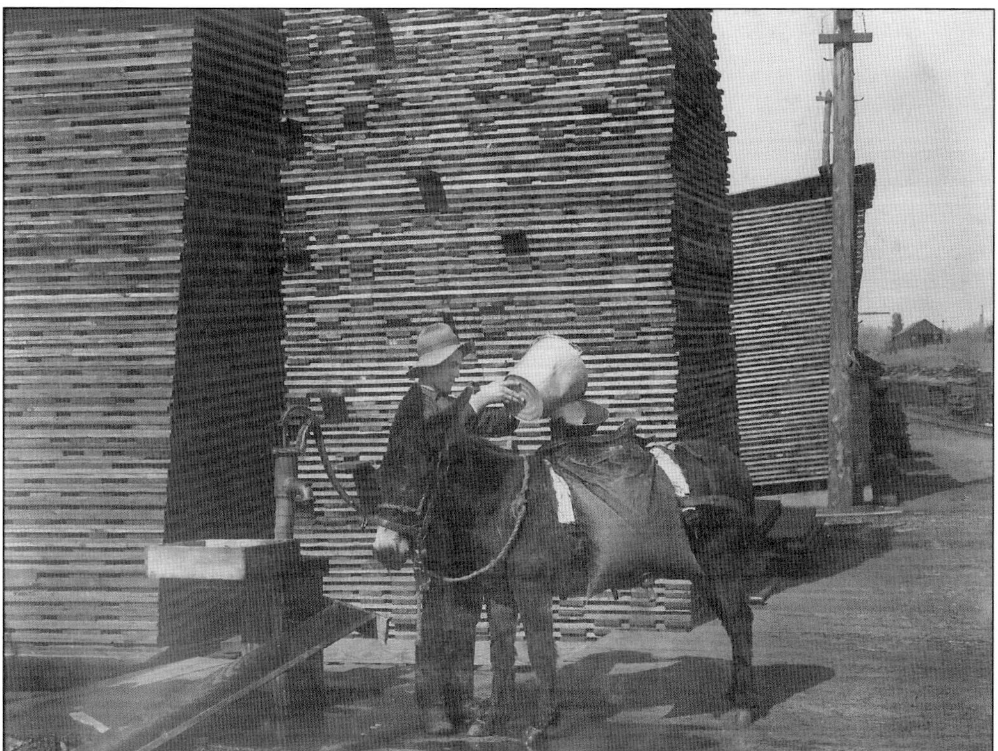

A West Side water boy loads water bags for the day's work ahead and places them on Tuolumne's reliable beast of burden, the burro. The slow, hand-operated well pumps were often all workers and firefighters had to douse flames.

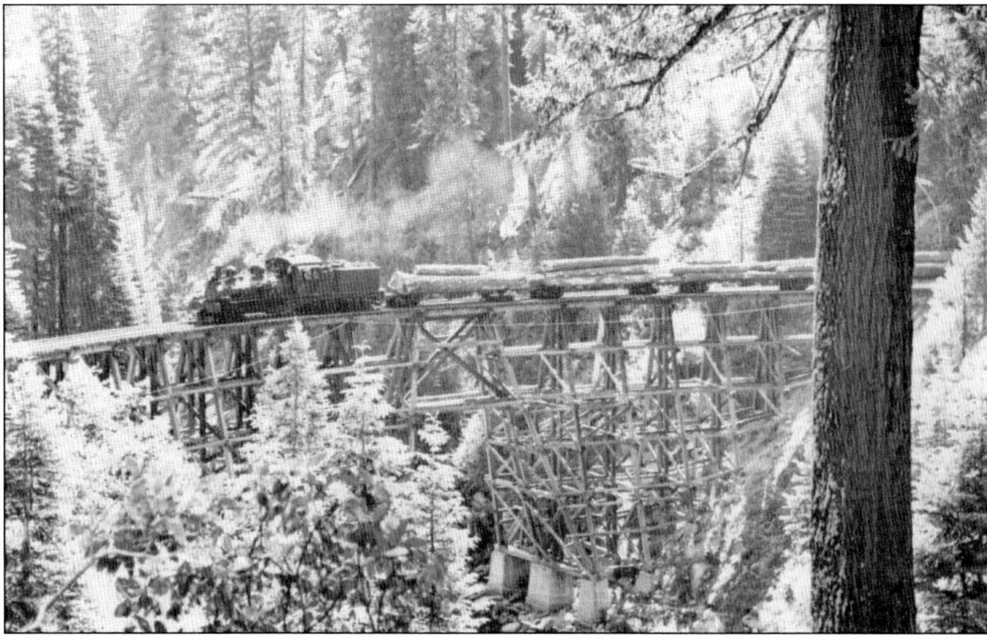

Along with the Bourland Trestle, the trestle bridge over the Clavey River was one of the more awe-inspiring (and nerve-wracking) routes for the West Side Lumber trains. A tributary of the Tuolumne River, the Clavey River is unique in that it runs north-south along the west slope of the Sierra Nevada. It is home to amazing swimming holes and some of the most pure, pristine water in the state.

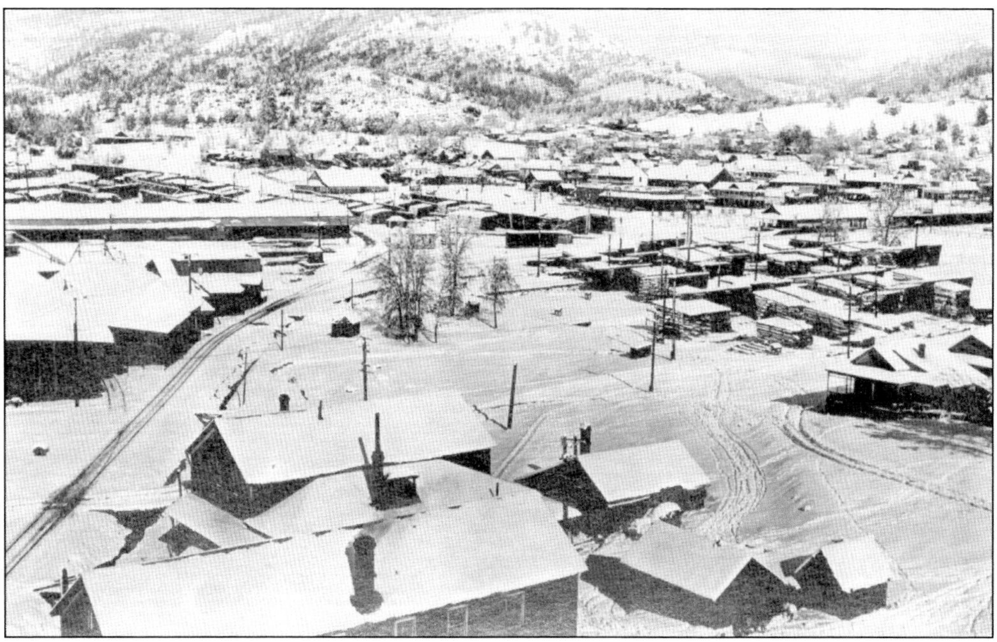

Snow on the ground was (and continues to be) a common sight in Tuolumne, and the West Side mill did not take snow days; it operated through the winter. Although it was generally slower than the peak summer seasons, mill workers and lumberjacks alike stayed busy during the colder months by processing the raw logs stored in the millpond.

An interior shot of the West Side mill and main log saw sheds a bit of light on how the log-to-lumber process operated. Logs came into the mill on the main conveyor belt before rolling down and being stopped by a set of massive claws, which then fed them into the main saw one by one.

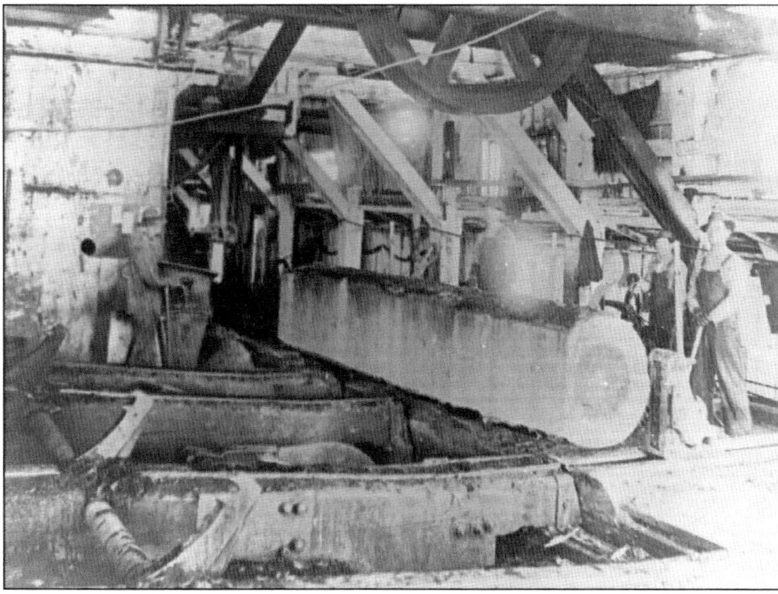

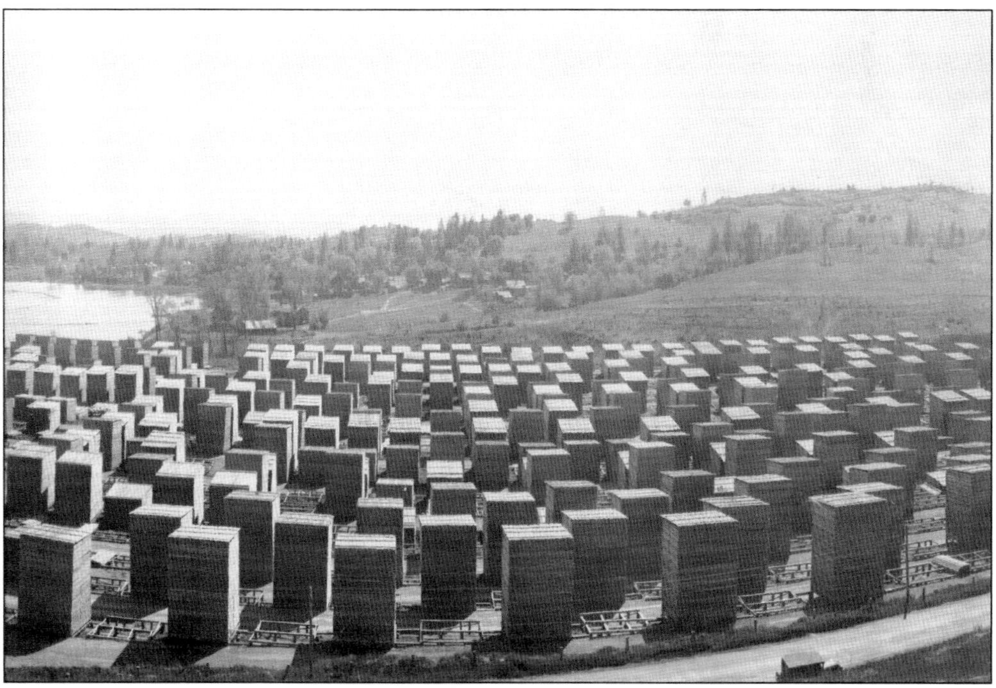

The sheer amount of raw lumber that West Side was capable of churning out was mind-boggling, as shown in this wide-angle shot of the drying yard. At its zenith—from the 1920s through the 1950s—West Side was one of the most productive and active lumber mills in the state.

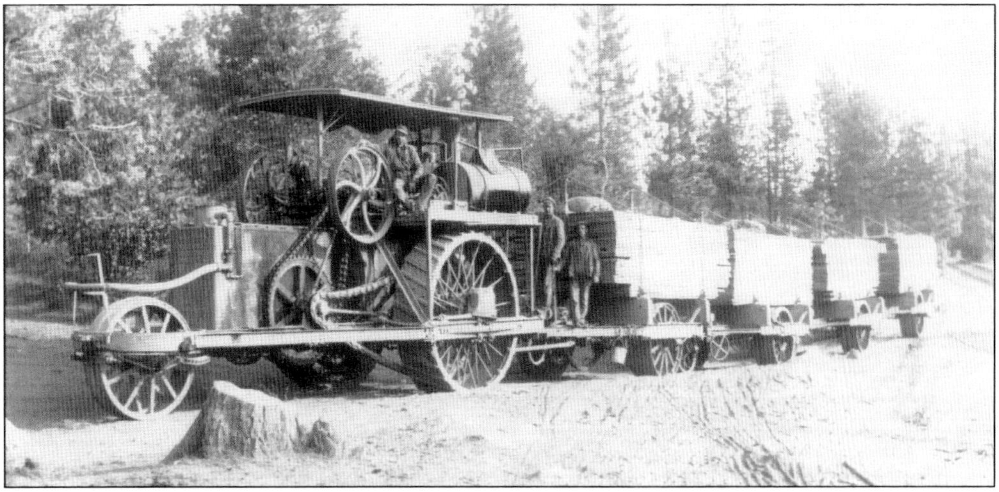

This unique three-wheeled vehicle (seen here near Confidence) was an early tractor used for short-distance supply in areas where tracks had not yet been laid. Driven by steam, these contraptions were exceptionally useful in ferrying supplies from the tracks to the logging camps and vice versa.

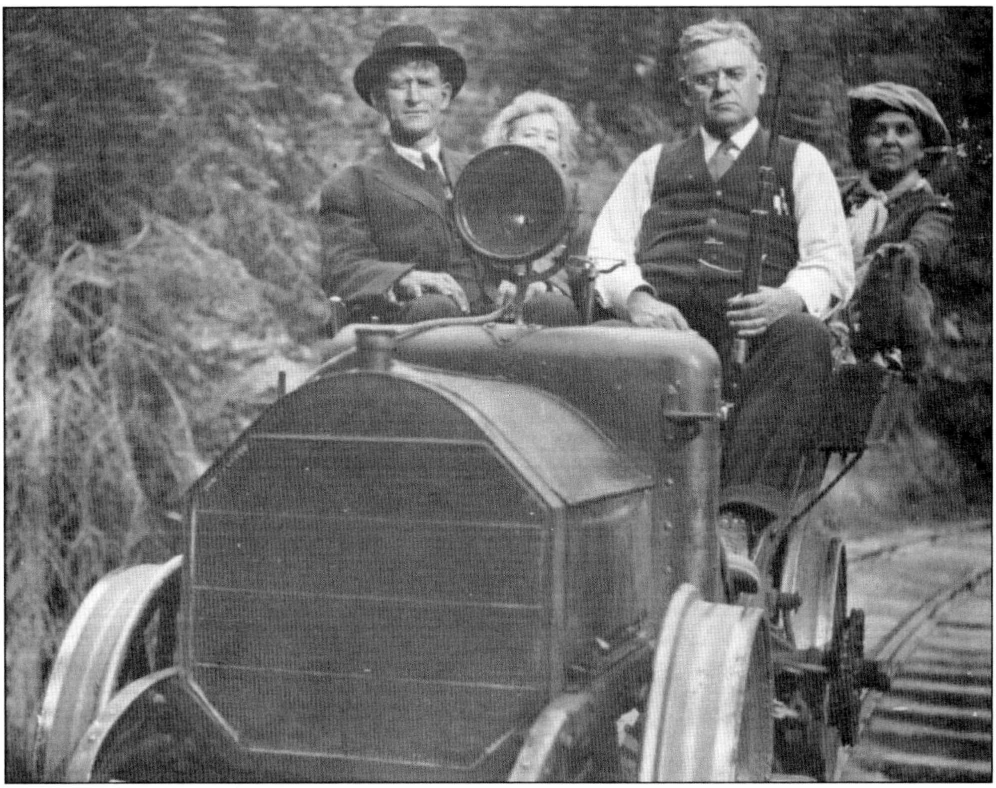

A railroad inspection car with a full crew rumbles along a section of West Side track in this photograph from 1910. Inspection cars played an important role in the development of West Side tracks. Chief among their responsibilities was inspecting the sometimes hastily laid narrow-gauge tracks for defects, since these were (and continue to be) the leading cause of railway accidents. Here, Supt. William Hanlon waits on a siding for a train to clear by, while escorting Mrs. J.R. Prince and Dr. Frank Nourse and his wife on a hunting trip.

The depot plaza in New Town, as it was initially known after West Side's completion, was a busy place with trains of all sorts coming and going. The standard-gauge line for passenger trains tied in here with lines to Jamestown and further into the Central Valley, as well as narrow-gauge lines for logging locomotives.

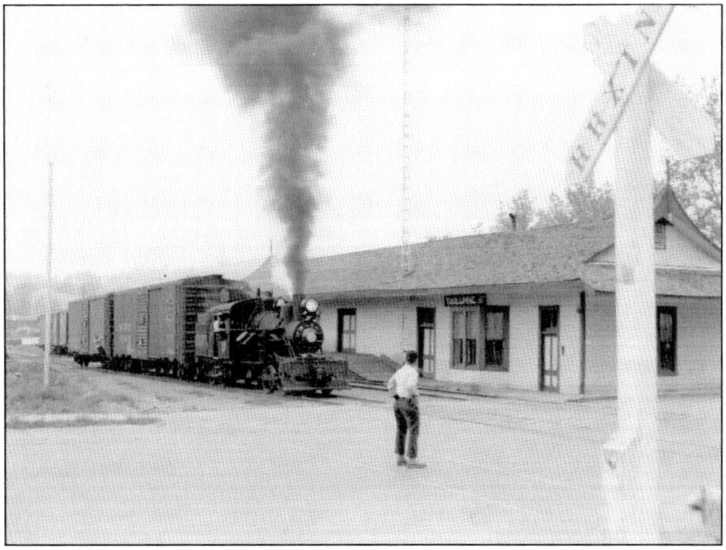

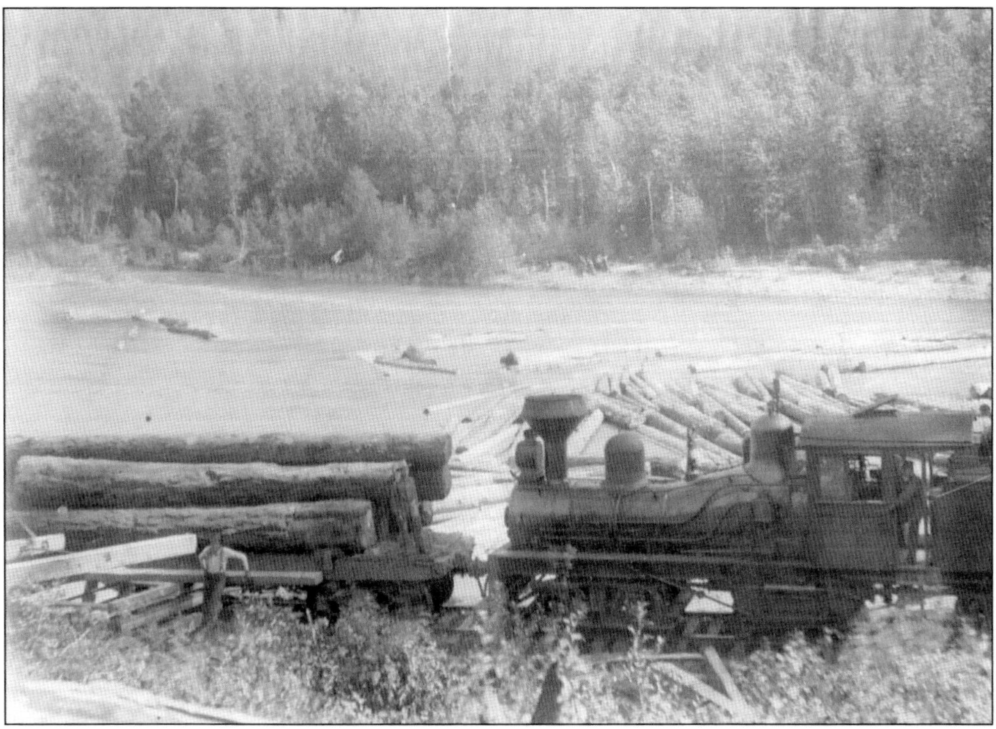

The track in the mill plaza circled around the millpond, offering easy access, although all logs were deposited at the main drop-off point near the dam, just off frame to the left. In this c. 1900 photograph, a locomotive pushes a flatbed car filled with logs down the track.

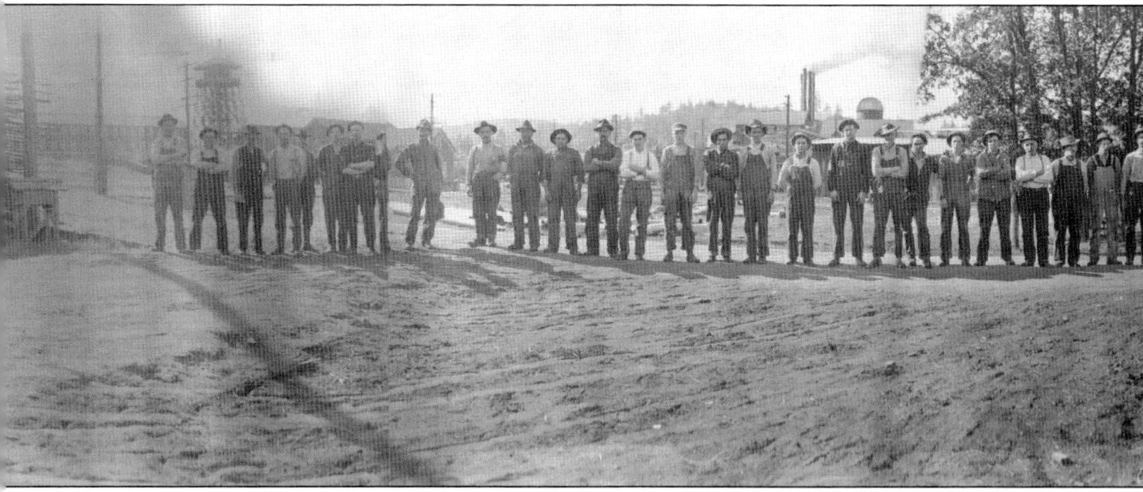

This panorama photograph of the West Side Flume and Lumber Company, taken sometime after 1900 when the mill was completed, shows dozens, but not nearly all, of the West Side employees. The mill was far and away the largest driving force behind Tuolumne's growth from a remote

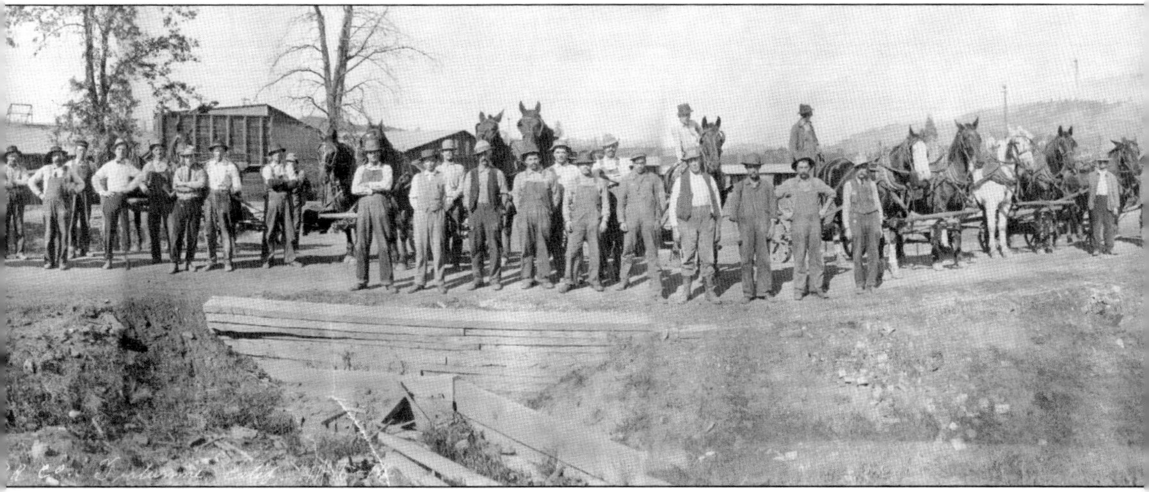

frontier outpost nestled in the foothills to an established and thriving community, and it would continue to fuel the town's economy until its closure in 1960 (the era between World War II and the closing of the mill is colloquially known as Tuolumne's golden age). At its height, the mill employed over 1,500 people.

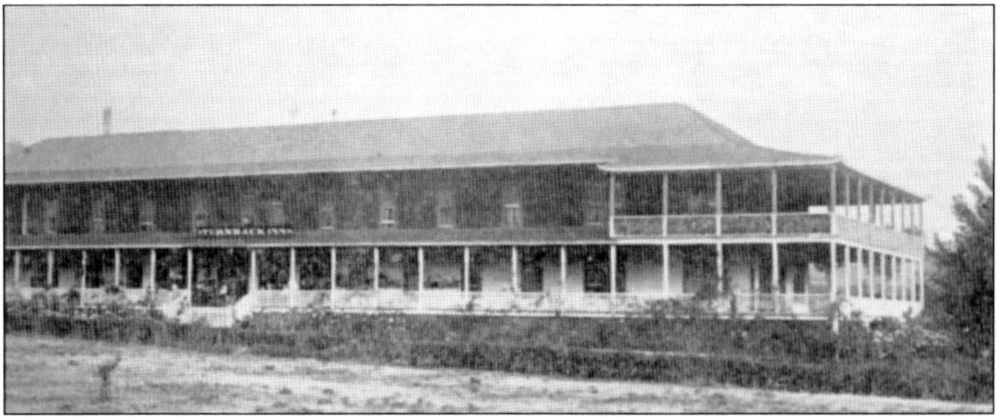

The Turnback Inn, which opened in 1901, was one of the most lavish resorts in Northern California at the time. The opulent two-story inn, located at the present-day intersection of Fir Avenue and Main Street (where the Memorial Hall is today), was originally designed and marketed as a gateway resort for tourists who had traveled considerable distances to stop over and rest before heading into nearby Yosemite National Park via the railroad depot, which was just a short walk from the inn. Sadly, the Turnback Inn was lost to fire in 1924.

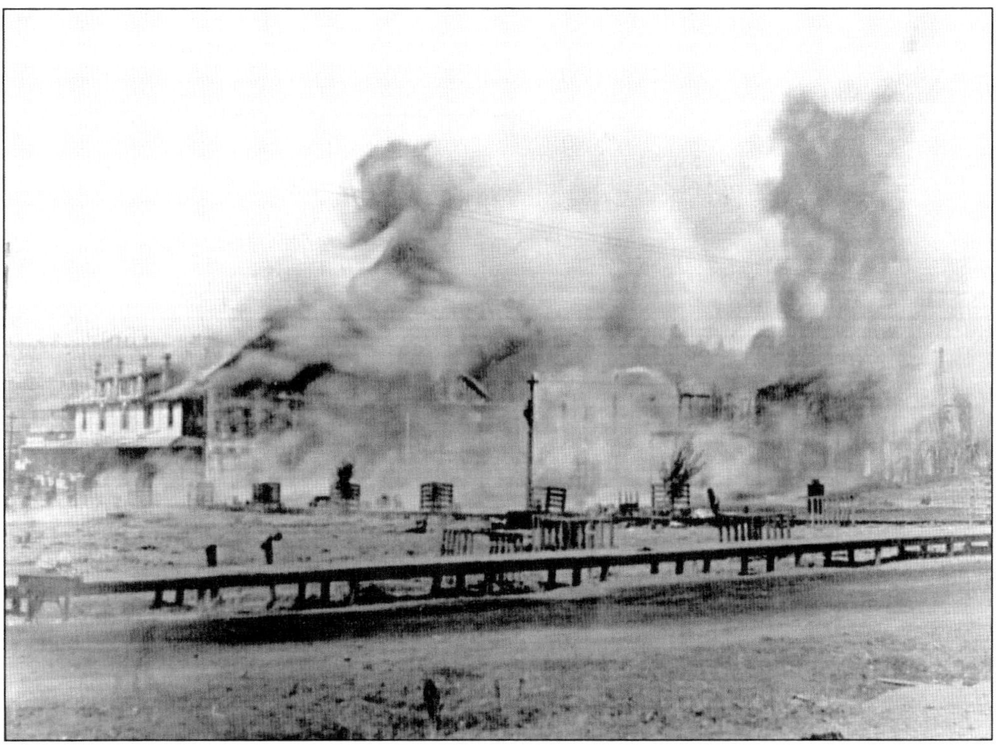

The West Side main office building was lost to fire in October 1902. It was rebuilt and changed locations; the old building was located on the corner of present-day Pine Street and Fir Avenue. This picture of the 1902 fire is the last photograph ever taken of the building.

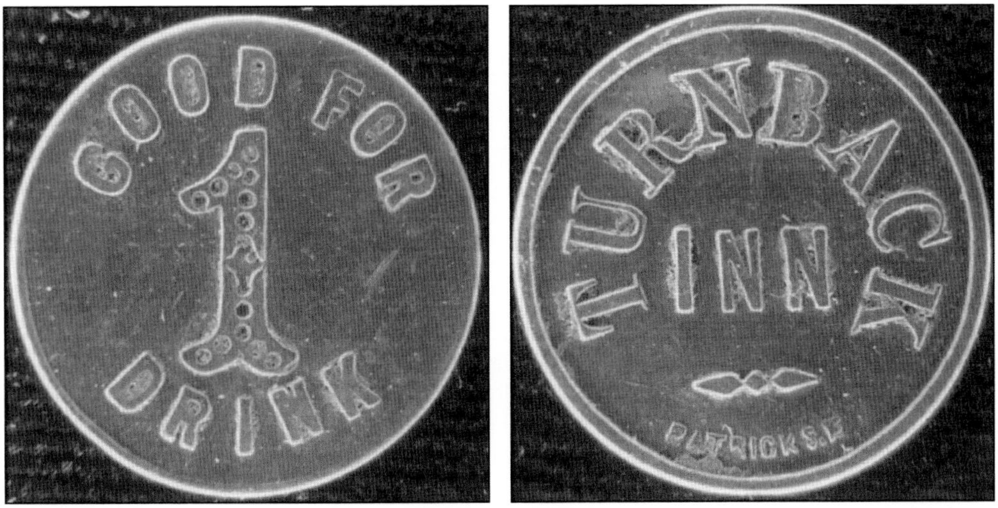

These drink tokens, given to patrons of the Turnback Inn, were good for one drink. Drink tokens could be bought for cash but were more commonly given away to locals to lure them in for one free drink and then loosen them up to buy several more.

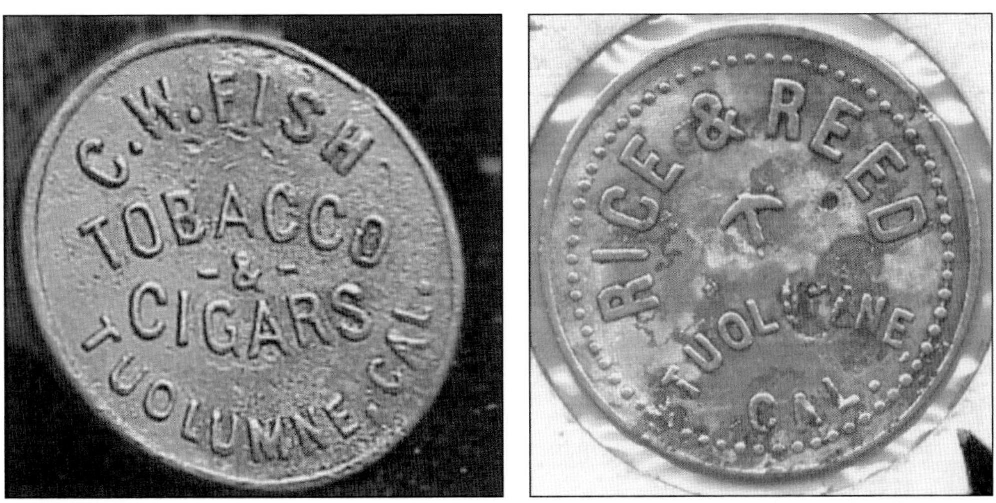

Other businesses besides hotels gave out tokens as well—as souvenirs. At left is a token from C.W. Fish Tobacco and Cigars, which was located on Main Street before the buildings on the block burned down, and at right is one from Rice and Reed Supply.

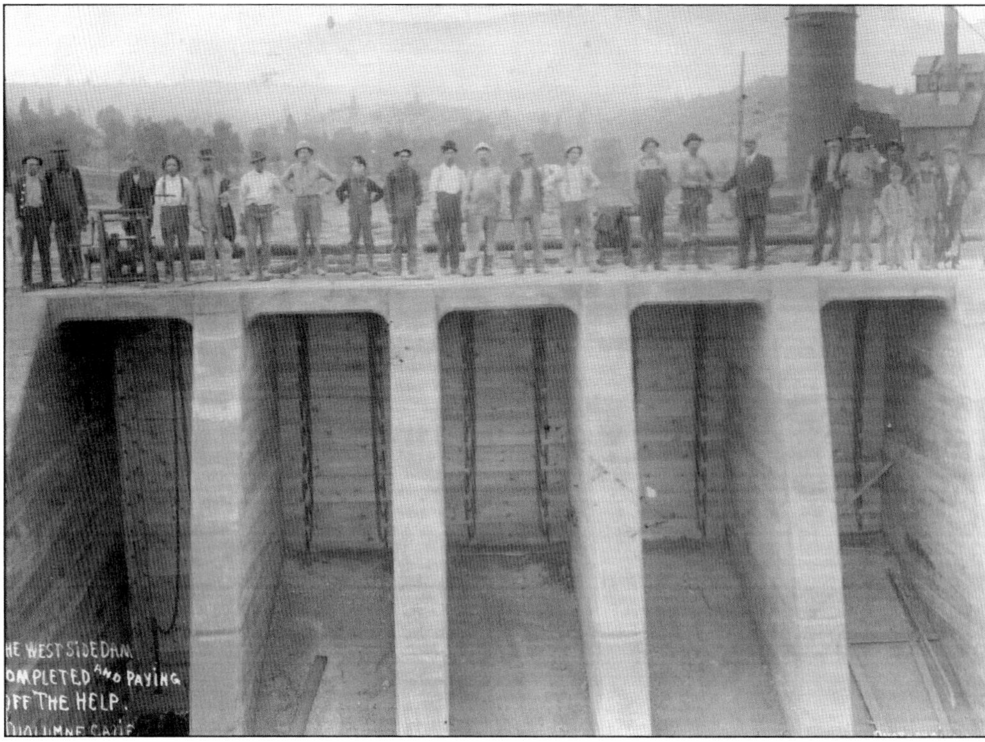

This picture shows the newly completed West Side Dam, constructed with both concrete and wood, with the proud employees atop it. This Turnback Creek dam formed the millpond that stored excess logs. The silo and mill facility are visible in the background at right. This dam gave way in 1911.

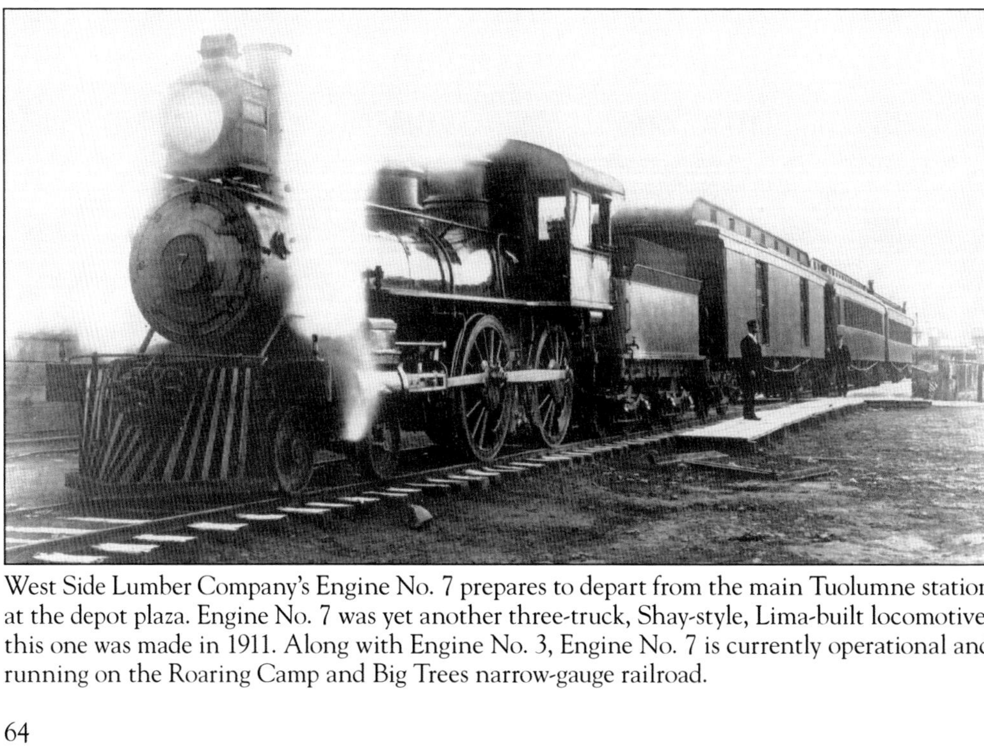
West Side Lumber Company's Engine No. 7 prepares to depart from the main Tuolumne station at the depot plaza. Engine No. 7 was yet another three-truck, Shay-style, Lima-built locomotive; this one was made in 1911. Along with Engine No. 3, Engine No. 7 is currently operational and running on the Roaring Camp and Big Trees narrow-gauge railroad.

Three

LIFE AROUND TOWN

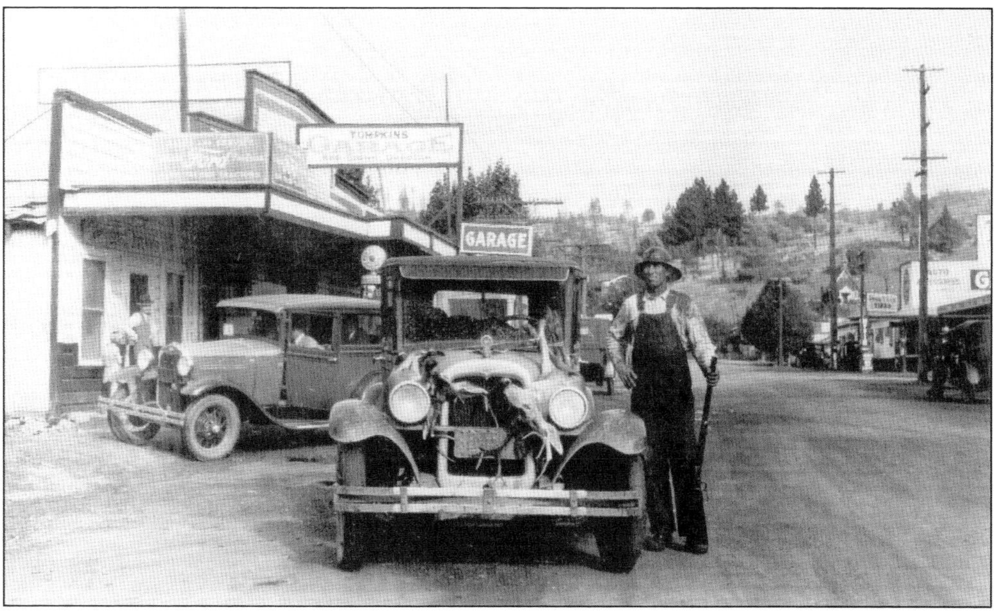

The folks of Tuolumne were (and continue to be) hardworking citizens who spend the day toiling away, first in the mines and then at the mill or in the forest; perhaps this is why Tuolumne is also known for cutting loose, having a good time, and celebrating. Here, a proud hunter displays two freshly killed bucks on the hood of his car. Deer are the most popular game animal in Tuolumne and the surrounding woods.

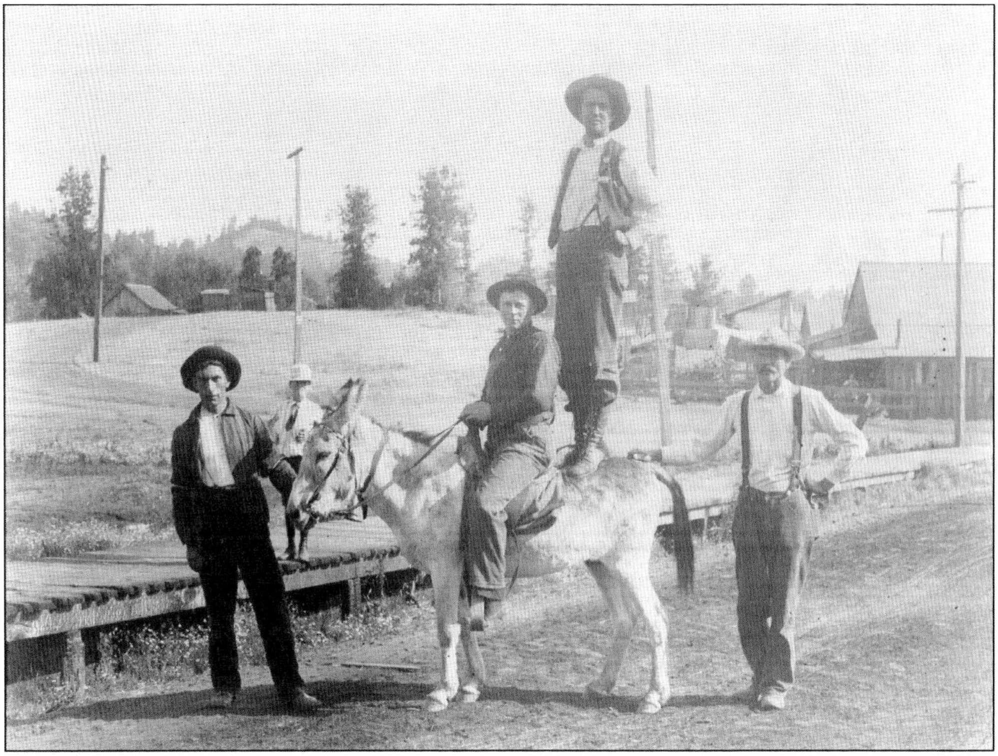

Burros, which became somewhat of a nuisance because of overbreeding and being left behind by miners in the gold-rush days, continued to be a viable means of conveyance for Tuolumne citizens through the 1940s. Some acrobatic men posed for this picture around 1920.

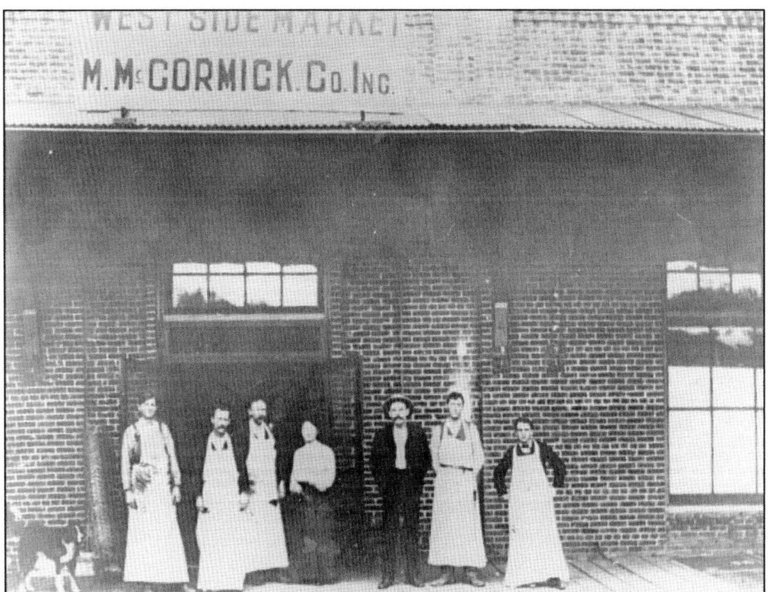

Not only did the West Side Market offer goods and services to West Side employees, it also served as the de facto grocery store in Tuolumne for many years. This 1905 picture shows a group of employees.

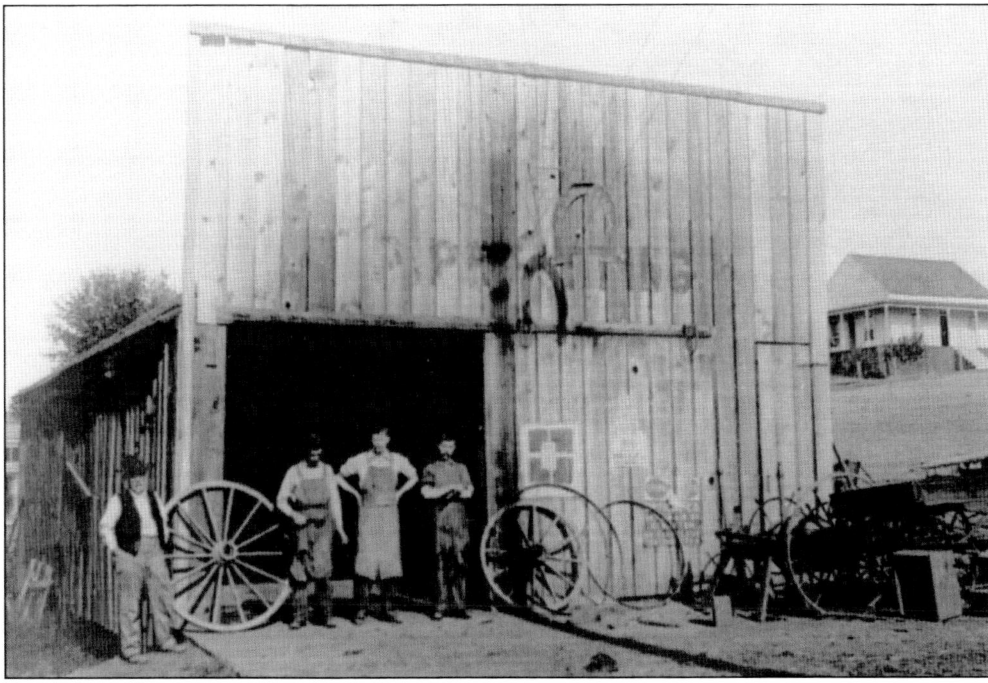

The Mullins' blacksmith shop, seen here in about 1910 and located on Carter Street, was Tuolumne's go-to place for any metal or woodworking needs. During the town's early years, the majority of Mullins' work involved casting and repairing wagon wheels for horse-drawn carriages, as seen in this image.

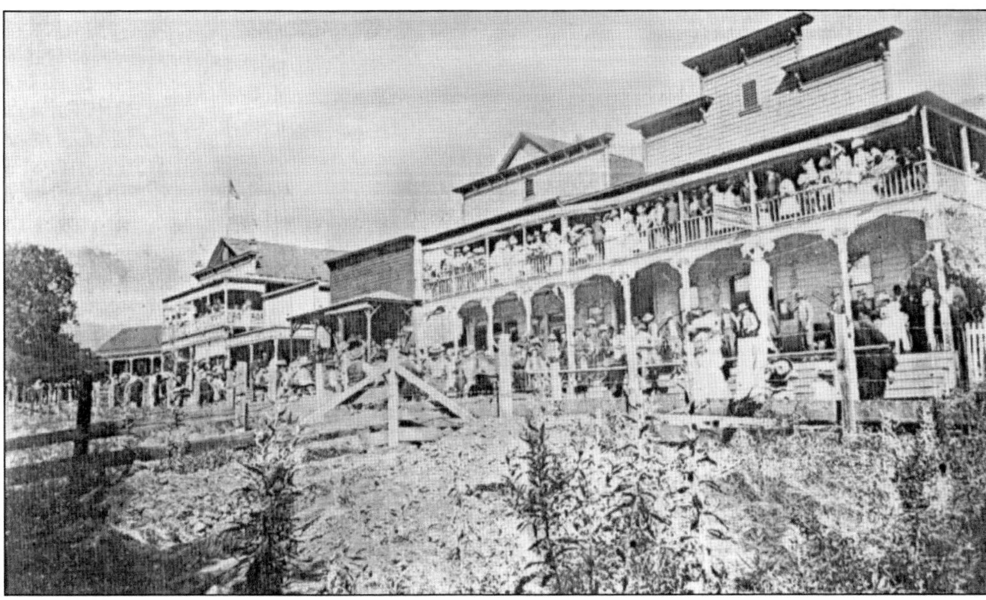

Before the construction of the Turnback Inn, the Summersville Hotel was the preeminent lodging for visitors to Summersville (as it was known in 1901, when this picture was taken). Like many of the area's early wooden buildings, the Summersville Hotel was lost to fire in 1905.

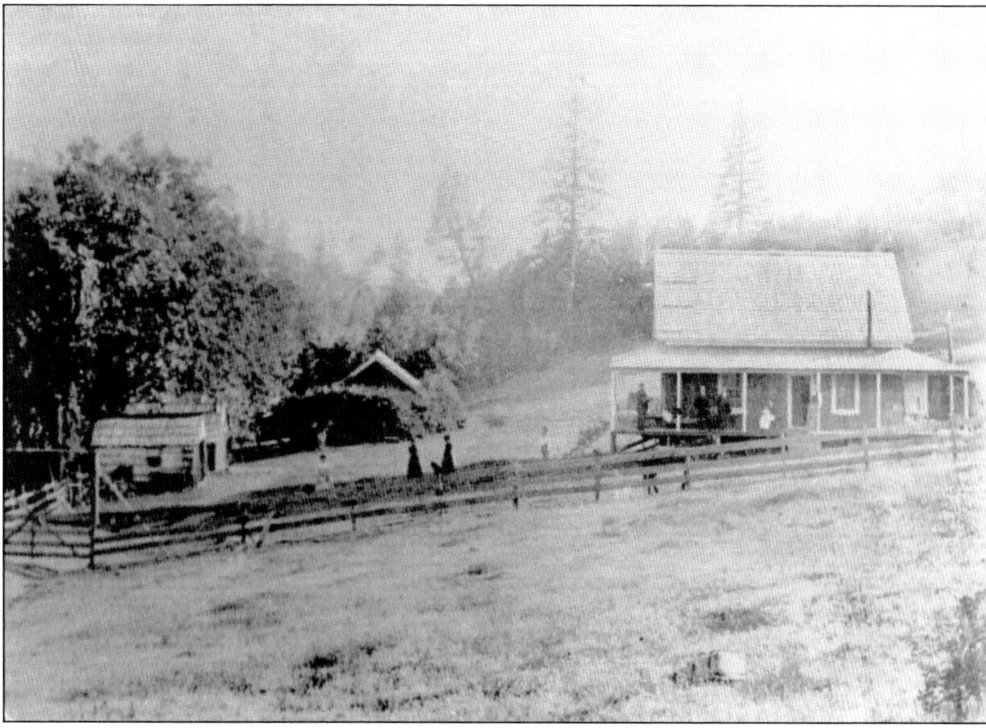

The Long Gulch Dairy Farm, located about a half mile north of town near present-day Mount Eaton Road off of Apple Colony Road, offered access to fresh milk and also made regular deliveries to town. It derived its name from the nearby settlement of Long Gulch, which predated even Carters.

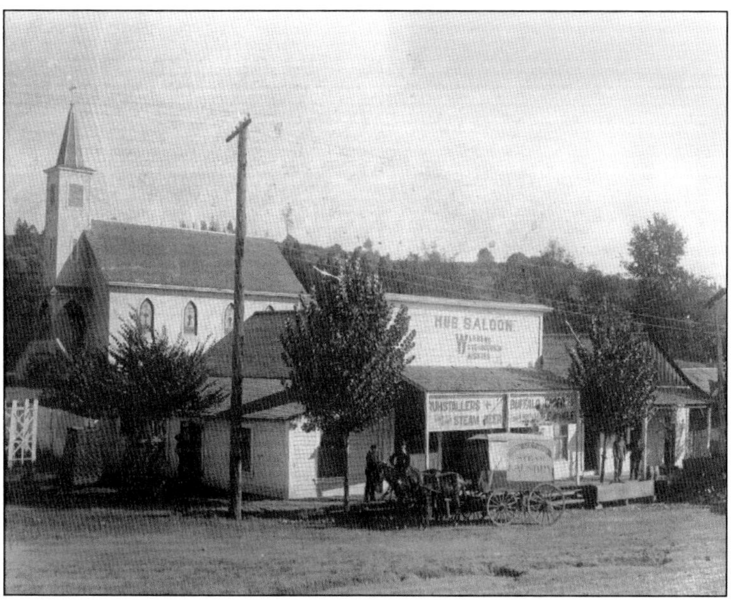

In an interesting example of juxtaposition, the Hub Saloon was located just a stone's throw from St. Joseph's Catholic Church, which is clearly visible in the background. The Hub Saloon was a popular watering hole that offered a variety of beer and spirits. In later years, the popular Tuolumne Frosty was located in this spot at the corner of Carter Street and Gardner Avenue.

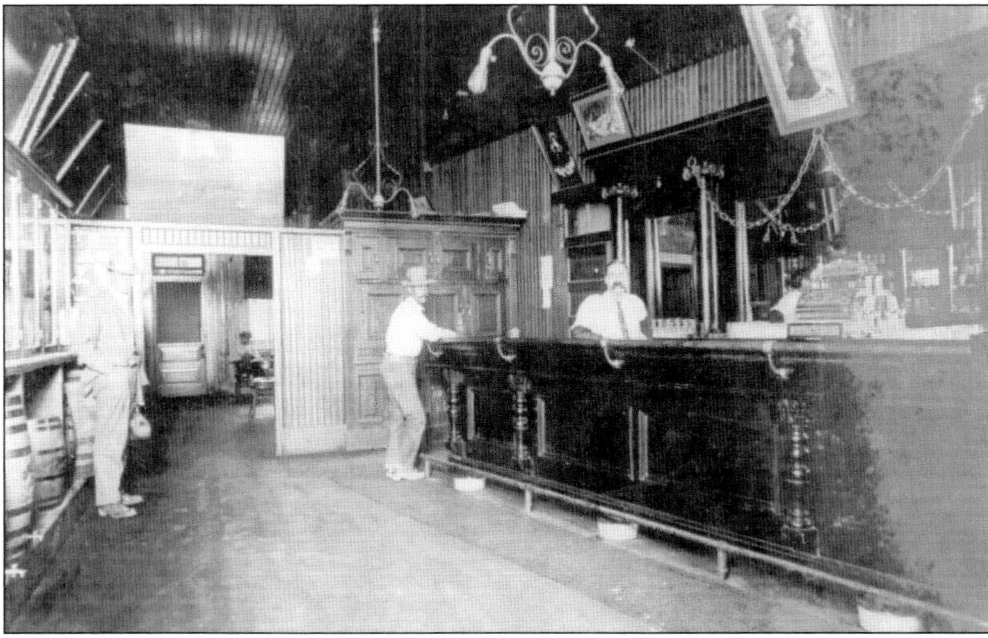

The interior of the Hub Saloon was simple, as with most bars and saloons of the early 20th century. Bars in Tuolumne, from the Hub to the Turnback Inn to Nick's and later businesses such as The Logger's and The Club, were some of the more popular social gathering places and remained so throughout Prohibition.

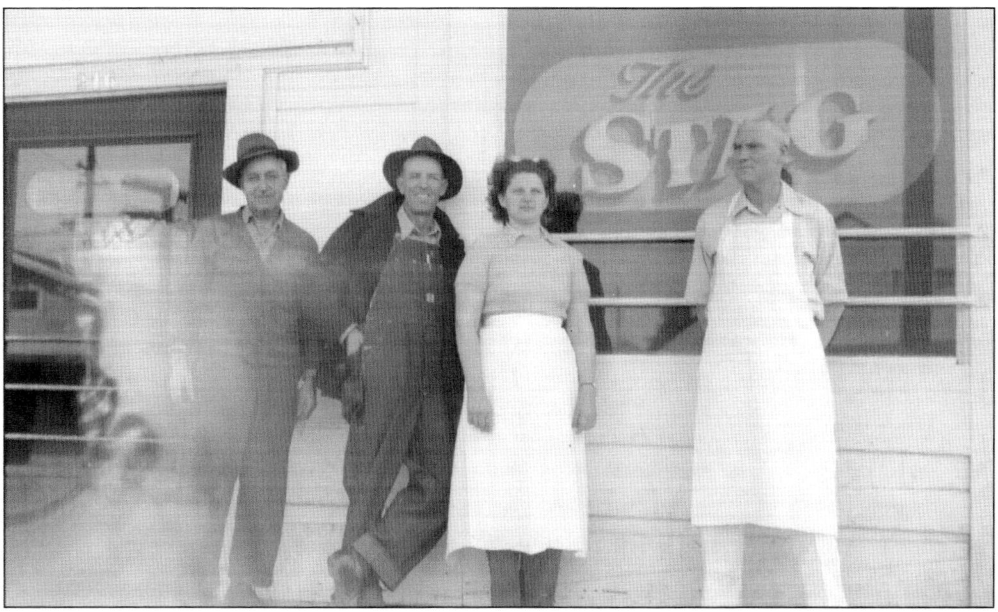

The Stag, located on present-day Chestnut Avenue between Pine and Main Streets, was a well-liked and long-lasting Tuolumne café that served patrons a wide variety of food and beverages. Although it changed ownership and names several times, it eventually turned into The Club, one of the more popular bars in Tuolumne County during the 1970s. Pictured here from left to right are an unidentified man, "Hap" Handy, Eleanor Carmack (who cooked at the café), and another unidentified man, also a cook.

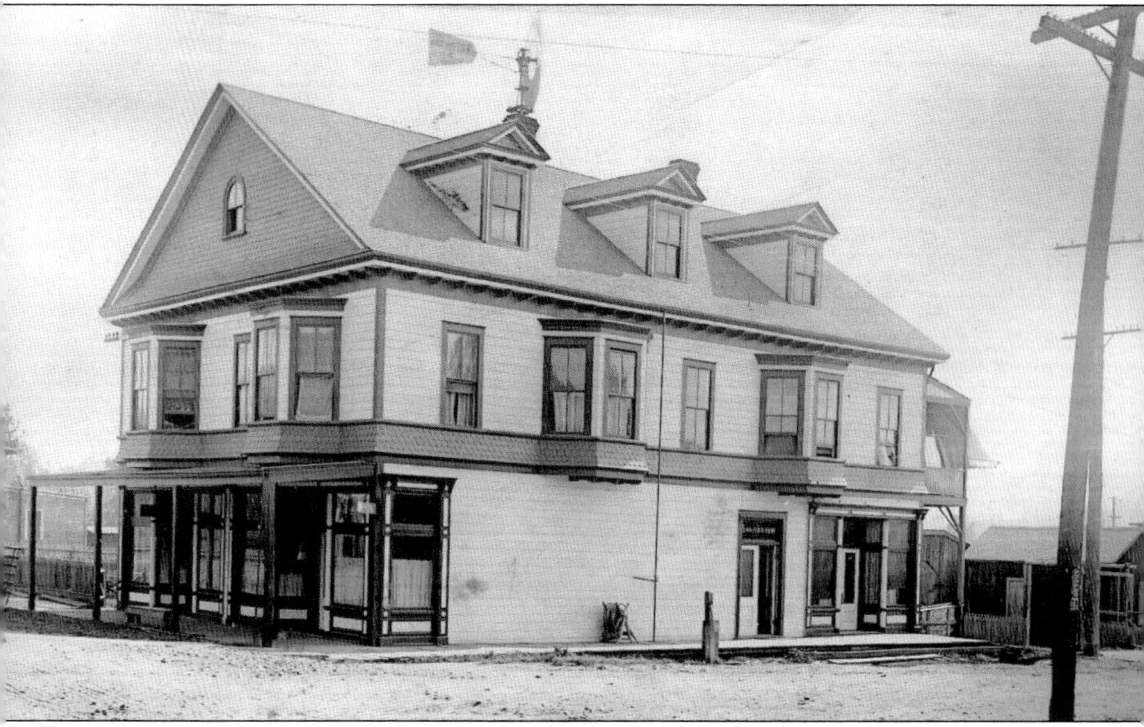

Dr. Eugene H. Reid's three-story sanitarium was arguably the best-known building in Tuolumne. An 1897 graduate of the Kentucky School of Medicine of Louisville, Reid completed his post-graduate studies in New York before moving to Madera, California, in 1901. He served as the physician and surgeon for the Sugar Pine Lumber Company for five years before moving to Tuolumne and setting up his private practice. The corner lot on Carter Street and Bay Street where the sanitarium once stood is now a simple grassy park appropriately dubbed Reid Park.

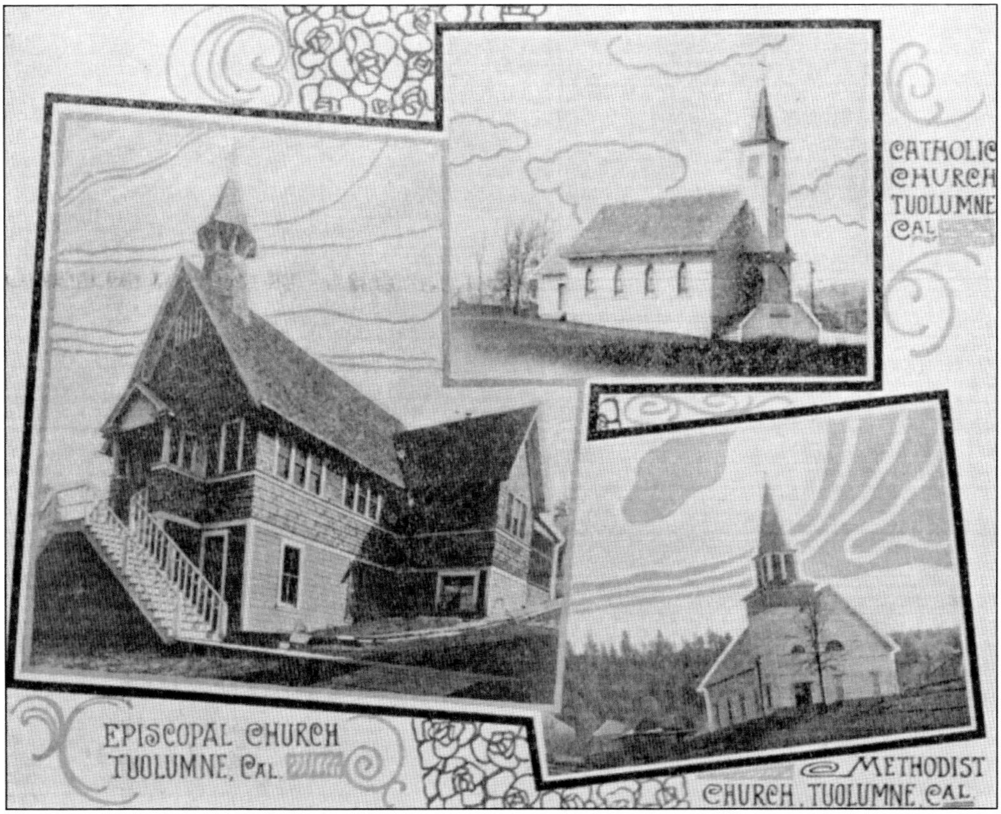

Worship and faith have always played a large part in day-to-day life in Tuolumne. This c. 1910 flyer shows the three churches this small town built in its infancy: the Catholic church (St. Joseph's) on Gardner Avenue, St. Michael's Episcopal Church on Cedar Street, and the Methodist church on Baker Avenue. All three are still standing today, although the Methodist church has been significantly rebuilt. St. Joseph's was built 1908, St. Michael's in 1901, and the Methodist church in 1902.

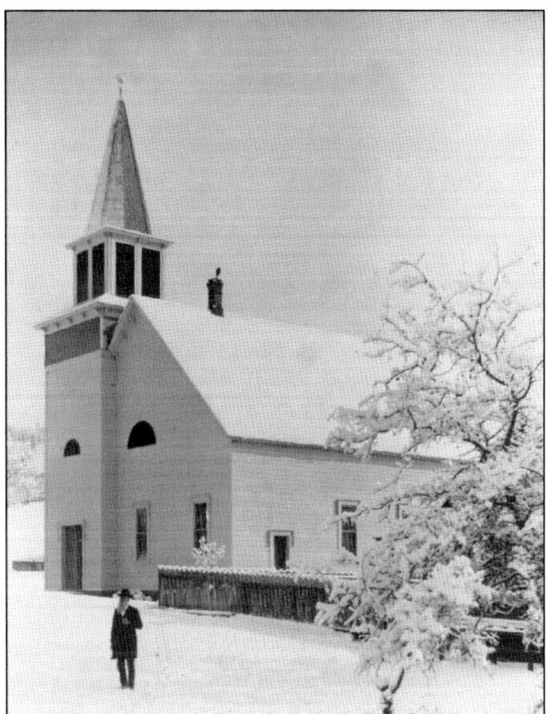

Standing in front of the Methodist church, one of the first houses of worship built in the town site, is C.H. Carter, who donated the land on which the church was built in 1902. The church burned to the ground after a flue fire during worship services on October 31, 1952. A new concrete block church was built on the same site in 1954 after several years of fundraising by the community and the congregation.

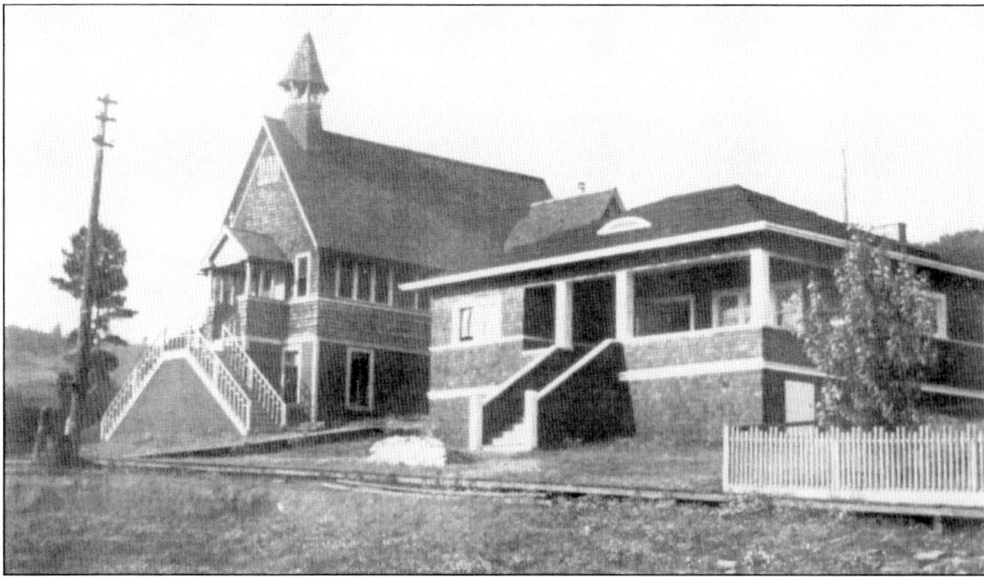

The Episcopal church on Cedar Street had a different fate than many other of Tuolumne's early wooden buildings; it was spared from the various fires that ravaged the town in the early 1900s. In later years, it became a Pentecostal place of worship, although it has not been actively used for decades and has fallen into a state of disrepair.

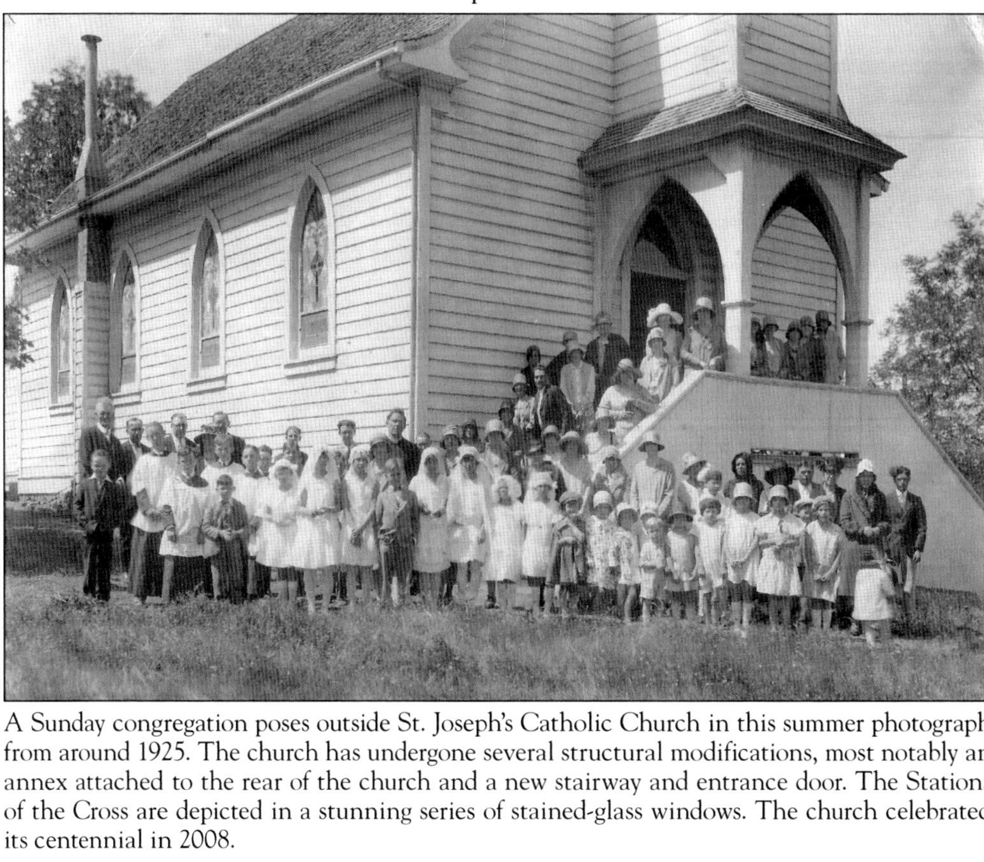

A Sunday congregation poses outside St. Joseph's Catholic Church in this summer photograph from around 1925. The church has undergone several structural modifications, most notably an annex attached to the rear of the church and a new stairway and entrance door. The Stations of the Cross are depicted in a stunning series of stained-glass windows. The church celebrated its centennial in 2008.

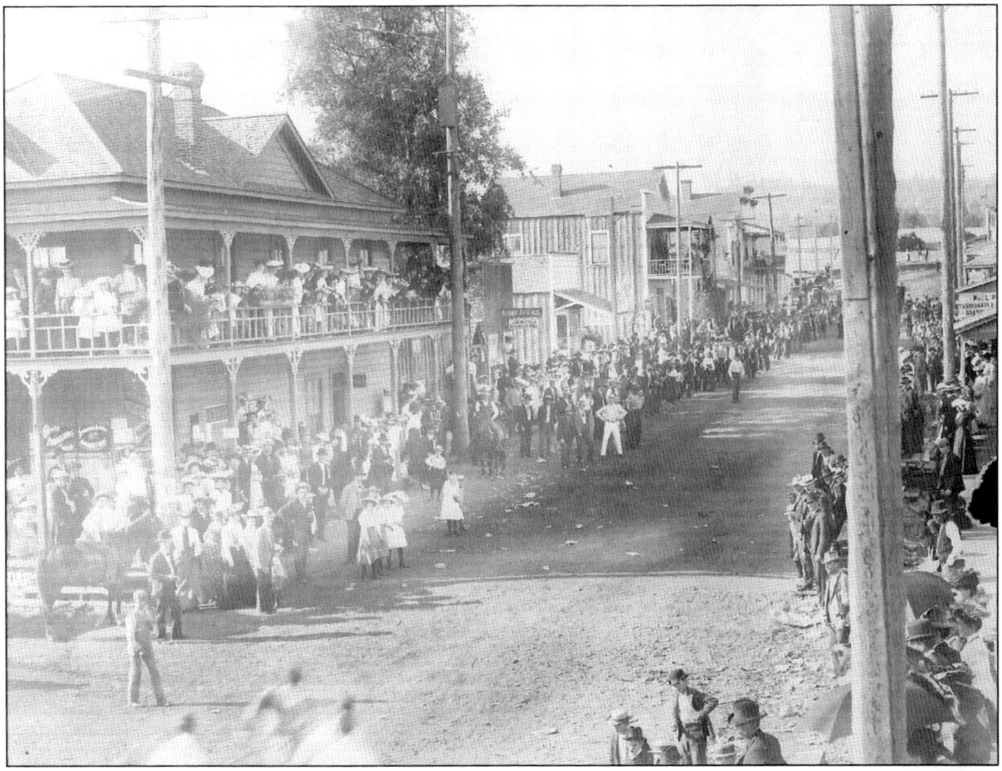

All of Tuolumne got dressed to the nines and decked out the businesses for this 1905 Labor Day or Fourth of July celebration. This is Carter Street, which, although Main Street is to its direct west, was and continues to be the main artery through town. All the buildings in this photograph were lost to a fire in 1918.

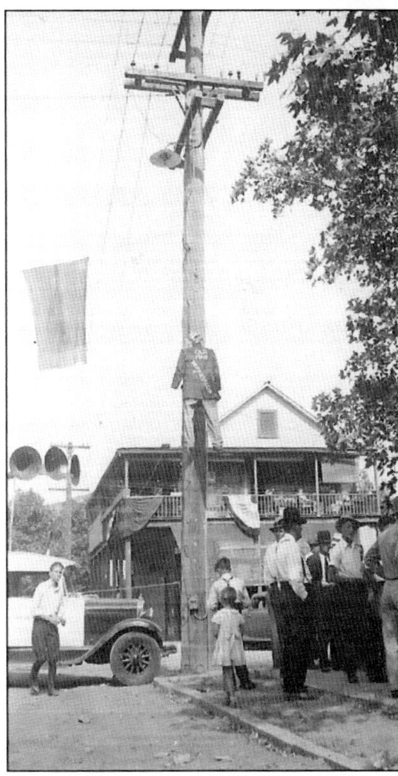

Like all cities across America in the 1930s, Tuolumne was hit hard by the Depression. The lumber mill, by far the town's largest employer, was forced to shut down from 1930 to 1935 due to economic hardship. In this photograph, taken during that time span, residents hang an "Old Man Depression" effigy from a corner telephone pole. This photograph was taken in 1935 during the first Lumber Jubilee that celebrated the reopening of the mill.

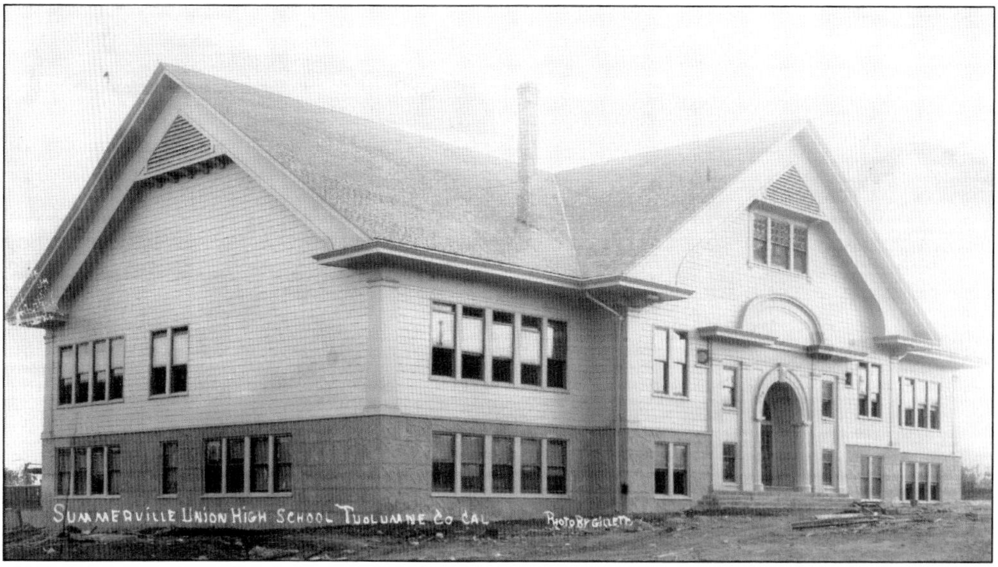

With help from the federal government, two public works projects kept the town on life support during the incredibly tough times when the mill was shut down. The first of these projects was the addition of an annexed gymnasium complex for the Tuolumne High School (pictured here before the addition). The high school was eventually relocated, but this building still stands and now serves as the private Mother Lode Christian School.

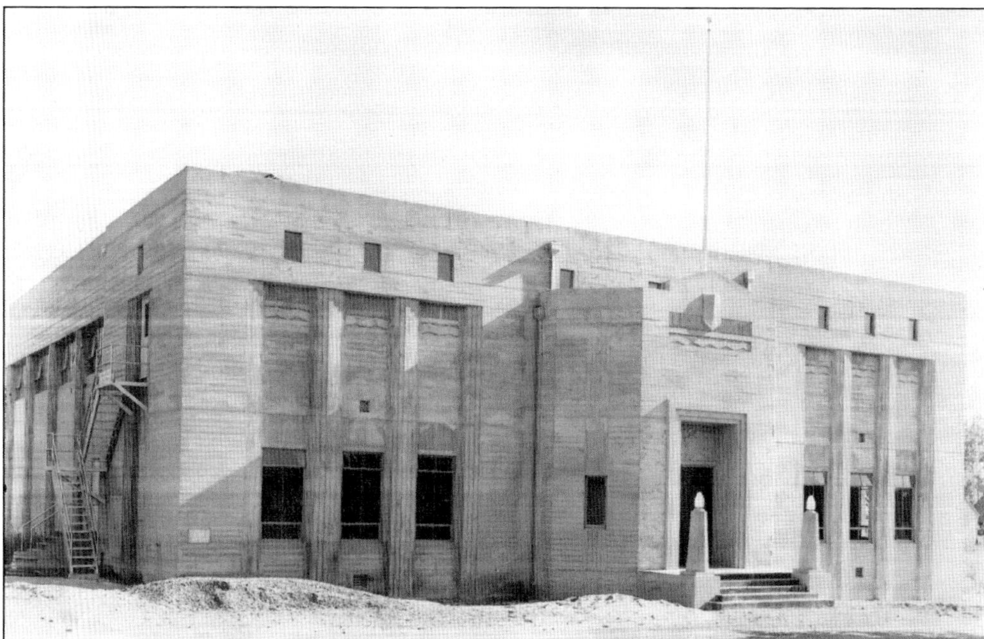

The second and larger of the Depression-era projects was the Tuolumne Veteran's Memorial Hall, which was completed in 1936. This tall, Art Deco–style multipurpose building, constructed with concrete and brick infill, is one of the more notable fixtures in downtown Tuolumne and was erected on the former location of the Turnback Inn (at the corner of Fir Avenue and Main Street). Both this and the gymnasium project provided much-needed work and wages to many members of Tuolumne's working force who were without employment when the mill was closed.

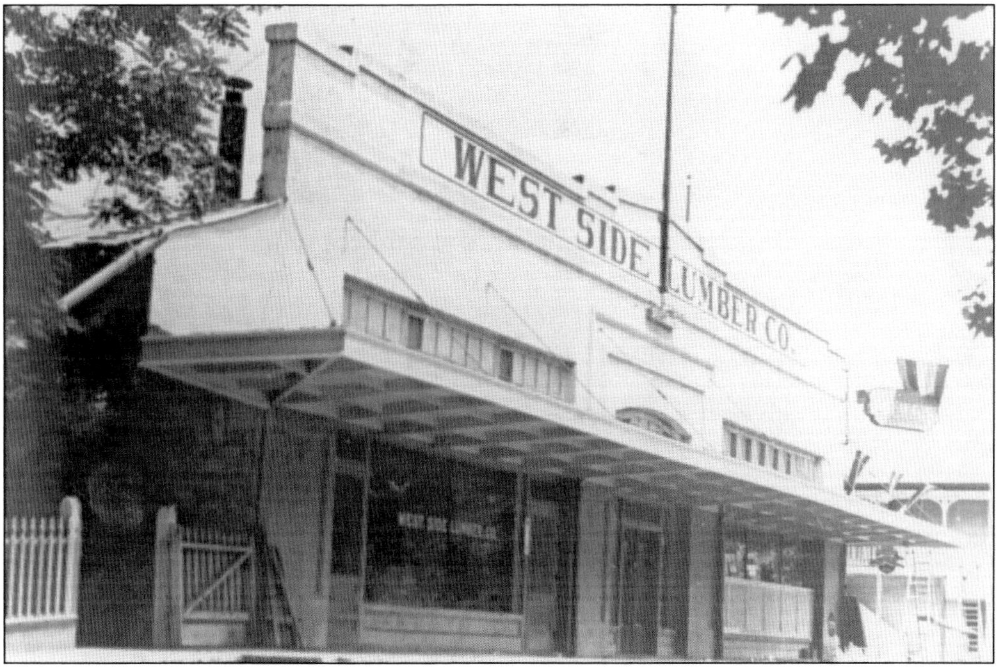

After much larger iterations kept being either severely damaged or destroyed completely, the latest and final West Side Lumber Company building was constructed in 1902 using materials that were more fire resistant on Fir Avenue west of Main Street. Although smaller than its predecessor, this building was still the heartbeat of West Side.

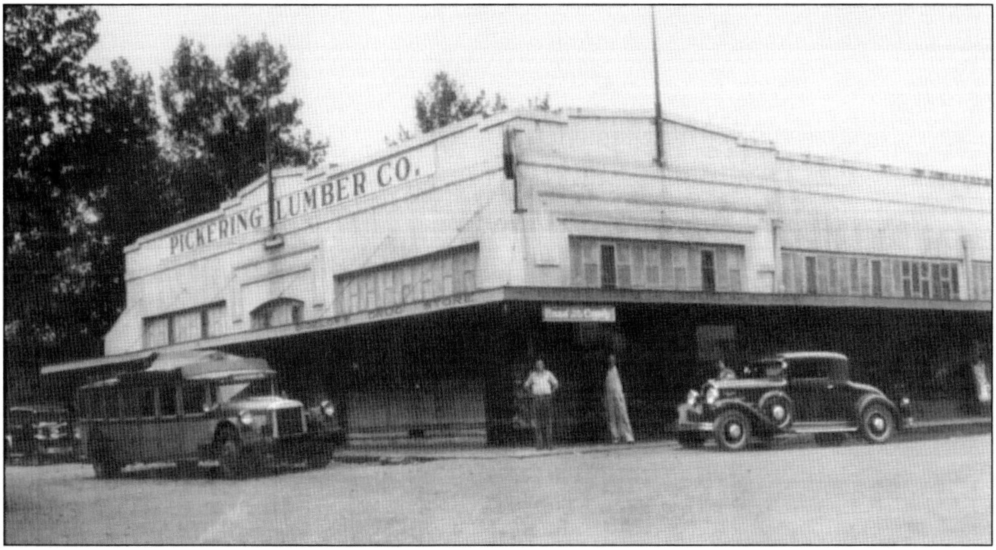

In 1921, Pickering Lumber Company acquired Tuolumne County's other major lumber operation, the Standard Lumber Company, which was originally based in Sonora and later in the company township of Standard. Pickering bought out West Side in 1925 but was forced to close down in 1930 because of the Depression; it gave the Tuolumne lumber operation back to its original owners. Pickering continued to operate as a lumber company until 1965, four years after West Side's closure.

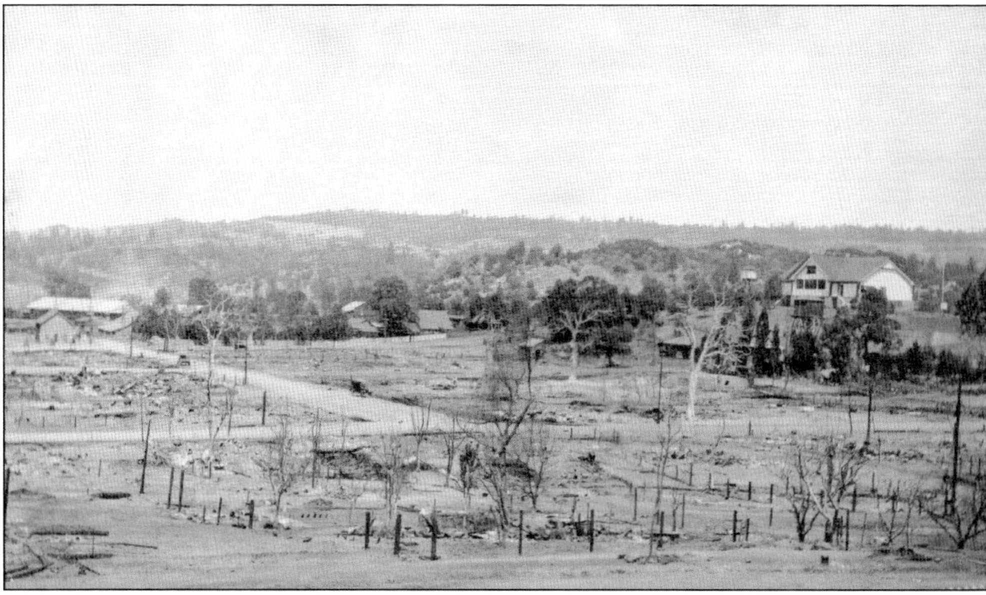

Fire was (and continues to be) a major threat to the township. This picture shows the near-total devastation from the massive fire of 1918. The vast majority of all-wood homes and businesses in downtown Tuolumne were turned into ashes in little more than two hours. The town rebuilt, however, and lined the streets that bordered the fire with sycamores to symbolize growth and rebirth; the trees are now fully grown and provide the town with summer shade and year-round beauty.

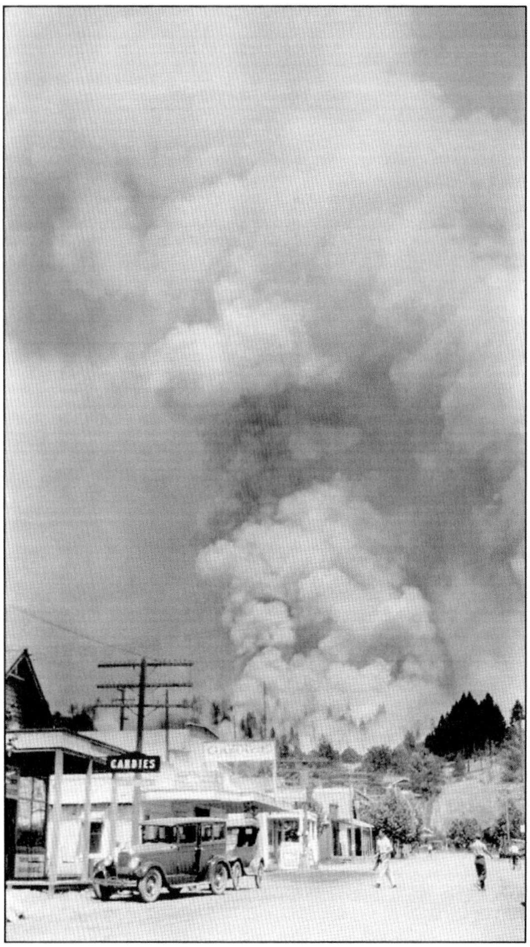

This shot, looking east along Chestnut Street, shows a large plume of smoke rising from an unnamed brushfire on the hillside (Mt. Havilah) above town. Citizens are emerging from homes and businesses to assess the size of the inferno.

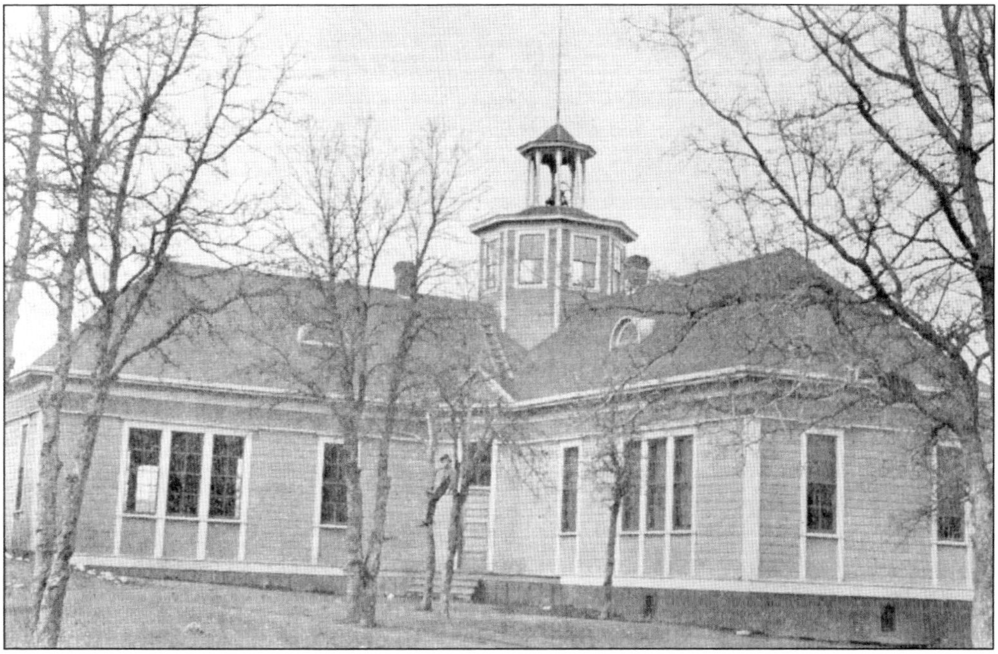

A lone schoolboy relaxes in a tree in the yard of the Summerville Elementary schoolhouse in 1905. This grammar school, located just south of Maple Avenue at the corner of Madrone Street, was built on a portion of the plot donated by Frank and Delia Baker in 1899. The school's structure was a four-armed cross with a large classroom in each arm, topped by an octagonal tower with a belfry. It was constructed in 1903 by the millwright, a Mr. Hiatt.

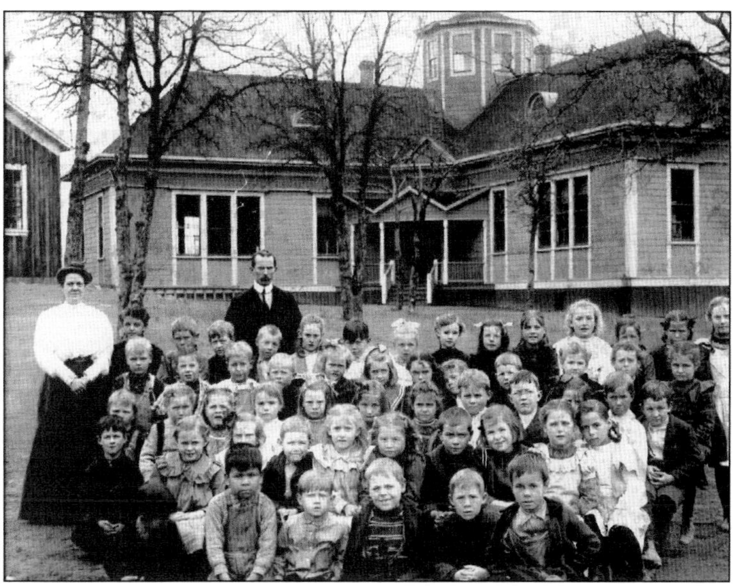

The class of 1906 poses for a school-wide photograph in front of Summerville Elementary. Principle James P. Gallagher (the stern-looking gentleman in the rear) and teacher Annie E. Teague joined the students for this photograph commemorating the school's third class.

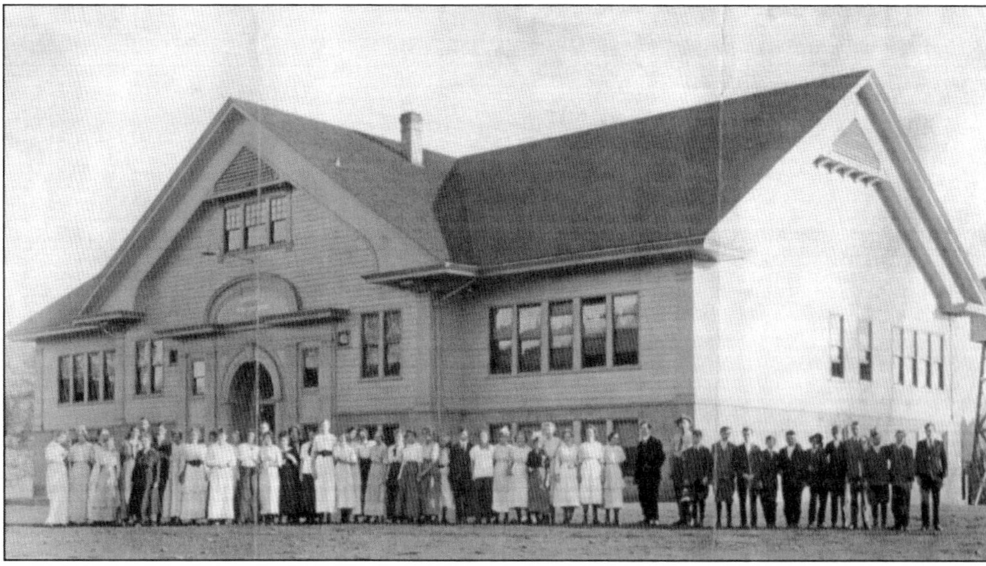

Although in the early years of Tuolumne the town got along with simply an elementary school, as the children grew up, their education needed to be continued. Up until 1912, Tuolumne children had to go to the train depot and ride into Sonora to attend high school. The wives of the mill owners (and mothers of the students) convinced their husbands to donate land and build a high school, and in this photograph, the class of 1914 (along with its teachers) stands in front of the two-year-old building.

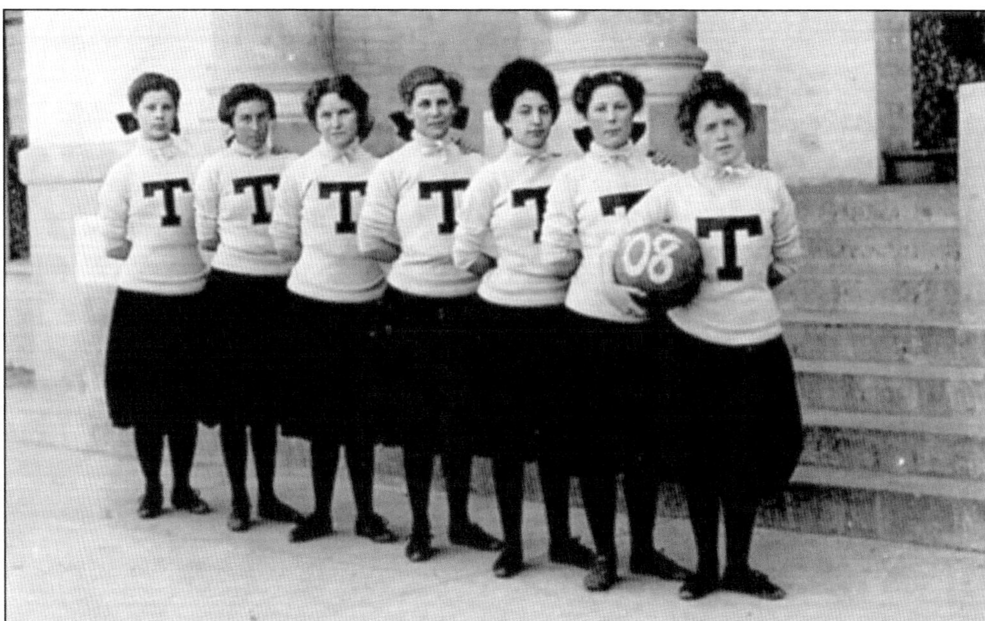

The girls of the class of 1908 pose for the team basketball photograph of Summerville High. Their letterman sweaters still bear the block "T" for Tuolumne, as was the case through most of the century. The name "Summerville" comes from Tuolumne's first name, Summersville, and only bears one *S* due to a clerical error on legal documents.

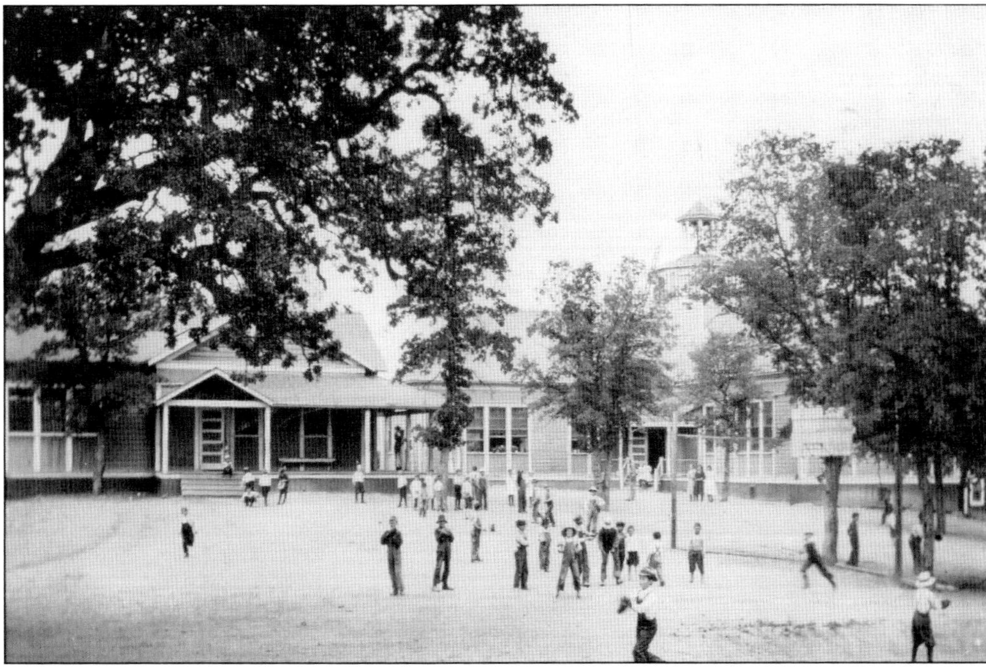

Students take a recess break at Summerville Elementary to participate in playground sports. Several young boys play a game of catch with baseball mitts, and a crude basketball hoop and backboard are nailed to a tree on the right side of the image.

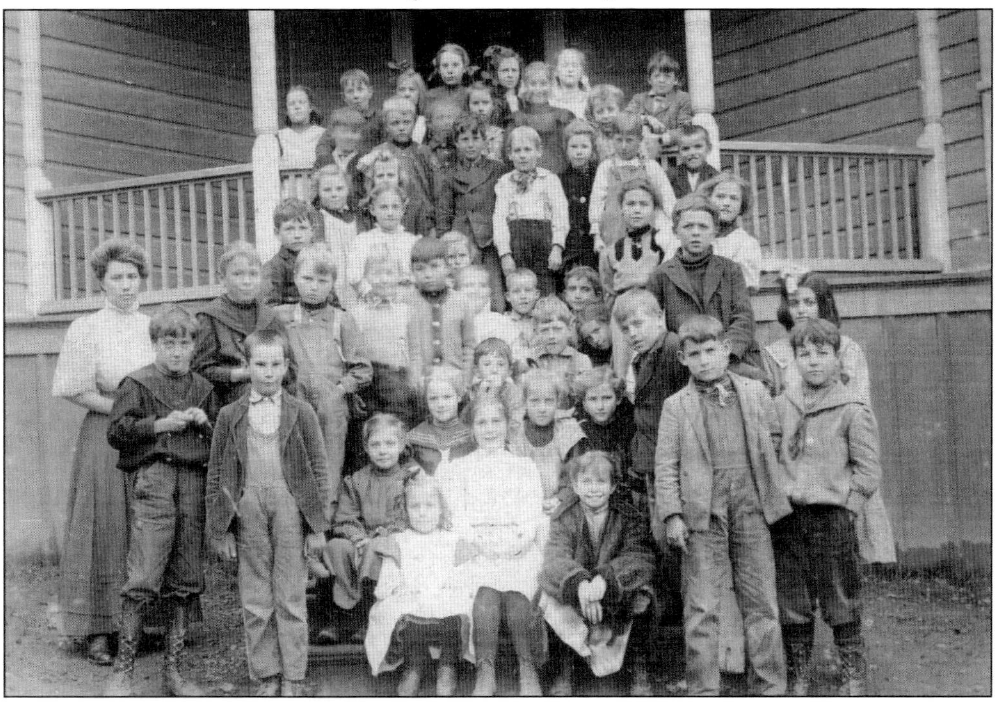

The noticeably smaller class of 1909 at Summerville Elementary assembles on the main staircase leading into the school. Today's Summerville Elementary School is located on the exact same spot. The current school retains none of the original buildings but is situated on the same lot.

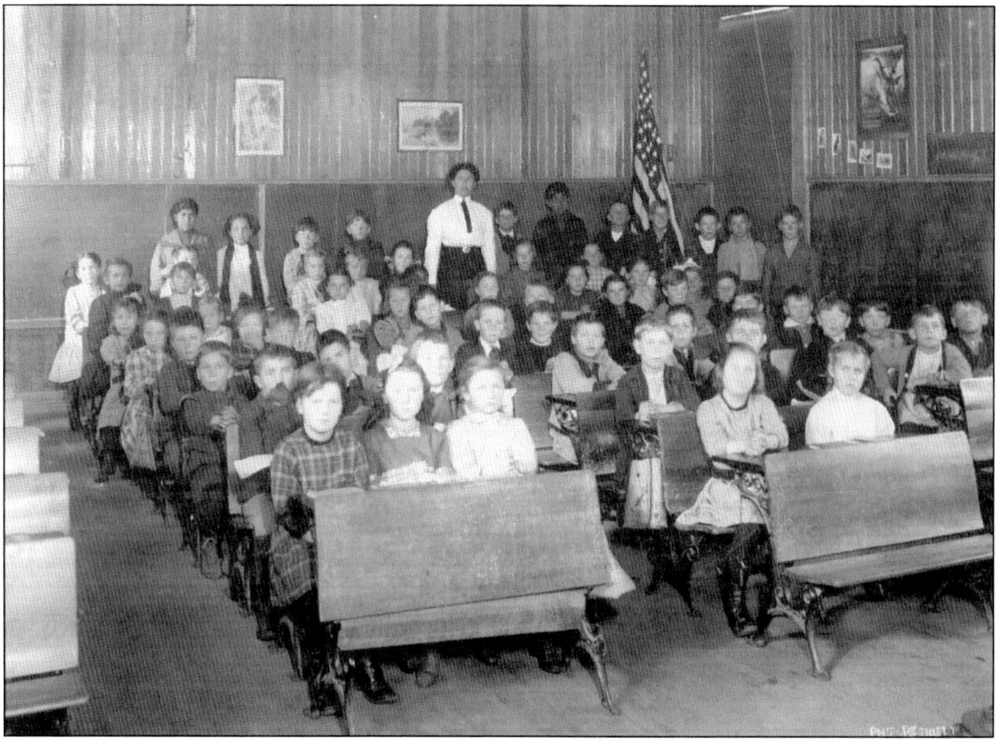

The classrooms at Summerville Elementary, like most grade-school classrooms around the country between the 1900s and the 1920s, were somewhat large, with upwards of 40 children in the same room. Younger students shared desks with either two or three students at a table and did not have their own desks and chairs until they got older (and larger).

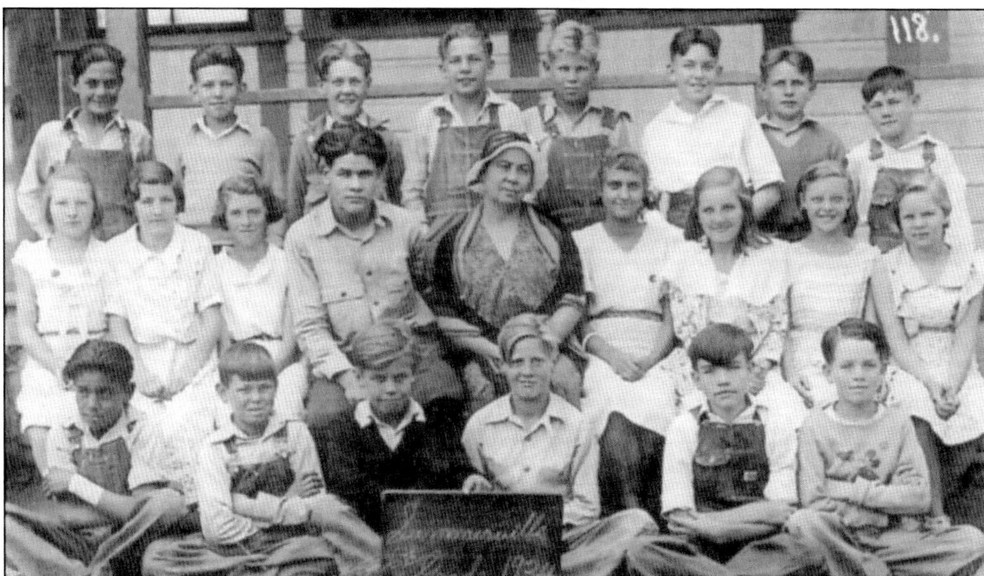

By the 1930s, Tuolumne had grown and enrolled enough children to offer different grade levels. Summerville Elementary featured grades kindergarten through eighth grade. Here, the sixth-grade class from 1934 poses for its annual photograph.

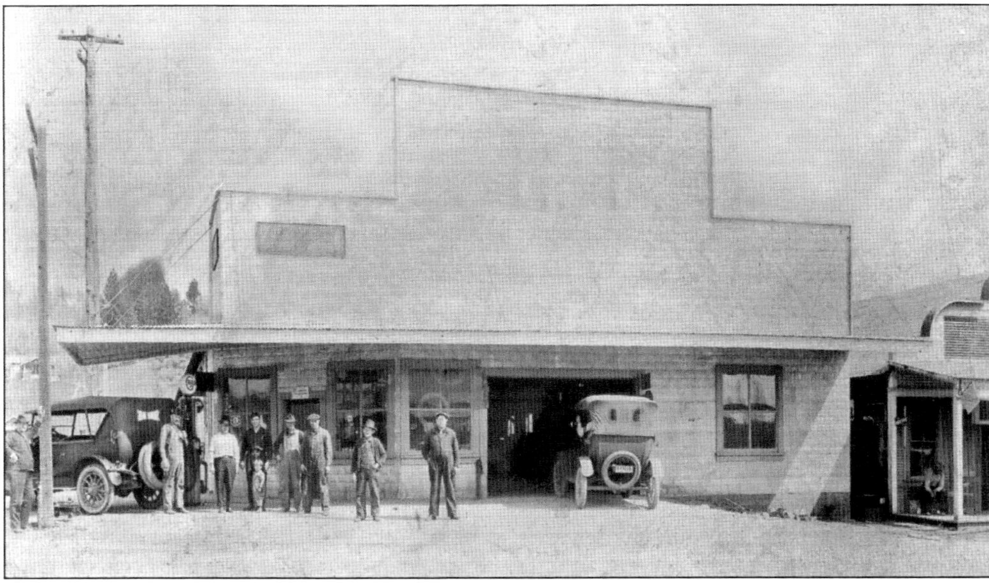

Opened by Sy Speaker in 1912, the Tuolumne Garage stood at the corner of Chestnut and Pine Streets until its demolition in June 2008. Sy operated the garage with a later partner, George Handy, until his adopted son, Joe Speaker, joined him in the business in 1946 when the name was changed to Speaker's Garage. The building was sold to entrepreneur Glenn Bell (the founder of Taco Bell) in 1976, and Joe continued working in the garage, restoring antique autos and trucks for the Bell enterprise at West Side. During its years in business, Speaker's was a favorite gathering spot for men to sit in the sun in the summer or around the oil stove in the winter, exchanging local news and tall tales.

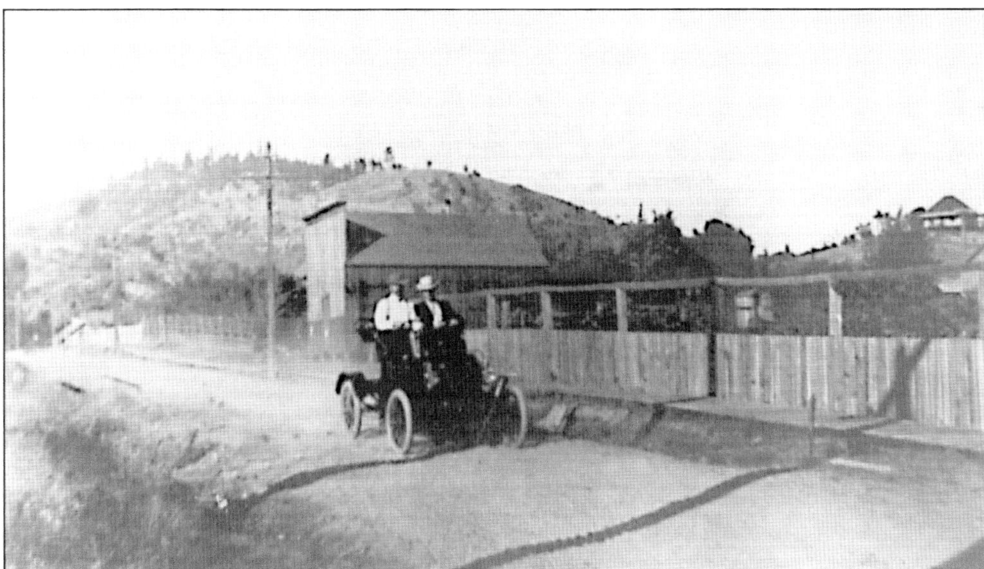

In this 1910 photograph, Sy Speaker (driving) speeds along Carter Street in what was reportedly the first automobile in town. Although he got stuck in mud on Yosemite Road and had to be pulled out by a team of horses on the way into town, Speaker knew that automobiles were the future and purchased his garage in 1912.

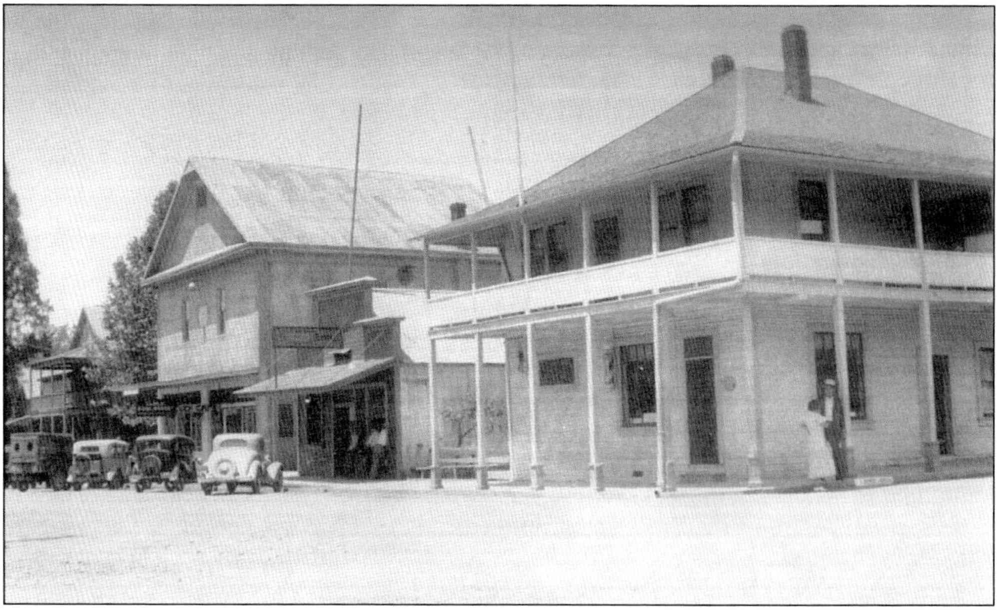

This c. 1915 photograph, taken looking northwest from the intersection of Pine and Bay Streets, shows the corner building (seen here, when it was the local barbershop owned by John Wittorf, also known as "Johnny the Barber;" currently a Sherriff Community Service building), a bar (currently The Logger's) selling the now-defunct Acme Beer, and the Tuolumne Grocery Store (which was the Public Food Market until the late 1990s).

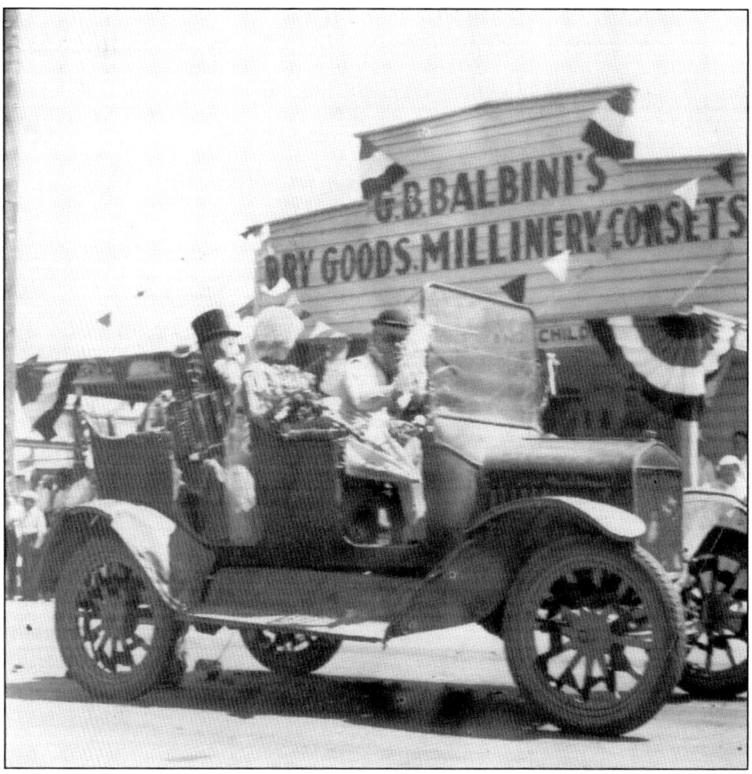

The biggest annual celebration in Tuolumne is by far the annual Lumber Jubilee. Started in 1935 after the West Side Lumber Company reopened, the Lumber Jubilee celebrates Tuolumne's rich tradition as a logging town with events, carnival rides and games, live music, and lumberjack-style competitive games. This photograph shows an entrant in the 1938 Jubilee parade motoring down Chestnut Avenue. The parade saw floats of all shapes and sizes.

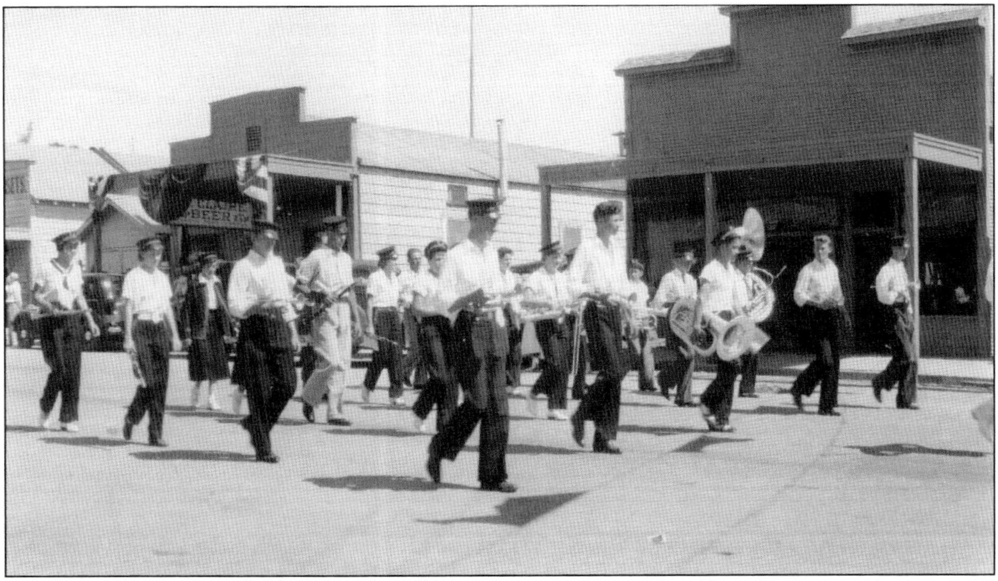

This photograph, also from the 1938 Jubilee parade, shows the Summerville Union High School marching band. The route of the march usually circled the outskirts of downtown and went along Carter Street and back down Main Street—nearly the entire area of town lost in the 1918 fire.

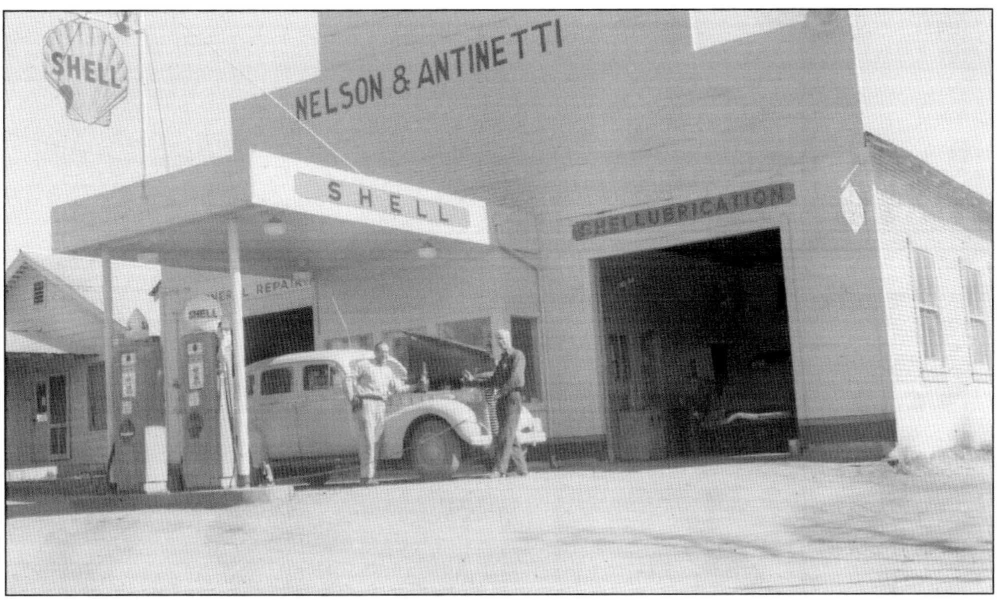

One of the other main garages, the Nelson and Antinetti Shell station (pictured here around 1940) was owned by Bruce Nelson and Adolph Antinetti and still stands today on the corner of Carter Street and Rozier Avenue. The two operated the station for 24 years. At one point, Tuolumne had four garages: the Blair, Speaker, Naegle, and Chevron, all of which offered full-service automotive work, as well as gasoline.

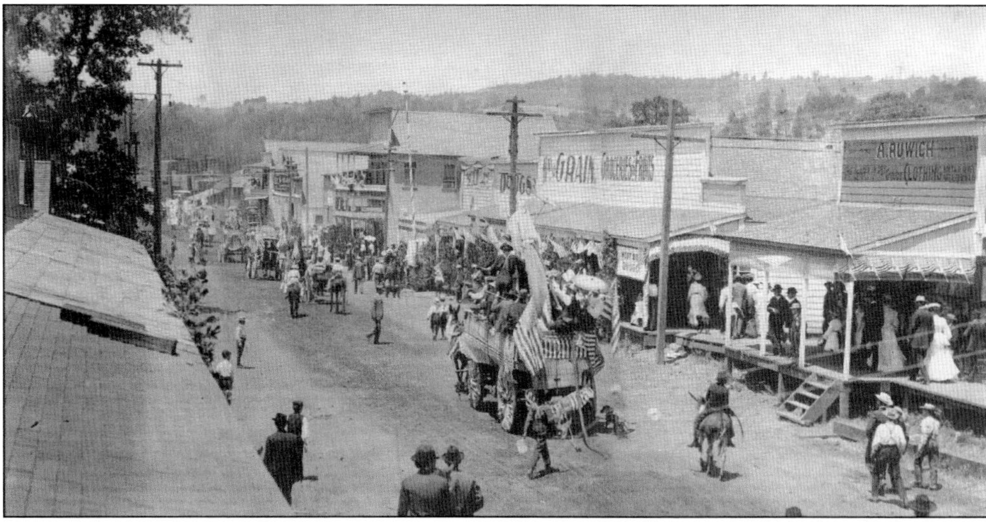

This photograph, taken from the roof of one of the downtown businesses, shows the 1904 Fourth of July parade rolling through downtown Tuolumne on Chestnut Avenue. All of this was lost in the 1918 fire. After the blaze, the Red Cross provided clothes and other necessities to the families most affected, and during that Christmas, Sears Roebuck distributed gifts labeled for each member of each family.

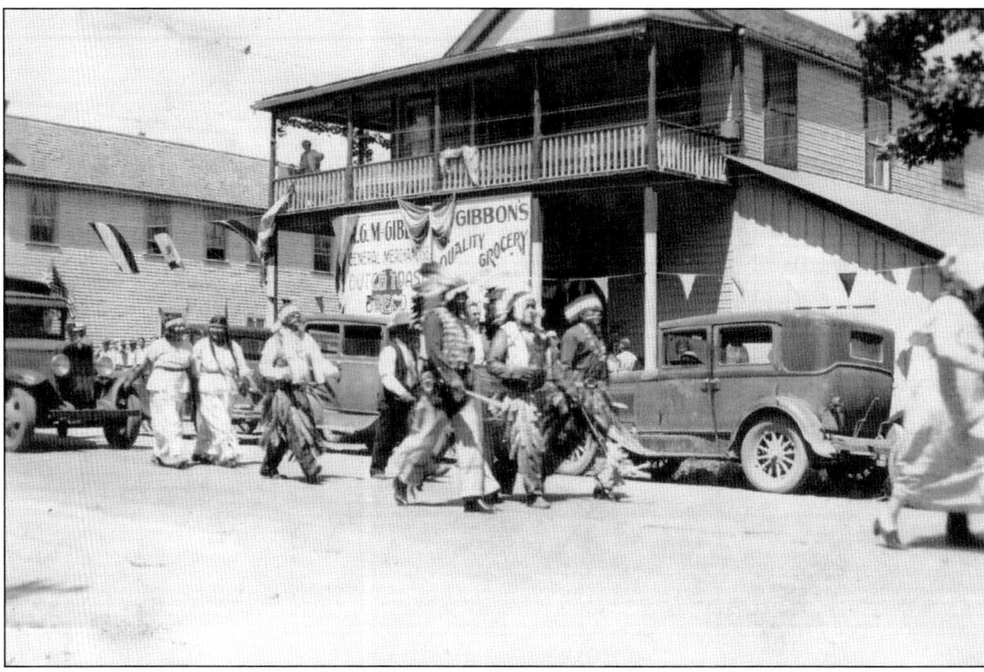

The Tuolumne Band of Me-Wuk Indians continues to play a major role in Tuolumne's history, and their heritage is also celebrated at town events. In a Lumber Jubilee parade from the 1930s, a group of local Me-Wuk Indians in ceremonial attire participates in the parade.

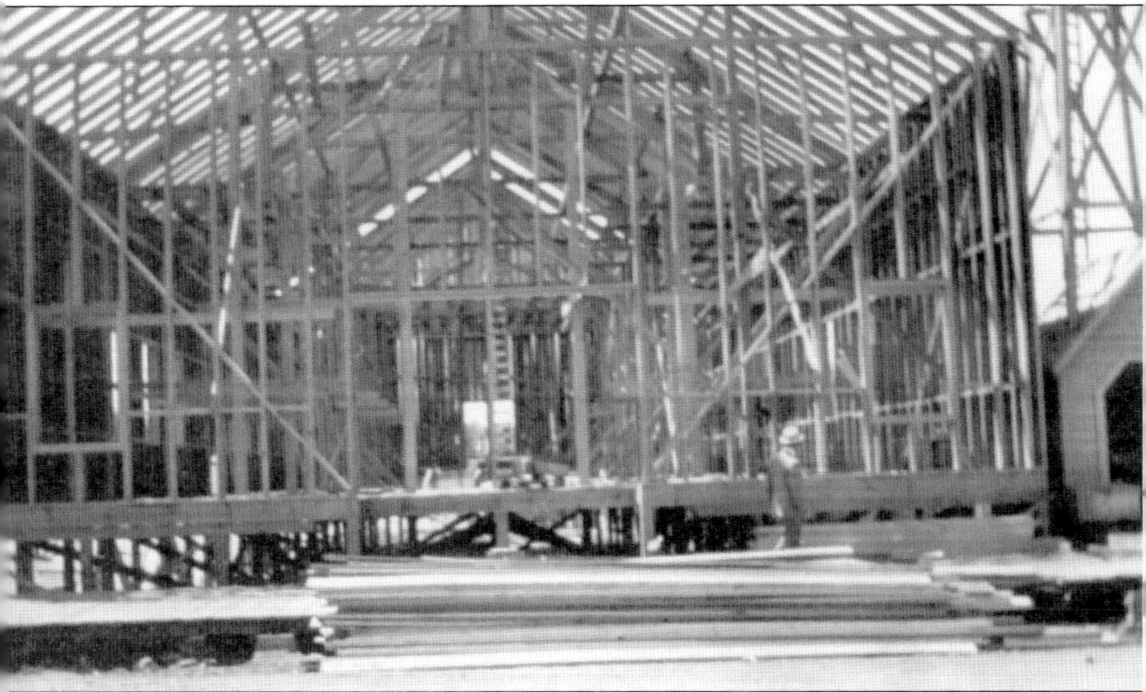

This image shows the initial construction stages of the Firemen's Opera House, located on the corner of Main Street and Chestnut Avenue. The opera house was built entirely by the volunteer firemen of the Tuolumne Hose Company No. 1, who ran it as a service to the community and to raise funds for their firefighting needs (which, as shown throughout this book, were extensive in a town as heavily reliant upon timber as Tuolumne). After the building was completed around 1906, it also served as a community town hall with its large basement and huge cooking range, at which many of the town's women would get together and make large dinners to raise money for various causes. It burned down several times (in 1916, 1918, and 1944) and was eventually repurposed into a movie theater.

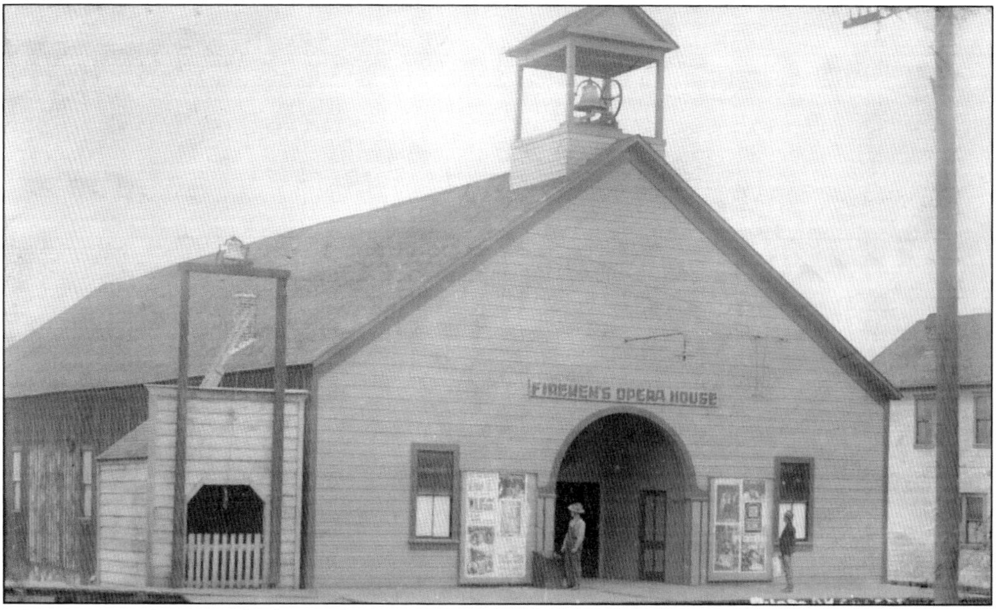

This c. 1915 photograph shows the completed Fireman's Opera House, which featured a belfry and arched gateway. A variety of productions put on by local amateur players rotated weekly and were advertised on the billings posted out front. This structure would burn down in 1916 and be rebuilt, only to burn down again in the massive downtown fire of 1918.

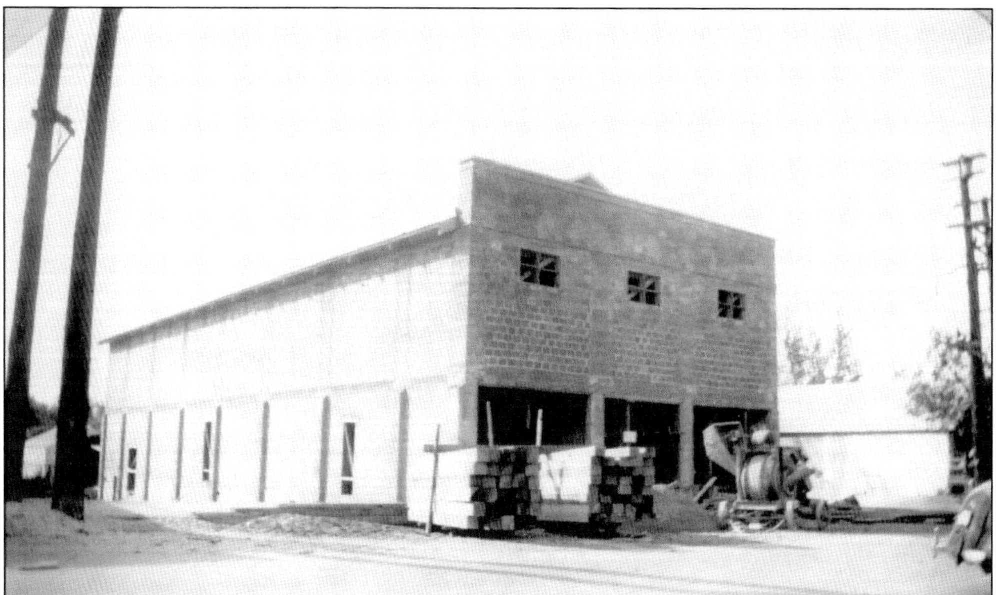

After burning to the ground yet again, the firemen finally decided to construct the opera house with concrete, cement, and brick in 1944. This picture from the very same year shows the project nearing completion as workers hustle to finish the parapet and marquee on the front of the building. Once motion pictures became popular in the 1920s, the opera house began showing movies. Once the Memorial Hall was completed in 1936 and took over as the primary town meeting space, the opera house was rebuilt specifically as a movie theater.

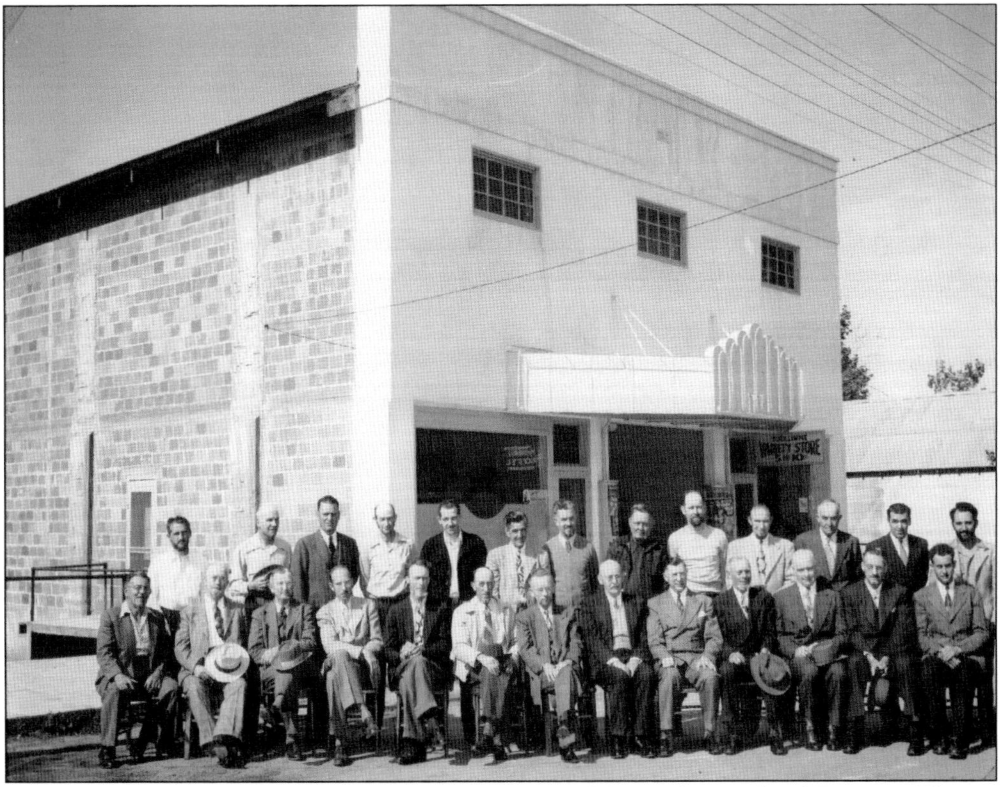

Workers, firefighters, and town patriarchs pose in front of the newly completed Firemen's Theatre in 1946. From 1946 through 1964 (when yet another devastating fire completely gutted the building's interior), the theater routinely showed movies on Wednesdays, Saturdays, and Sundays, with ticket prices ranging as high as 25¢ and as low as potatoes or other vegetables.

This interior view, taken from the front of the theater toward the back (facing north), shows the raked (tiered) floor and seating arrangement. This was new to the movie theater in 1946, as previous iterations of the Firemen's Opera House had one large, flat floor with removable seats so that the well-attended community dances could be held there.

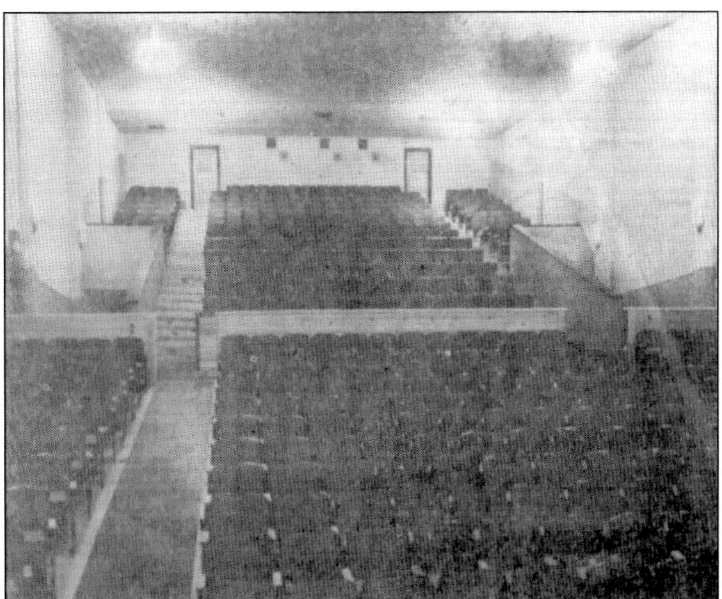

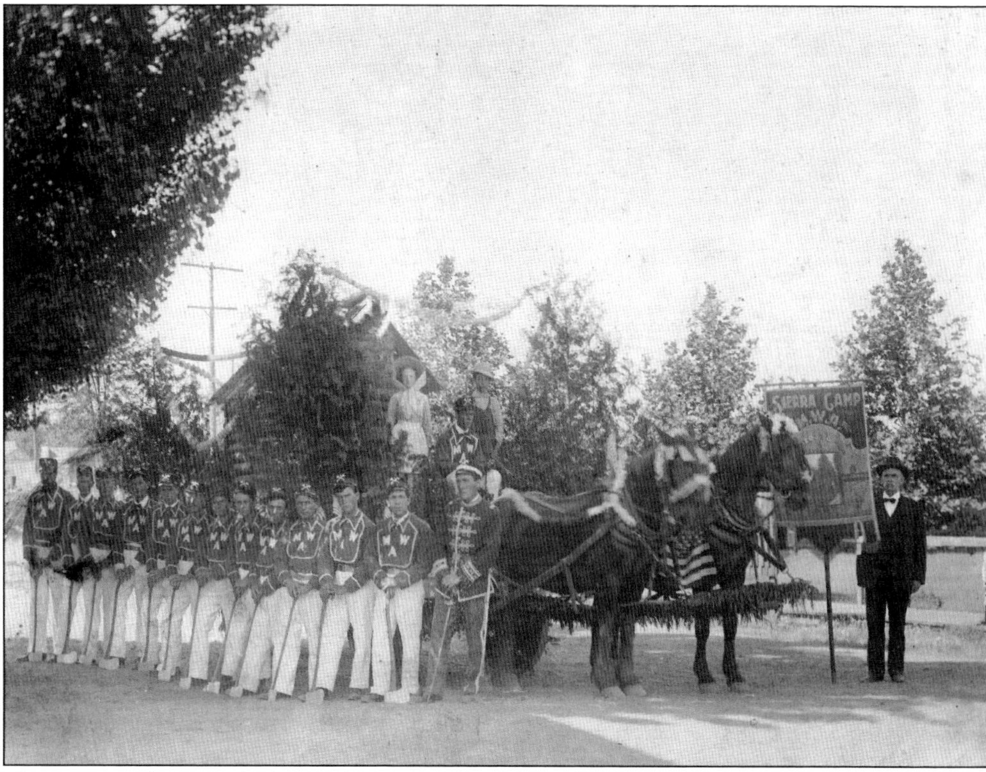

This c. 1910 photograph shows the Sierra Camp branch of the Modern Woodmen of America (MWA). Tuolumne is nestled in a fairly remote and heavily wooded area, so the MWA proved to be a popular fraternal club. The group held regular meetings and participated in a wide variety of games and activities for the entire family. According to the MWA website (www.modern-woodmen.org), the group "honors the pioneering woodmen who cleared the forests to build homes, communities, and security for their families."

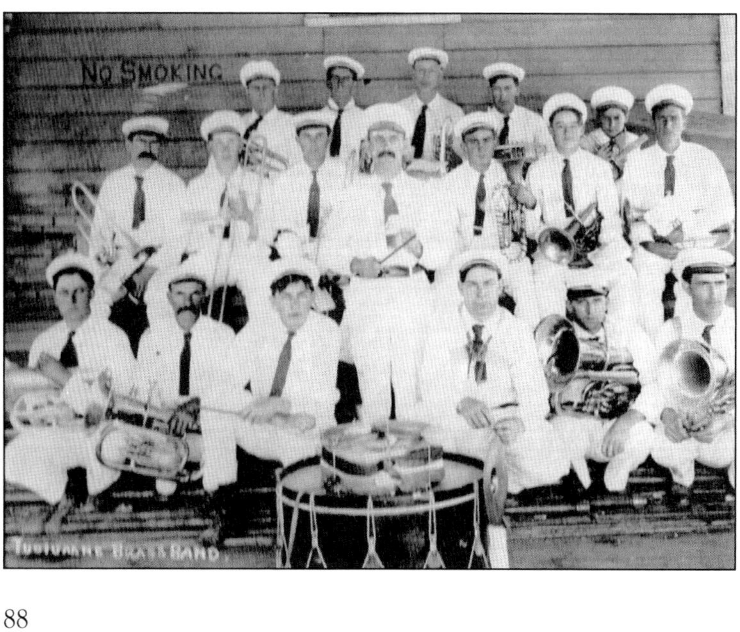

The Tuolumne Brass Band, pictured here around 1915, played for a variety of town functions, including town dances and social gatherings at the Firemen's Opera House. The group led a host of parades by pulling marching-band duties and serenaded the participants and spectators at each year's Lumber Jubilee festivities.

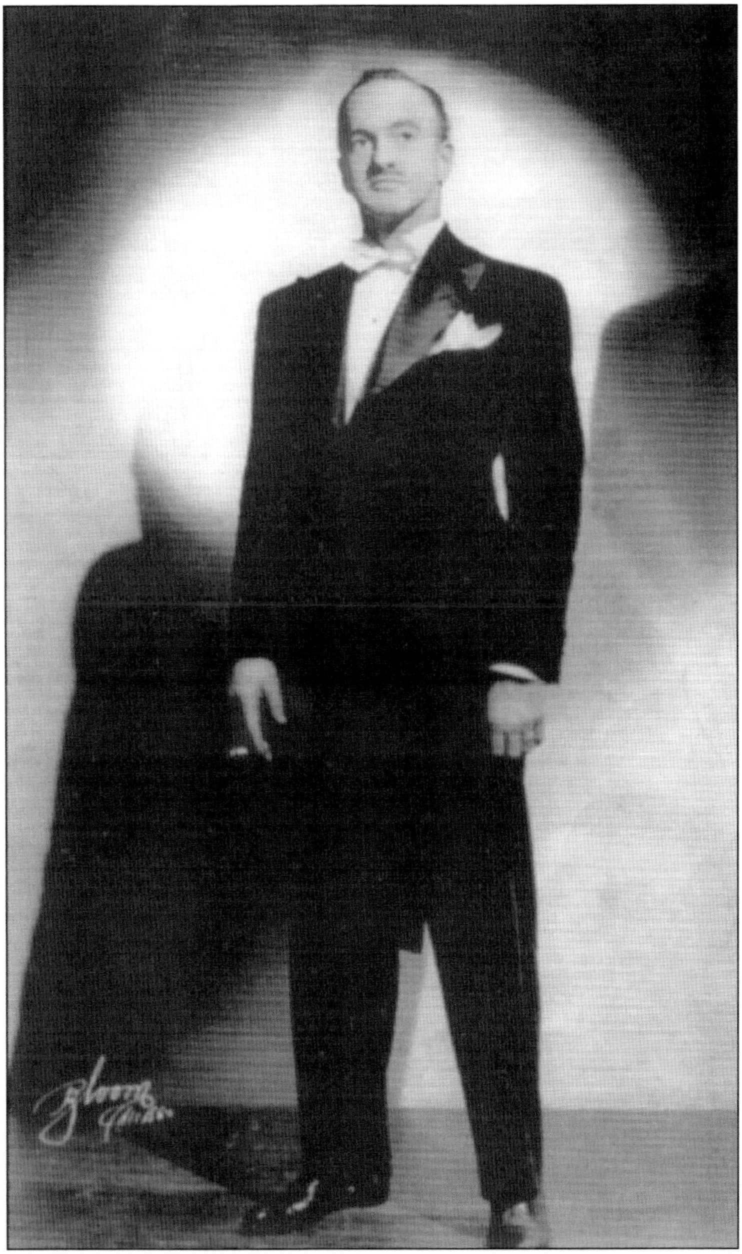

Arguably Tuolumne City's most famous citizen, Lord Buckley (born Richard Myrle Buckley on April 5, 1906) was a prolific recording artist, stage performer, monologist, poet, and comic. He has been mentioned as an influence by a wide variety of figures, such as George Harrison (of the Beatles), Bob Dylan, Tom Waits, and Dizzy Gillespie. Born to British immigrants, Buckley grew up in Tuolumne and worked for West Side as a lumberjack before eventually leaving in the early 1930s. His scat monologues and hipster dialect were at the forefront of the beatnik movement, and some of his recordings are beatnik/hipster retellings of famous speeches (the title of his first album was *Hipsters, Flipsters and Finger Poppin' Daddies—Knock Me Your Lobes*, a play on the speech by Mark Antony in Shakespeare's *Julius Caesar*). He appeared on several major television shows, including *The Ed Sullivan Show* and Groucho Marx's *You Bet Your Life*.

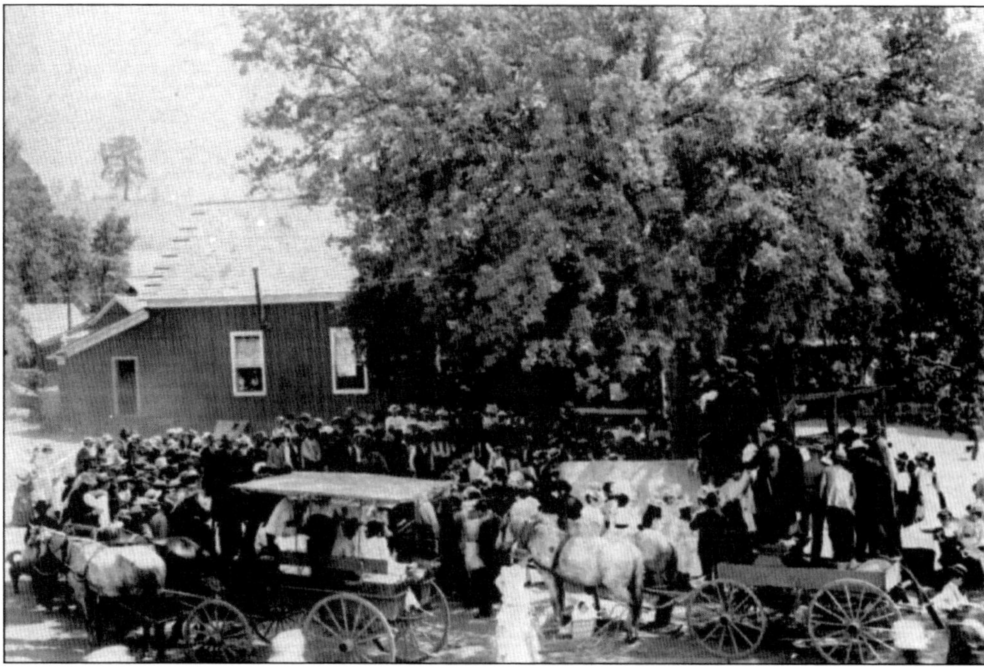

This is one of the earlier celebration photographs the museum has on record, from around 1900. This was snapped near the west end of Buchanan Mine Road in old-town Carters. In frontier towns such as Carters around the early 1900s, it did not take much for citizens to get together.

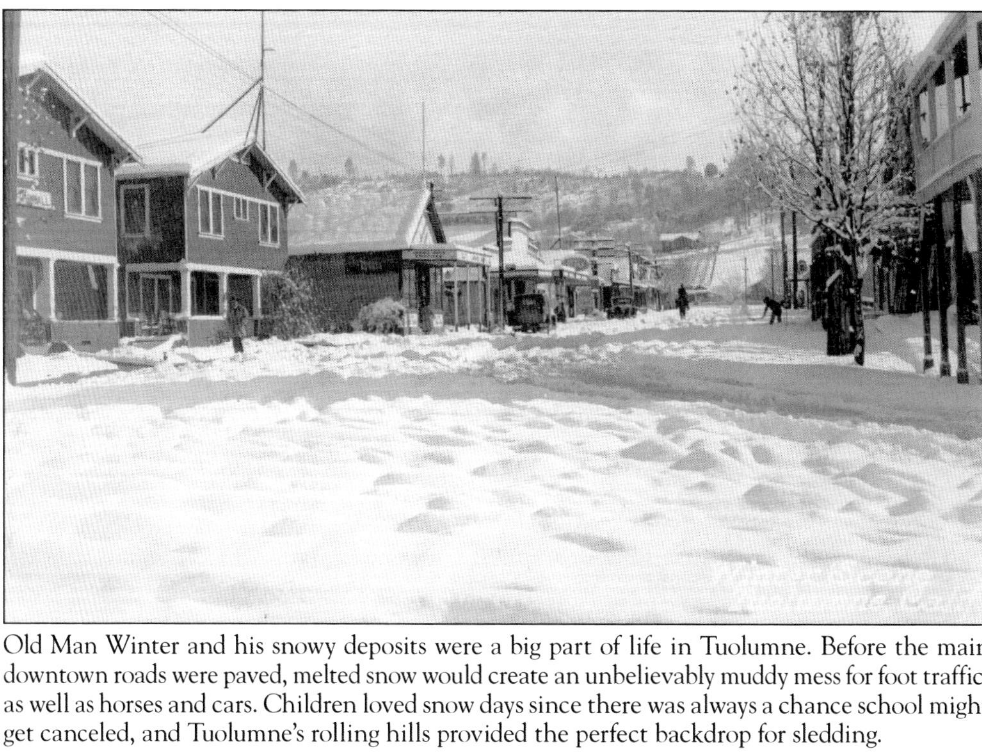

Old Man Winter and his snowy deposits were a big part of life in Tuolumne. Before the main downtown roads were paved, melted snow would create an unbelievably muddy mess for foot traffic, as well as horses and cars. Children loved snow days since there was always a chance school might get canceled, and Tuolumne's rolling hills provided the perfect backdrop for sledding.

Four

The Golden Years and Present-Day Tuolumne

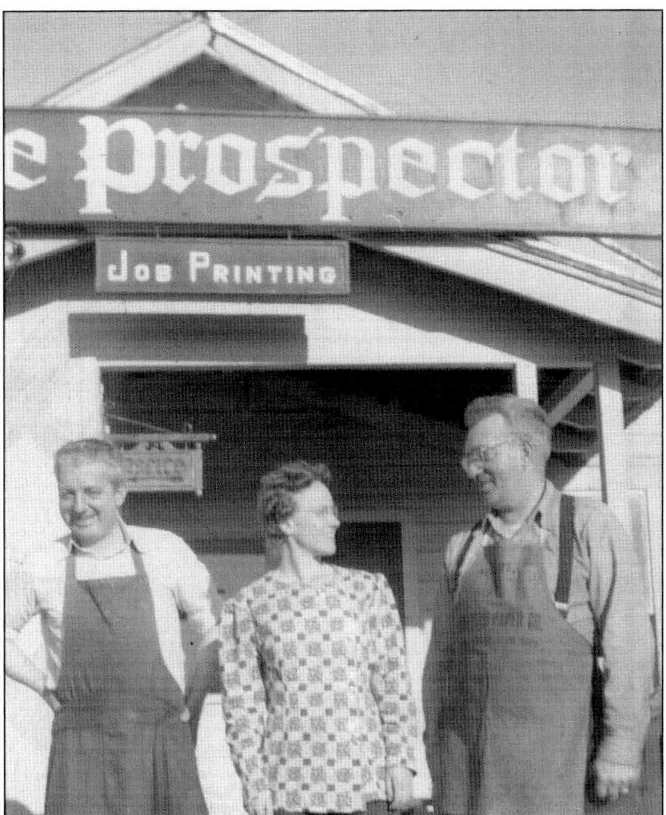

During Tuolumne's heyday, from the early 1940s through the 1960s, the city was one of the busiest and most unique in the entire Mother Lode. For a while, the town supported its own newspaper, *The Prospector*. Although it could not compete with the county's leading—and only—daily newspaper, *The Union Democrat* (which has been printing since 1854), *The Prospector*, which was published weekly, provided Tuolumne-centric news in a whimsical manner. The printing office also carried out a variety of print jobs to supplement income before it closed in the mid-1960s. Employees Wes and Dorabell Howard are seen in center and at right.

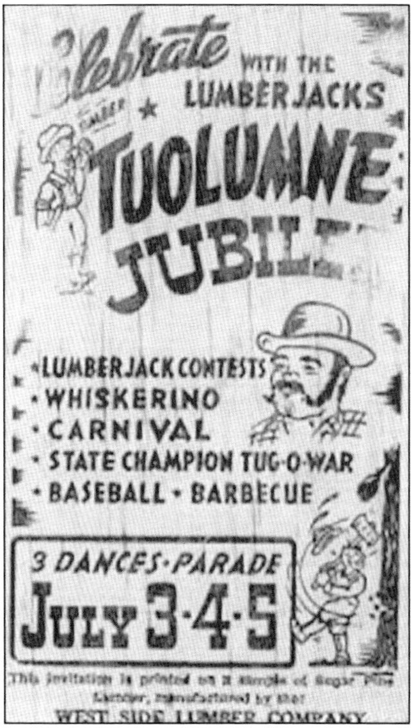

This is one of the earliest wooden postcards printed on West Side sugar pine and distributed to promote the Lumber Jubilee. The annual summer festival began in 1935 to celebrate the West Side mill and lumber facilities opening back up after being closed for five years. The men in town were thrilled to have work again, and to many, it signaled the beginning of the end of the Great Depression. Jubilees are held every year in Tuolumne with a variety of contests and games, many of which date back to the first Lumber Jubilee.

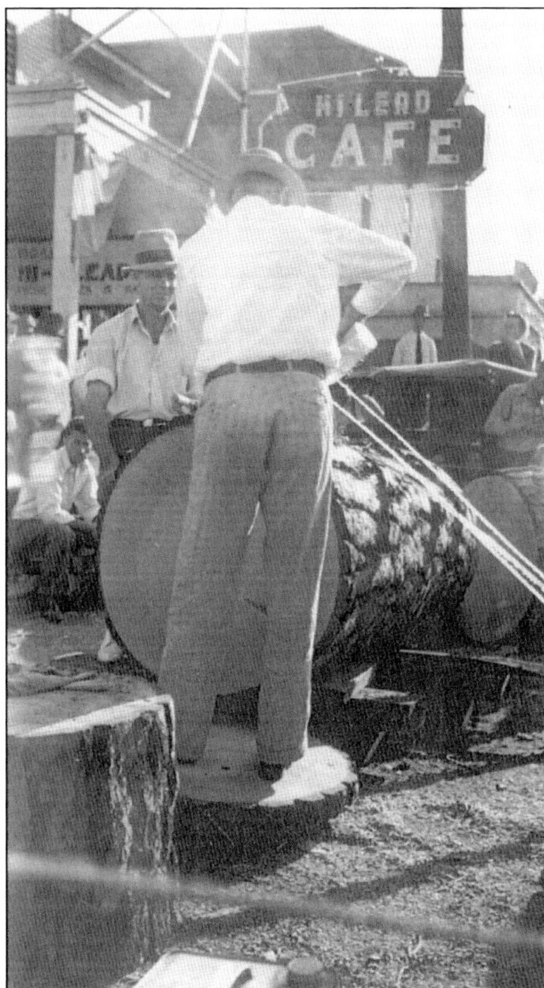

One of the competitions held at the Lumber Jubilee is the hot saw contest, in which lumberjacks or aspiring amateurs are timed to see who can saw through a massive log the fastest. In the early days, participants used handsaws, but as the years progressed, chainsaws became the weapon of choice. Here, a log is prepped in front of the Hi-Lead Café on Chestnut Street.

Without a doubt, the most popular event at the Lumber Jubilee is the tug-of-war. Tuolumne would round up its biggest and strongest men to take on rival teams from neighboring towns of Sonora and especially Jamestown. Teams would oppose one another on a board filled with wooden slats for foot holes, and the first team to pull the other team beyond a certain point was the winner. Here, Tuolumne's team practices before the 1955 Lumber Jubilee.

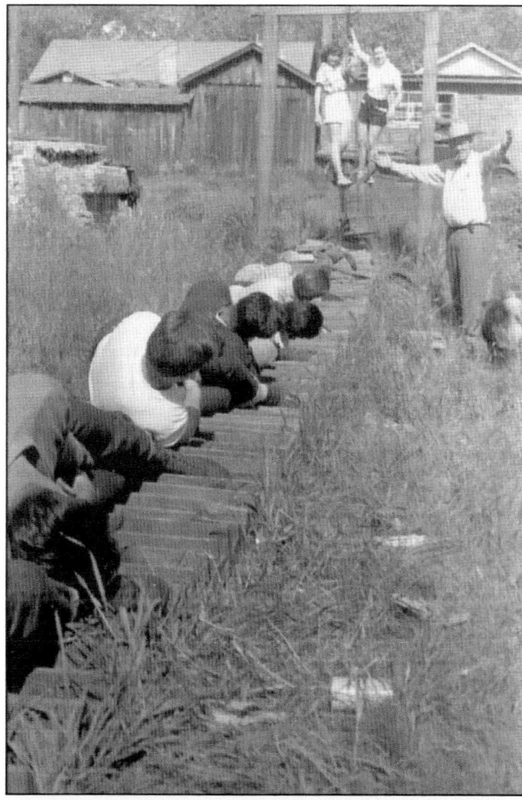

This picture shows Tuolumne's winning team from the 1948 Lumber Jubilee tug-of-war. Pictured here are, from left to right, Gibby Dahl, Marlin Heldstab, Robert Ingals, Walt Clungen, Pinkie Bamber, Jerry Norman, Ray Thornburg, and Felipe Penida. This particular team went on to win the state championship.

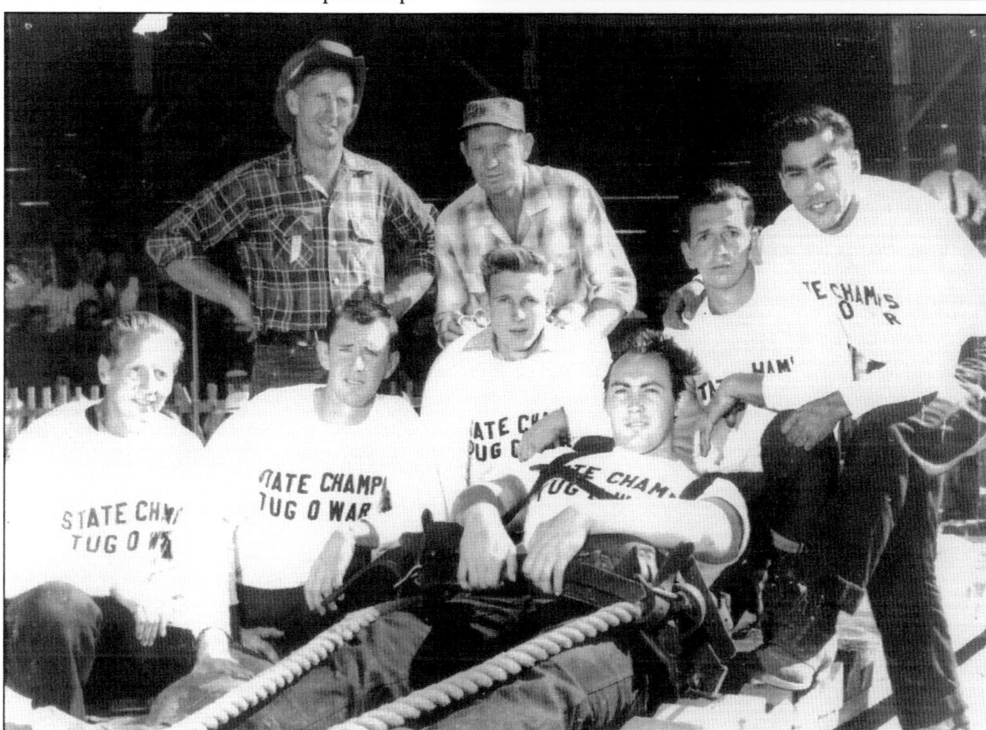

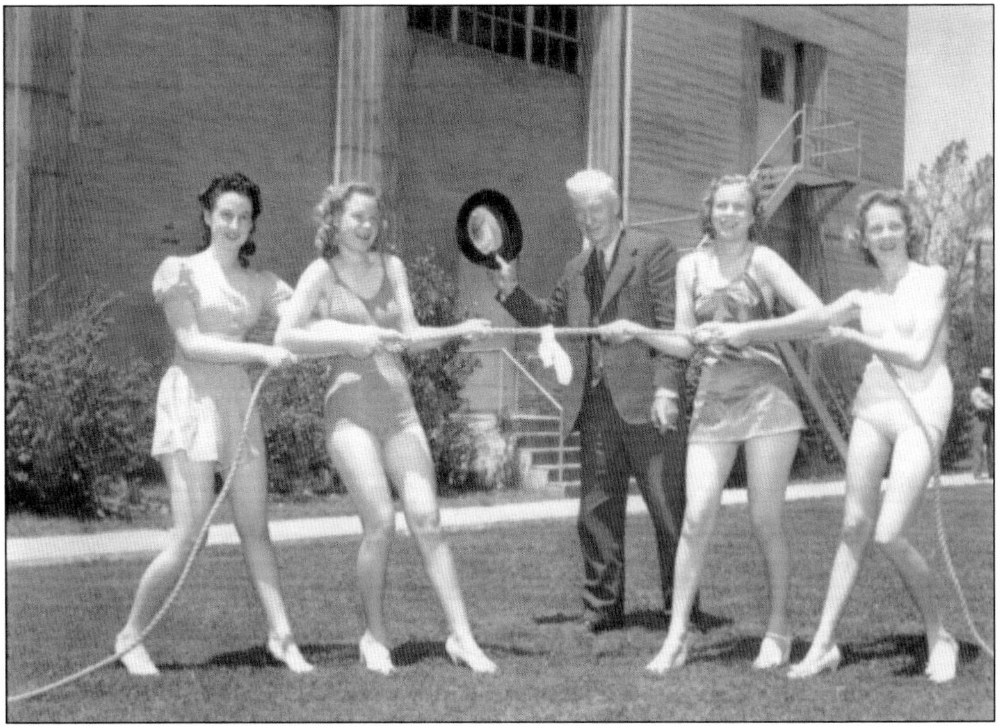

Never ones to be left out of anything, Tuolumne's ladies got in on the tug-of-war action in this promotional shot from the 1950s. The picture was taken on the east lawn of the Tuolumne Veteran's Memorial Hall, which by this time was the town center, along with the Memorial Park, which was located across Fir Avenue. Judge Ed McDow presides over this mock tug-of-war.

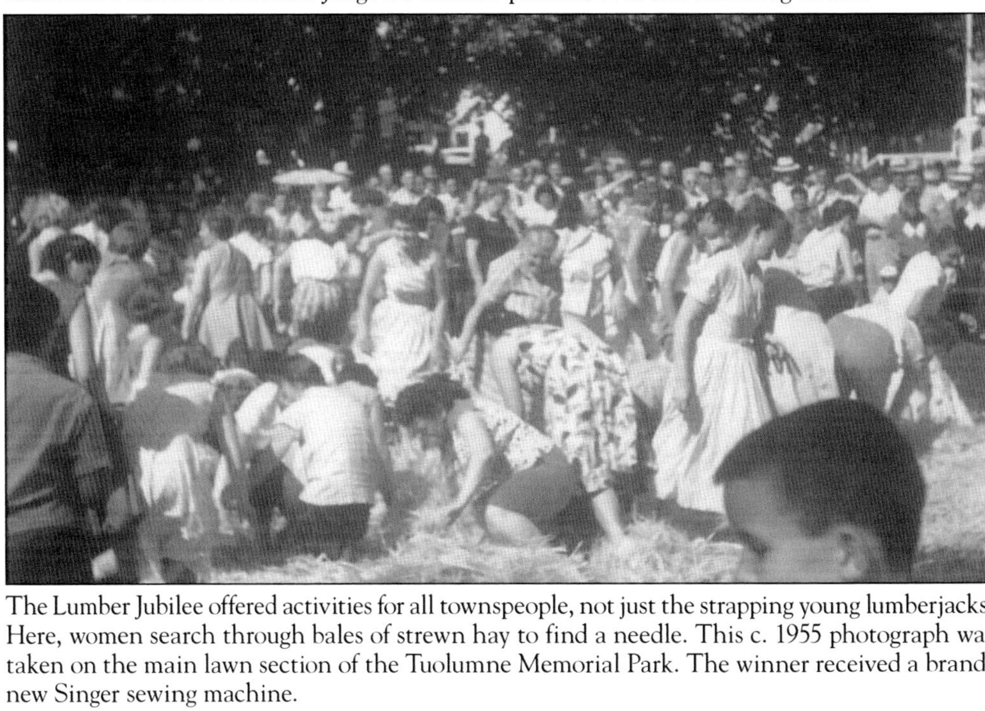

The Lumber Jubilee offered activities for all townspeople, not just the strapping young lumberjacks. Here, women search through bales of strewn hay to find a needle. This c. 1955 photograph was taken on the main lawn section of the Tuolumne Memorial Park. The winner received a brand-new Singer sewing machine.

As technology advanced, so did the competition at the Lumber Jubilee. The hot saw contest evolved from handsaws to chainsaws, greatly increasing the speed at which cuts could be made. To compensate, contestants had to make multiple cuts starting from both the top and the bottom of the log.

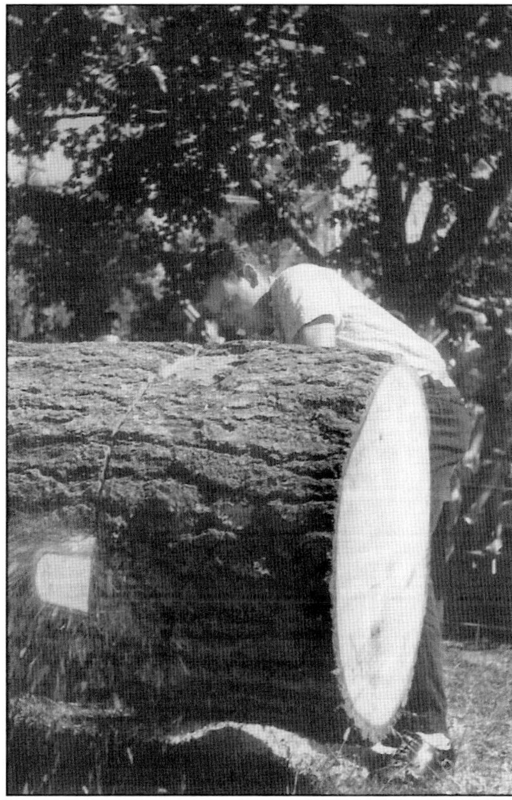

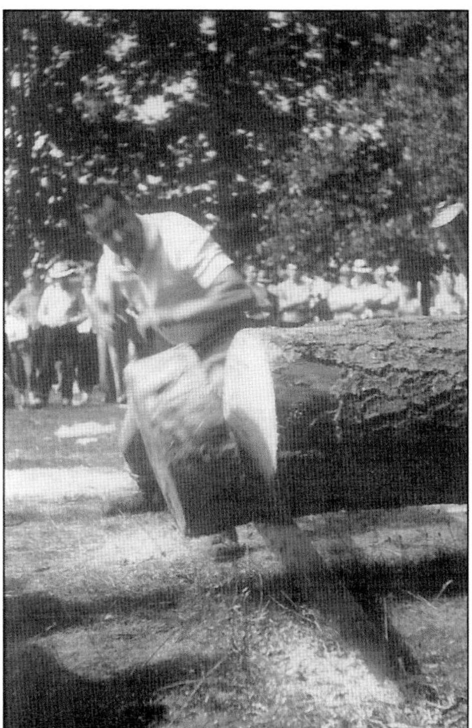

Handsaws do remain a competition category during the Lumber Jubilee, either operated solo or in teams of two. Logs for the handsaw competitions, especially for the solo variety, tended to be from thinner, younger trees than those used for the chainsaw or team handsaw events.

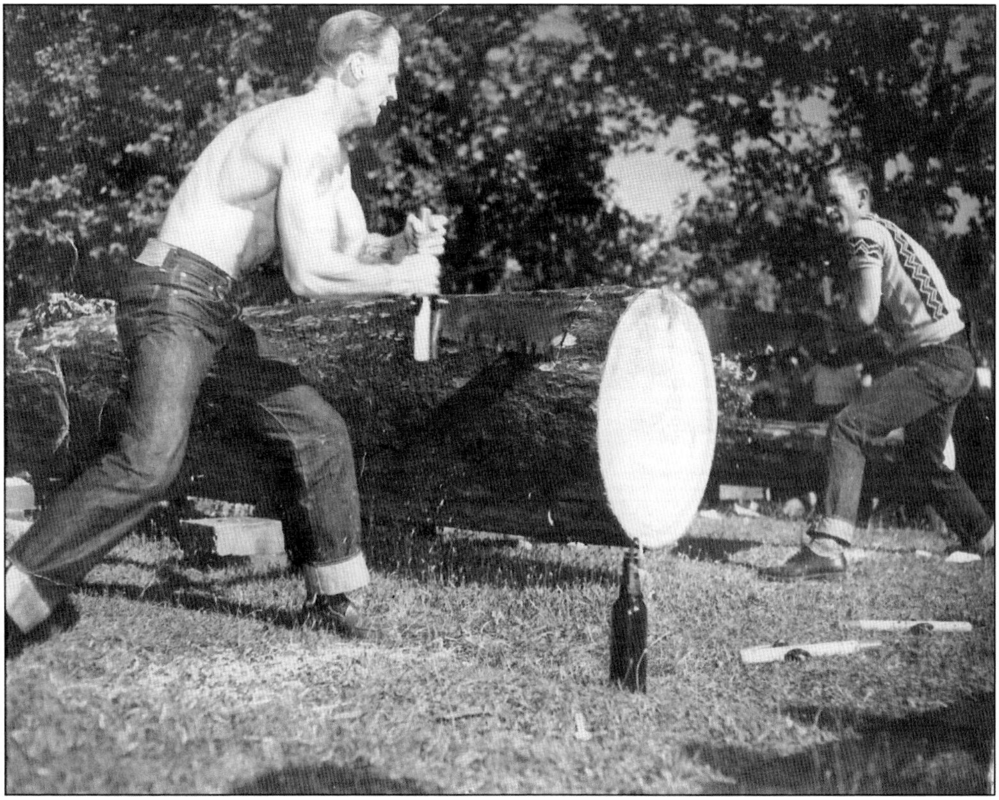

A team of jacks operates a two-man saw in this competition photograph from around 1949. Timing and rhythm were key in posting quick times, so teams that either worked together in the field or practiced beforehand often walked away with top honors.

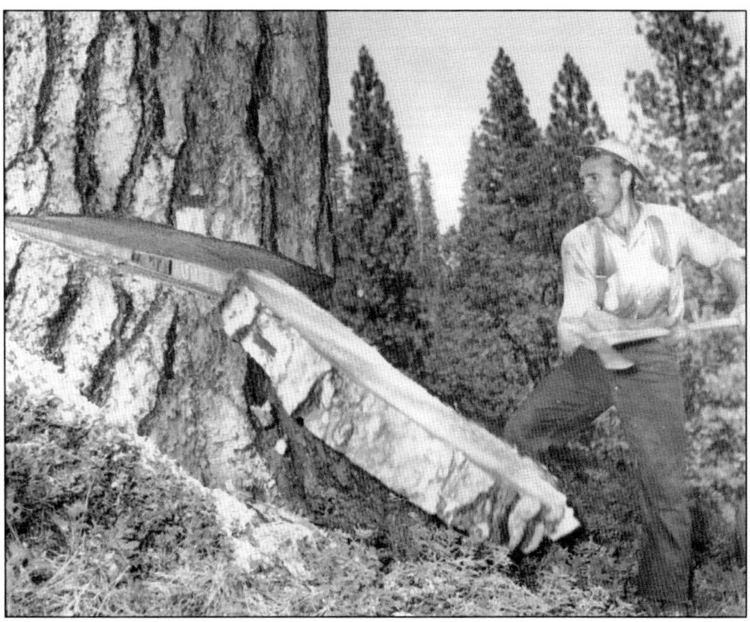

Although slightly antiquated by the time this picture was taken in the late 1950s, hand axes still played a crucial role in West Side's timber-harvesting operations, as demonstrated here by lumberjack Walt Adams. This lumberjack takes out a wedge of a massive sugar pine in order to direct the fall. With trees that were over 200 feet tall and weighed tons, precision was important.

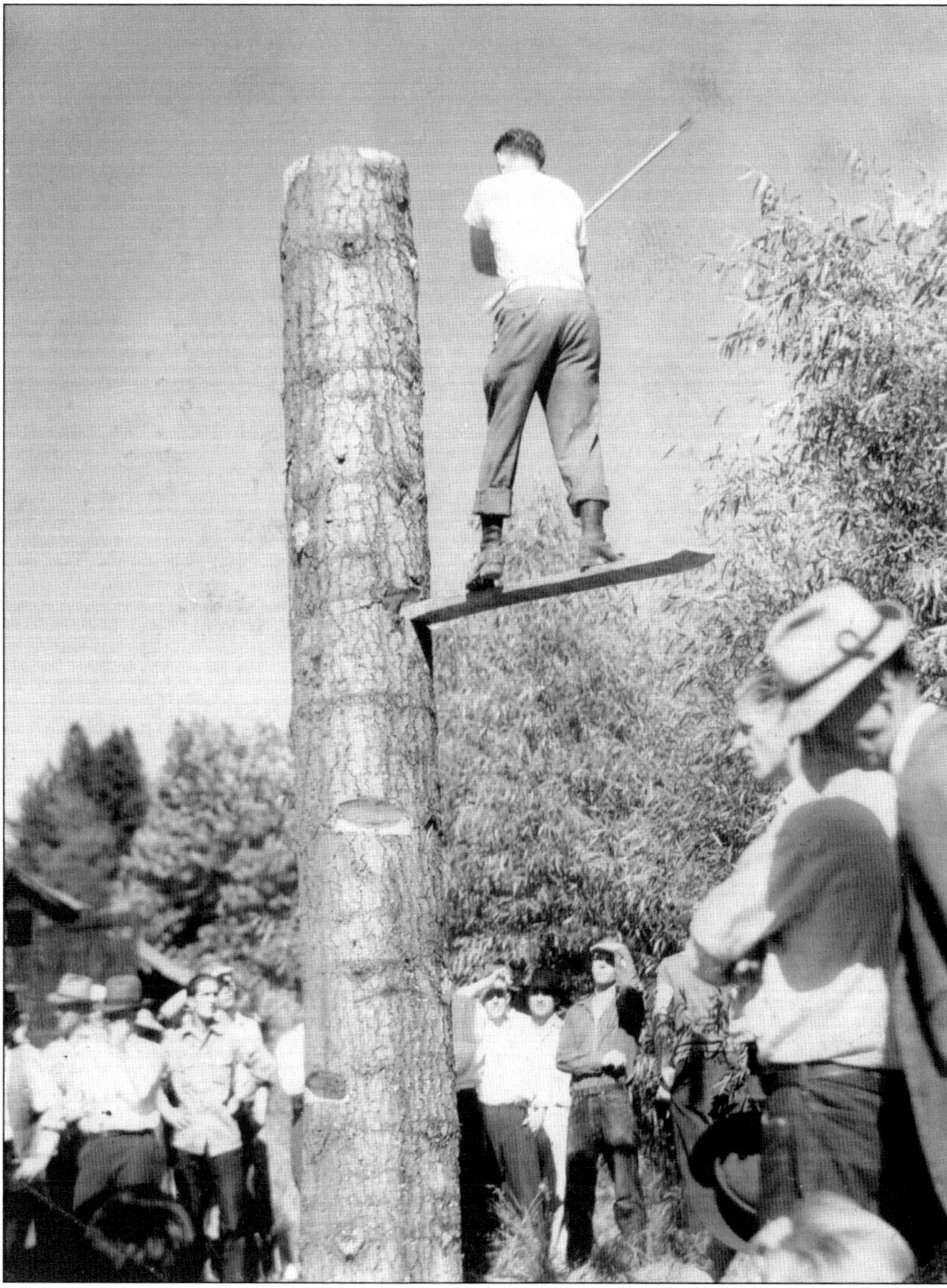

One of the more exciting and dangerous events at the Lumber Jubilee is the springboard chop, demonstrated here by a daring young lumberjack around 1950. This event requires tremendous axe skills, impeccable balance, and speed. In the forests around Tuolumne, West Side lumberjacks would often employ the techniques used in the springboard chop to enable them to reach the softer, more forgiving wood above the sometimes knotty and gnarled base of a tree marked for clearing. Climbing to a height of nine feet, contestants would make two chops for springboards to stand on before chopping through the diameter of the top of the tree. This event is still held today.

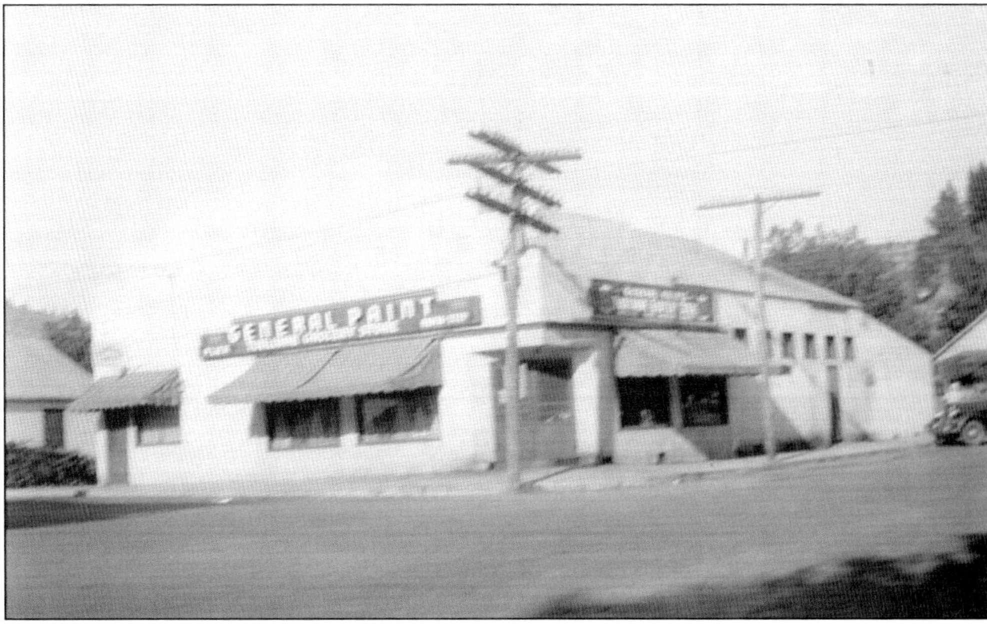

Boasting one of the best locations in town at the corner of Pine Street and Bay Avenue, the Tuolumne Hardware store was originally a grocery store operated by Bill Talbert from the 1940s through the 1960s. It eventually became a paint store (as seen here), before being converted to a hardware store in 1969. As of 2012, this building is vacant.

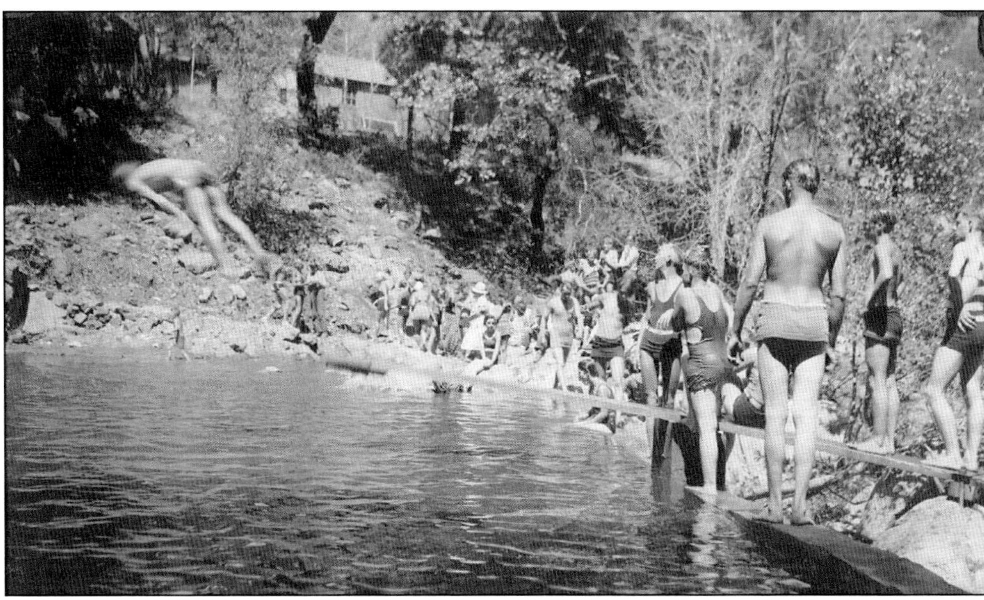

In the summertime, one of the more popular hangout spots for youngsters was Riverside Pool, which was just down Buchanan Mine Road along the North Fork of the Tuolumne River. Located only a few minutes' drive from town, this particular swimming hole was the place to be when school was out and featured a makeshift diving board.

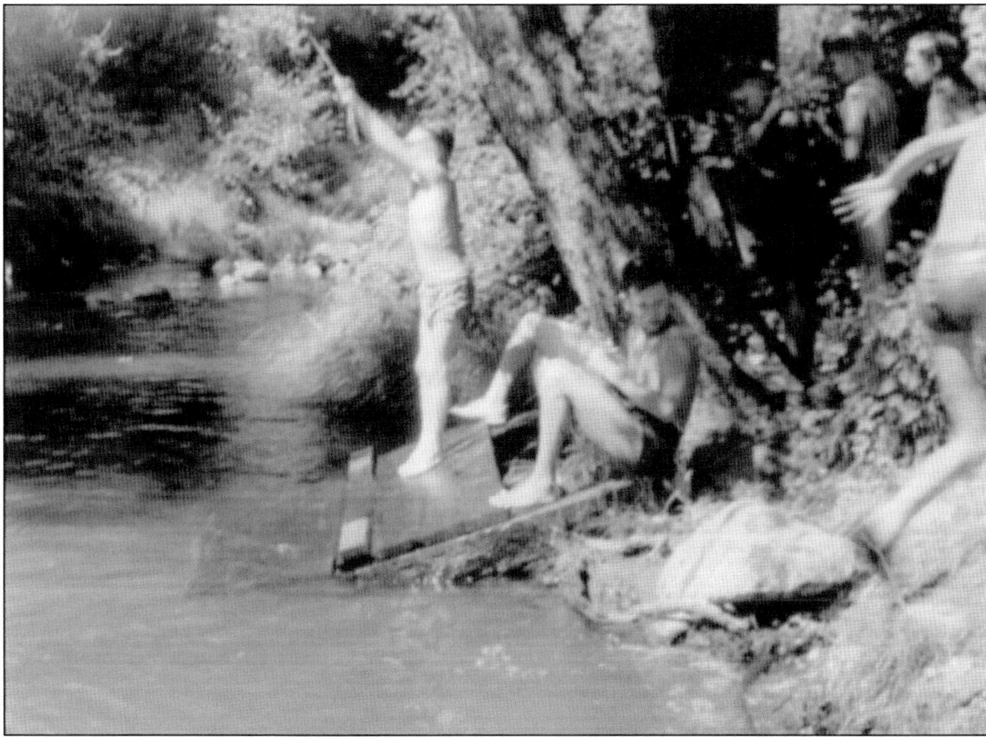

Rope swings were also a popular addition to Riverside Pool and other swimming holes by the Tuolumne River. The stretch along the Tuolumne down Buchanan Mine Road remains one of the most popular camping and recreational destinations for residents of Tuolumne County.

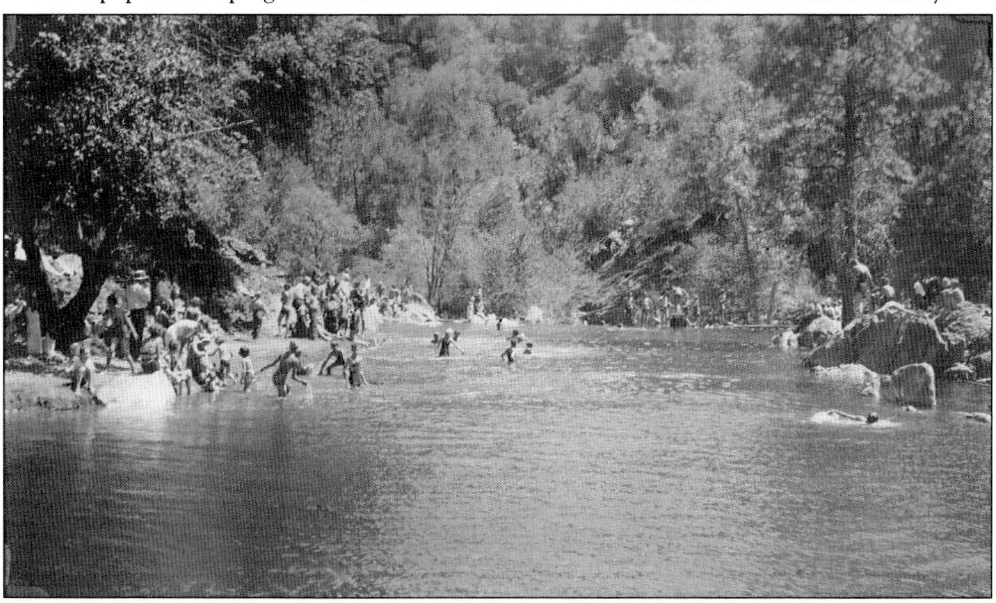

Most Tuolumne children walked or rode bicycles to the swimming holes along Tuolumne River; some even hitched a ride on a stray burro (during the very early 20th century) or with a rancher. Oftentimes, entire families would drive down to the river and spend the day or camp overnight in the hot summer days before air-conditioning.

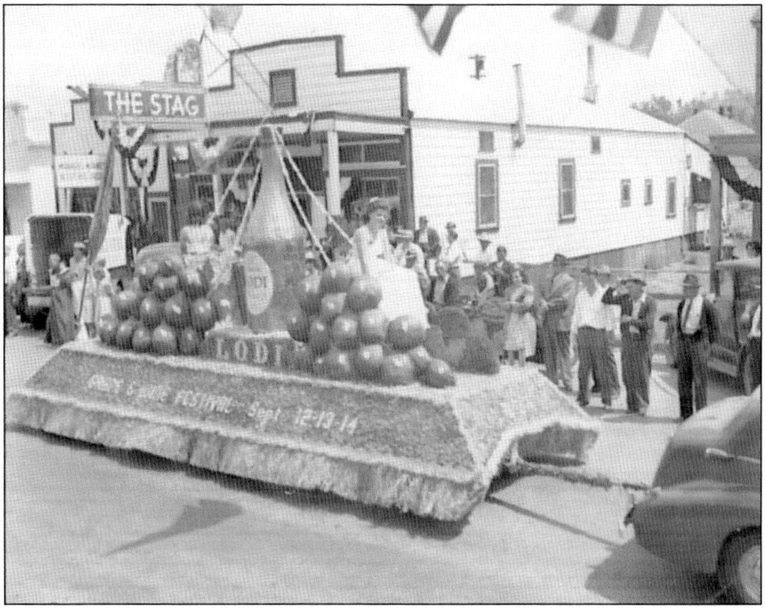

During its zenith in the late 1950s, the Tuolumne Lumber Jubilee parade featured floats from all over Northern California. Here, a young lady promotes the upcoming Lodi Grape and Wine Festival occurring during that late-1950s summer. Lodi is over 115 miles away from Tuolumne City.

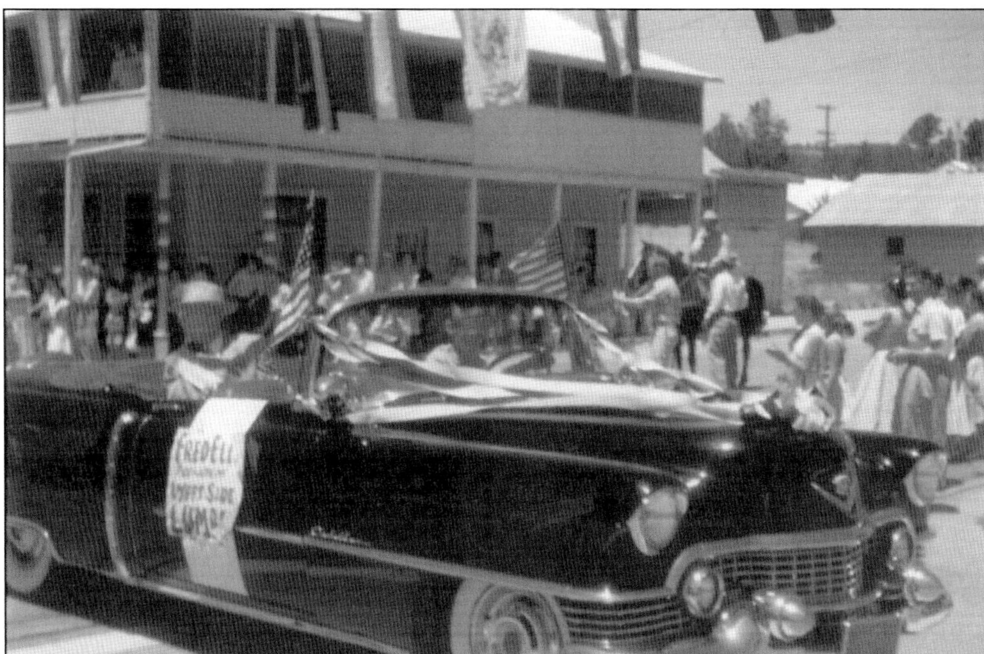

Although some came from out of town, local floats were far more common. Here, Fred Ellis, the president of the West Side Lumber Company, rolls through the Lumber Jubilee parade down Bay Avenue. Ellis was one of the longest-serving presidents of the West Side Lumber Company.

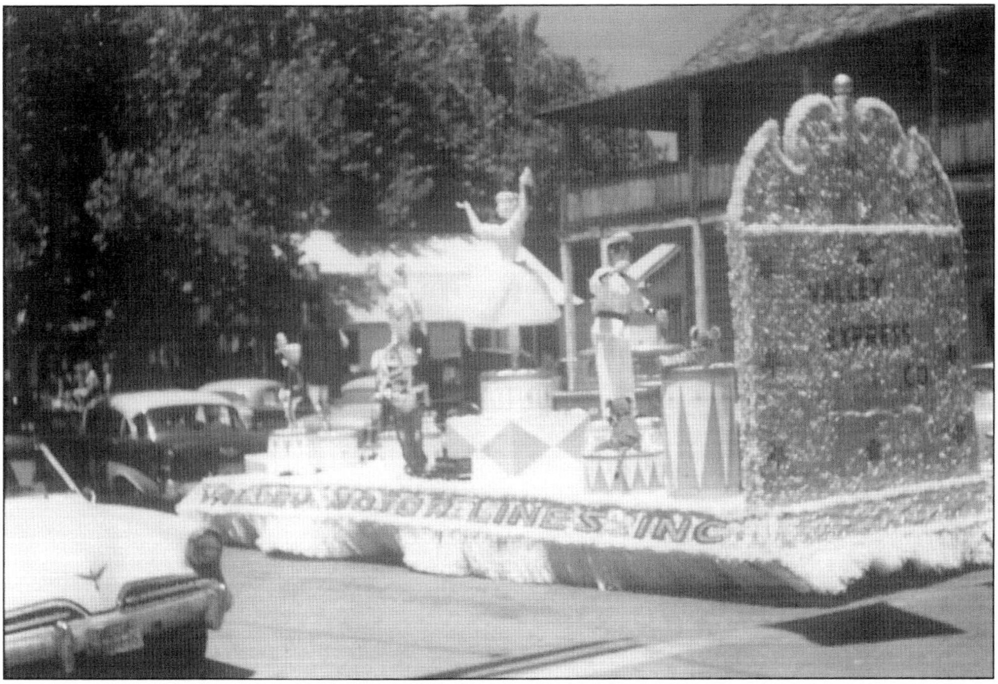

Lumber Jubilee floats became quite extravagant as the years went on, as evidenced by this Valley Express Company float from around 1960. Complete with full-color animatronic characters and many moving parts, this float was sure to catch eyes as it traveled down Main Street.

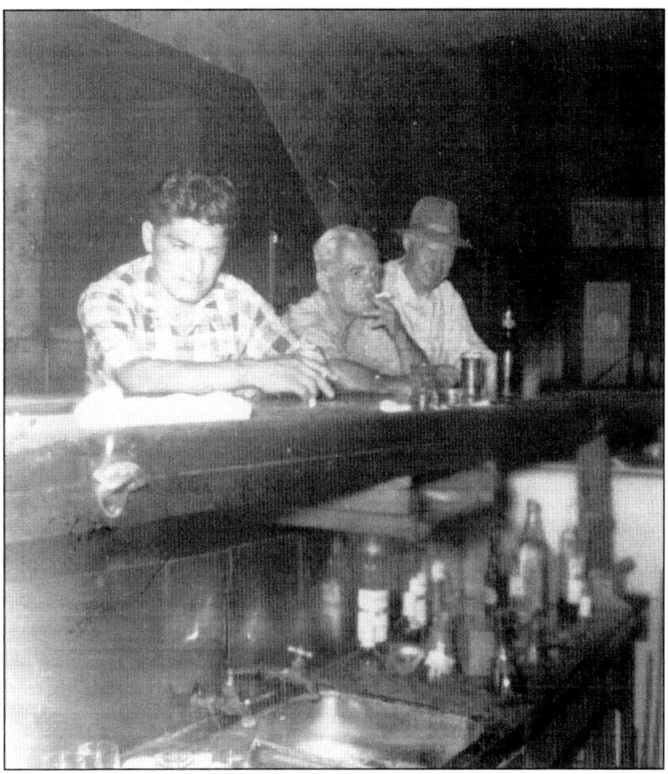

A popular stop during any Lumber Jubilee celebration was one of Tuolumne's several bars. This c. 1950 photograph, taken at what is now The Logger's, shows three patrons unwinding after a long day. The Logger's is currently the only remaining bar in Tuolumne City.

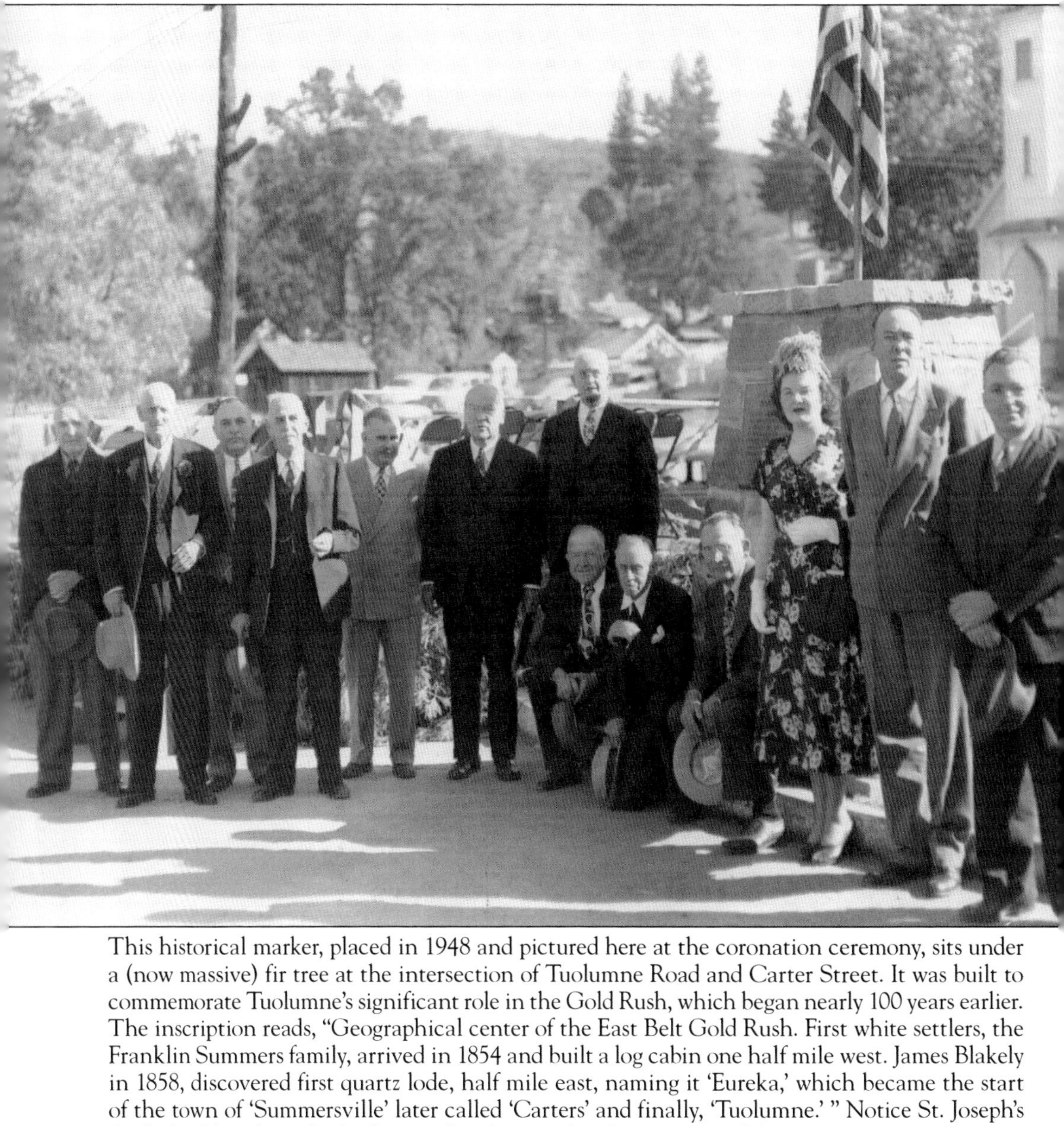

This historical marker, placed in 1948 and pictured here at the coronation ceremony, sits under a (now massive) fir tree at the intersection of Tuolumne Road and Carter Street. It was built to commemorate Tuolumne's significant role in the Gold Rush, which began nearly 100 years earlier. The inscription reads, "Geographical center of the East Belt Gold Rush. First white settlers, the Franklin Summers family, arrived in 1854 and built a log cabin one half mile west. James Blakely in 1858, discovered first quartz lode, half mile east, naming it 'Eureka,' which became the start of the town of 'Summersville' later called 'Carters' and finally, 'Tuolumne.' " Notice St. Joseph's Catholic Church in the background with its updated entrance and front staircase.

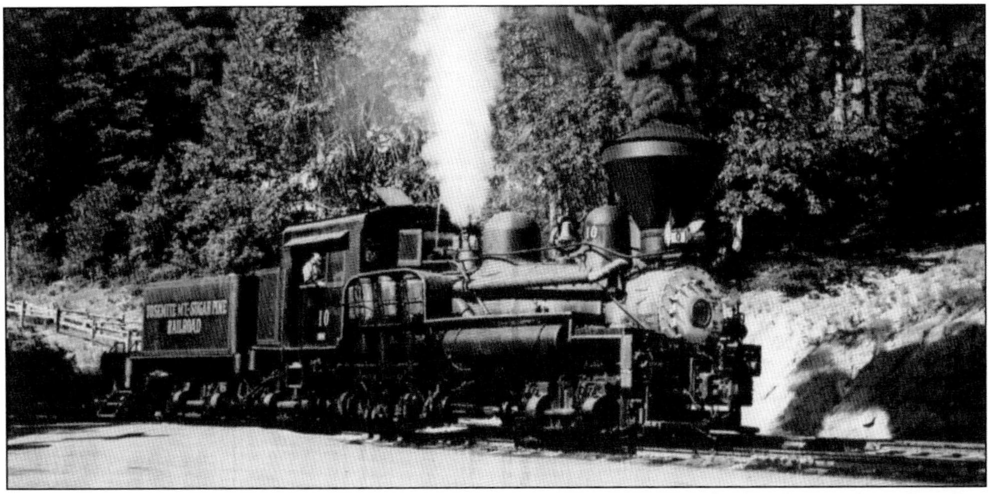

When "Shorty" Maddox drove the last West Side logging train to the lumberyard on October 28, 1960, it sounded the death knell for many of West Side's unique and prized narrow-gauge locomotives. However, Engine No. 10, a Lima-built, three-truck Shay constructed in 1928, avoided that fate by being picked up by the Yosemite Mountain Sugar Pine Railroad, which is pictured here in the 1980s.

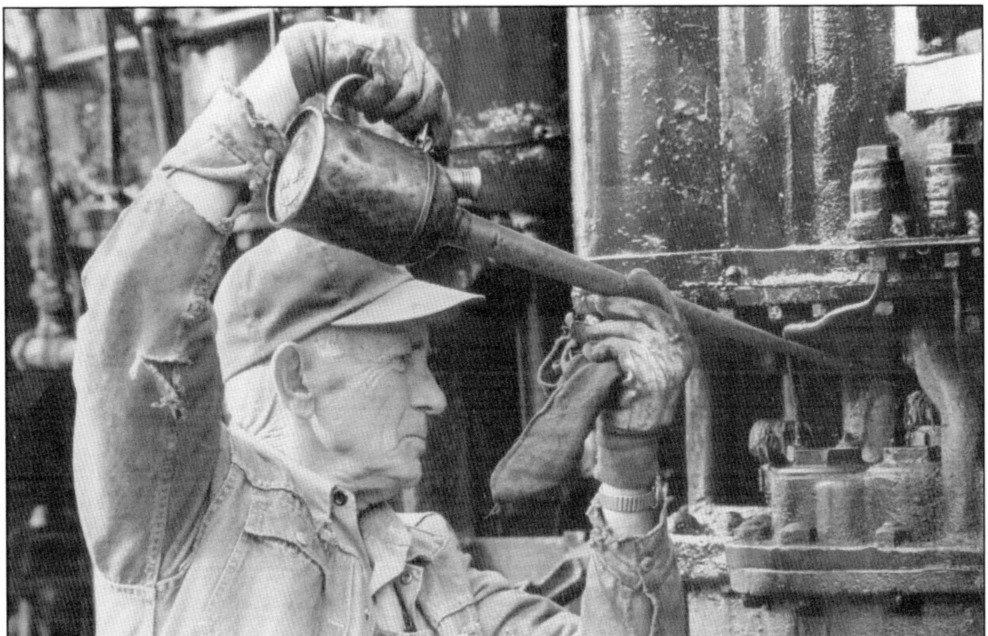

Seen here using a long oiler for regular maintenance is Ed Sullivan, who started his career with West Side at 13 years of age, working in the box factory to help support his family after his father died. He then became a water boy, hauling water by burro to lumber pilers and mill workers, who later gave him a gold watch for his remarkable service. Sullivan went on to become a West Side Railroad fireman and then an engineer when he was 18, learning his trade by hitching a ride on the West Side trains at the end of the day when his duties as water boy were over. Sullivan continued to work at West Side as an engineer and later in the engine house, maintaining the locomotives until his retirement in 1960, when he received a second gold watch from the company.

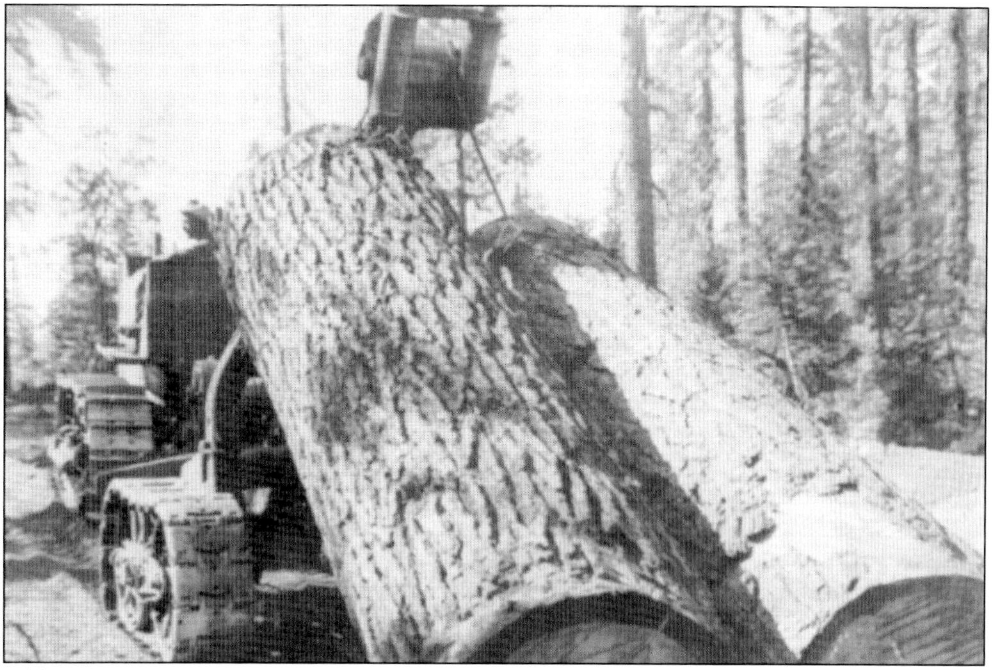

Although it officially shut down in 1960, West Side's death was slow and prolonged. A combination of factors led to the closure, and one of them was the advent of new technology. As equipment like bulldozers became available, more trees could be harvested faster by fewer people, initiating the loss of some of the mill's labor force.

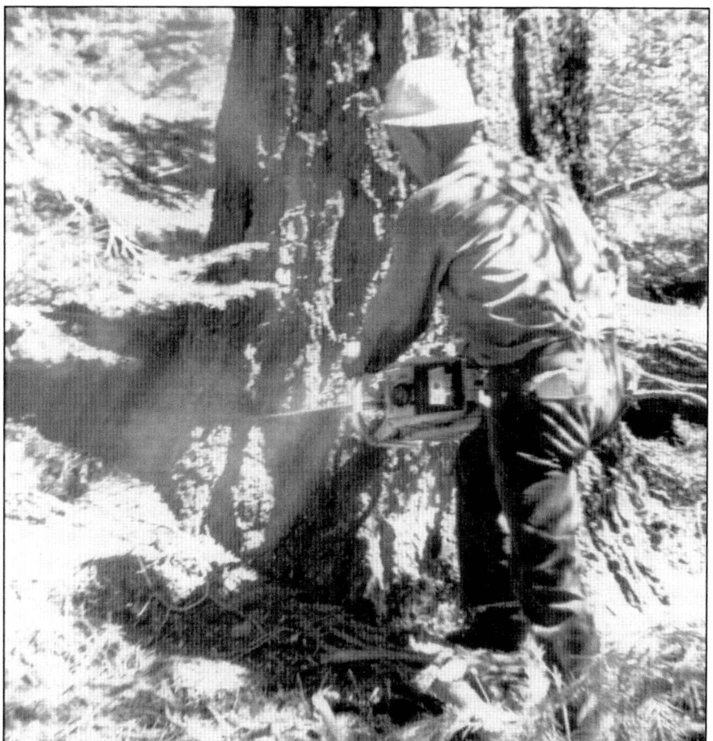

Another cause for West Side's demise was the decreased availability of the huge stands of virgin timber for which the mill was built. As smaller trees were harvested, most mills were refitted to handle the smaller timber, but West Side's huge saws became obsolete. Pickering sent more of its timber to the Standard mill, and West Side handled increasingly fewer logs. In this 1940s photograph, a lumberjack preps a large tree with a chainsaw.

The advent and eventual dominance of logging trucks was another key component that hastened West Side's demise, as the system and infrastructure was set up to be reliant upon trains. Trucks were cheaper to run, quicker and easier to load, and able to reach to most of the locations trains could. Here, a West Side employee double-checks a strap before sending the truck off with its payload.

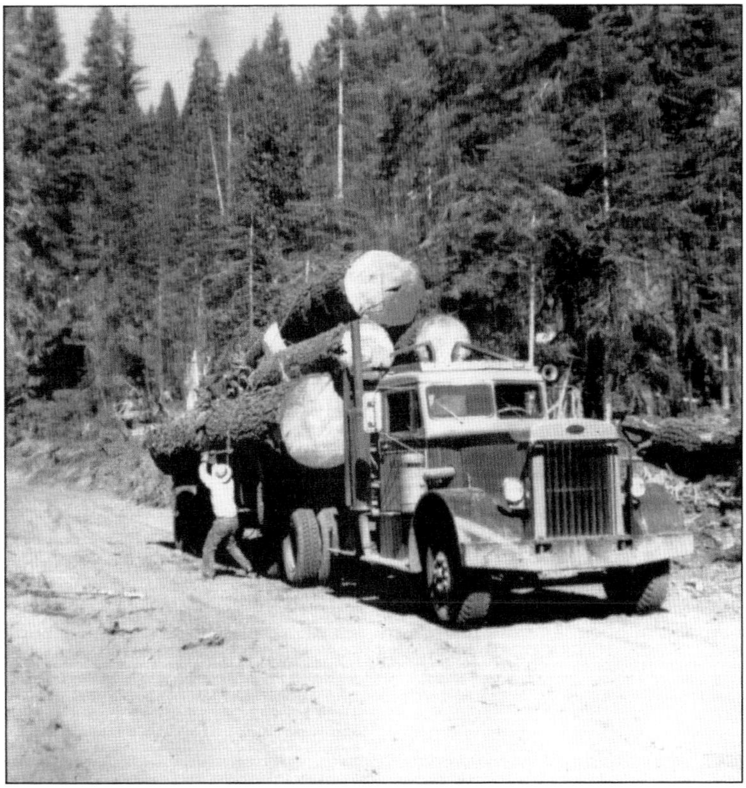

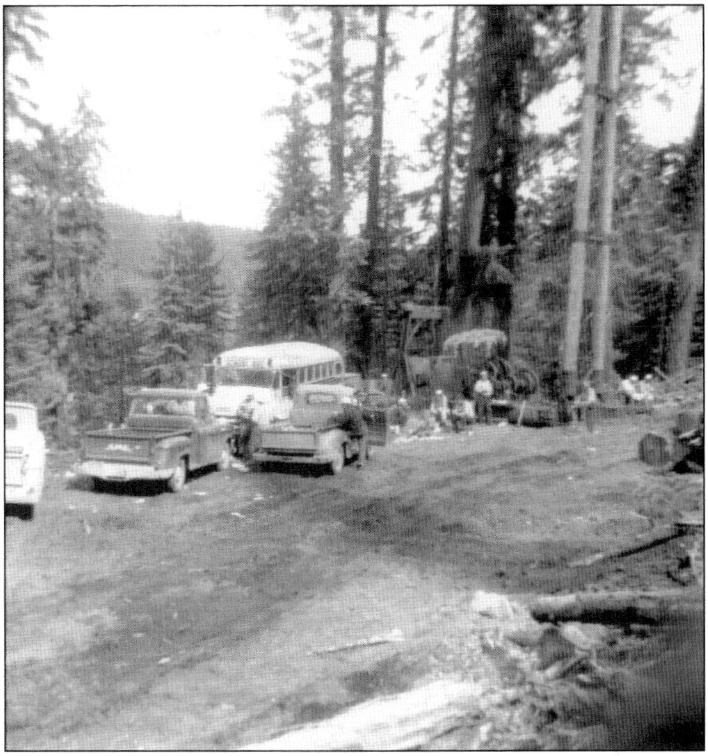

Another casualty of technological progress was the logging camp. For years, lumberjacks—and sometimes their families—would move out to logging camps set up in the forest during the summer to avoid long and economically unfeasible train rides to and from the site. With the explosive growth of the automobile, however, employees could ride in and out to work in a fraction of the time. Unfortunately, many of the logging camps were simply abandoned and left to mar the landscape.

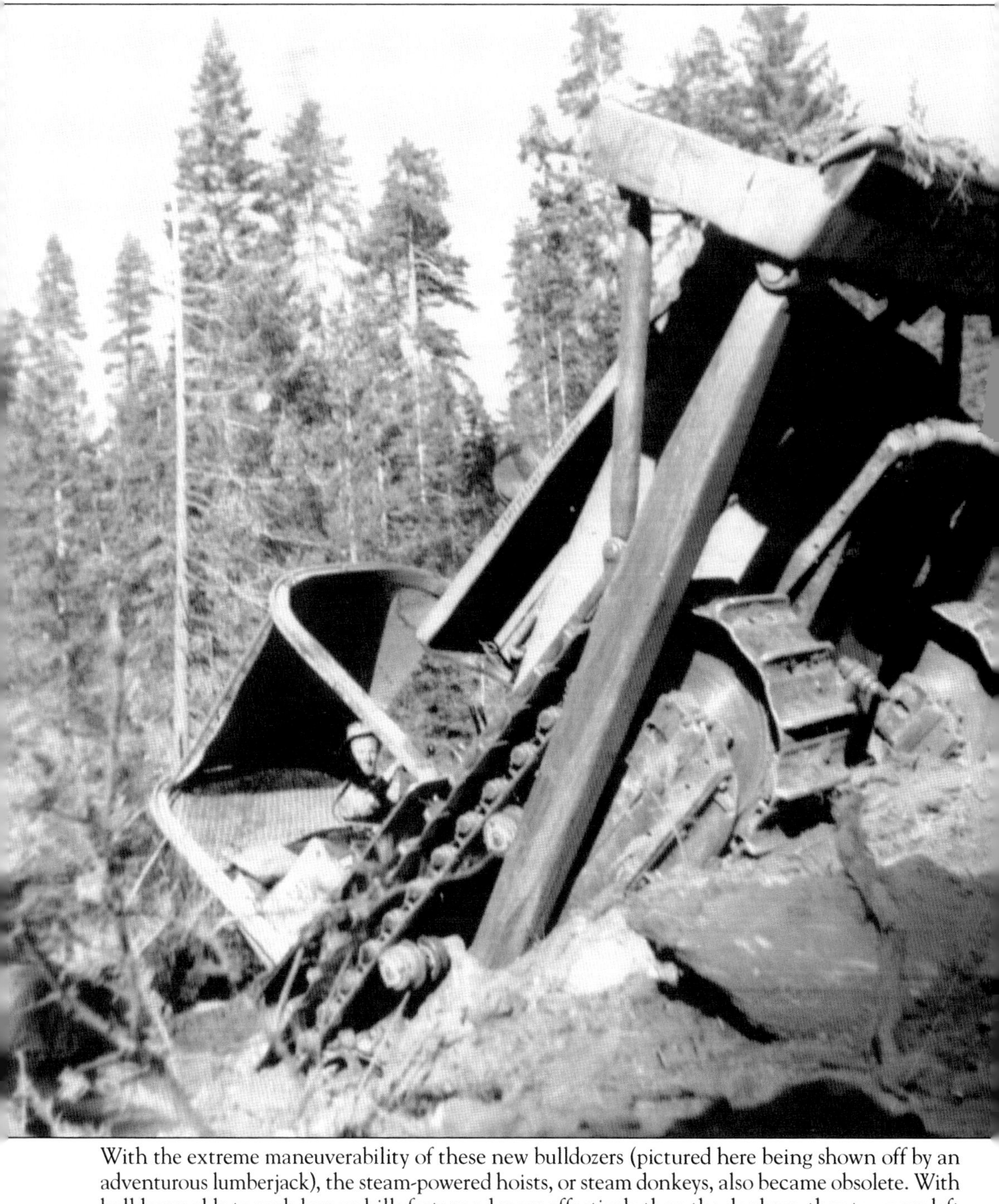

With the extreme maneuverability of these new bulldozers (pictured here being shown off by an adventurous lumberjack), the steam-powered hoists, or steam donkeys, also became obsolete. With bulldozers able to push logs up hills faster and more effectively than the donkeys, they too were left to rot and rust and can still be found in many areas throughout the forest surrounding Tuolumne. The steam donkey remains a popular cultural image in Tuolumne County today, as several are preserved and on display in various locations. A popular bar and restaurant near Lake Pinecrest (located approximately 25 miles northeast of Tuolumne) is named the Steam Donkey.

One of the reasons the narrow-gauge train and rail system of West Side remains so popular today is its quaintness. In this 1955 photograph, the bridge-tender of the logging camp of Camp Niagara, Frank Smith, hands a letter to train conductor Earl Shields for prompt delivery to Tuolumne City.

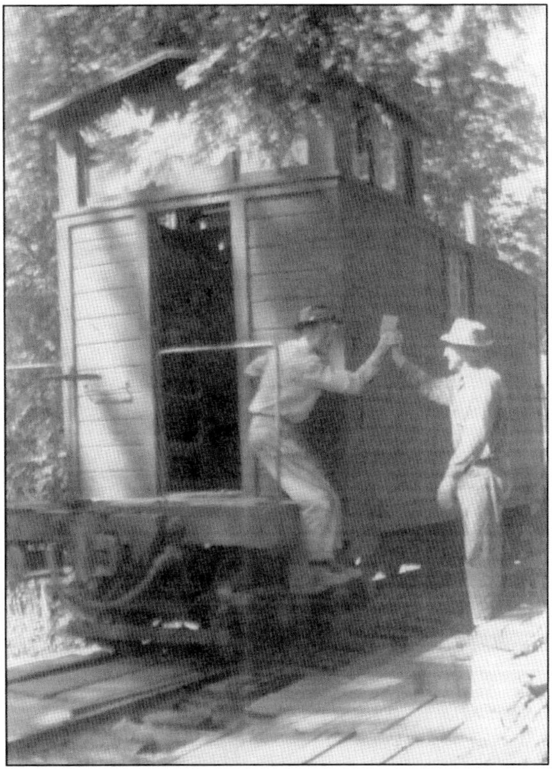

This c. 1940 image shows the early Tuolumne Post Office, housed in the West Side building for nearly 60 years. The post office was later moved to a building at the corner of Pine and Fir Streets (which is now Tuolumne Parks and Recreation District building) and again to its current location on Carter Street.

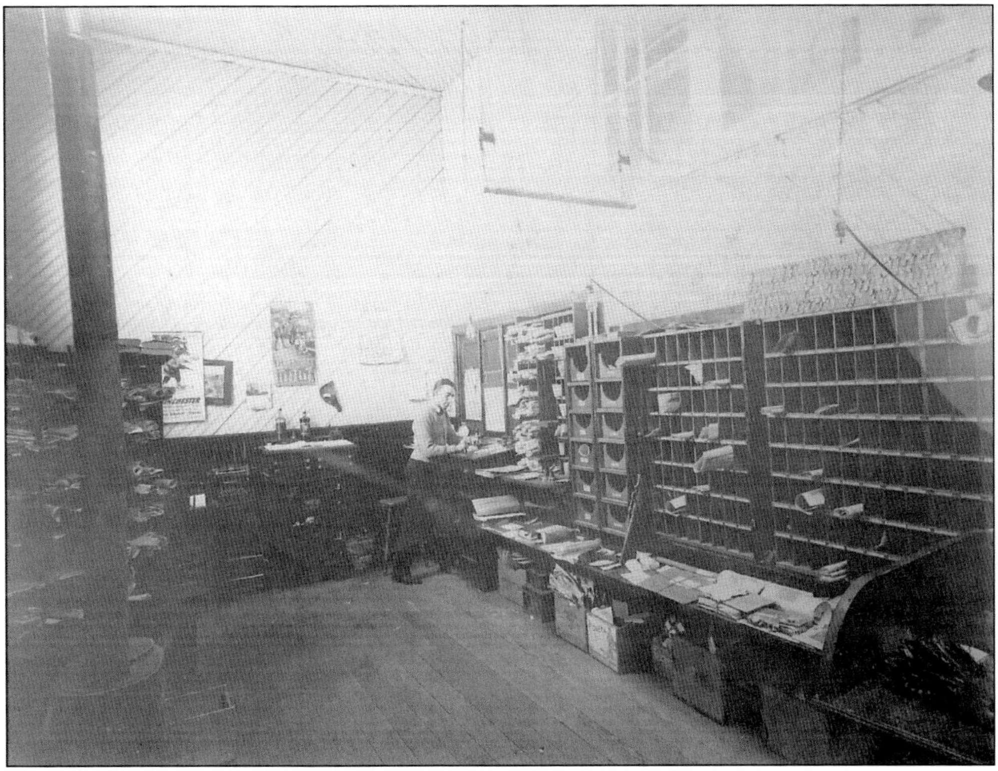

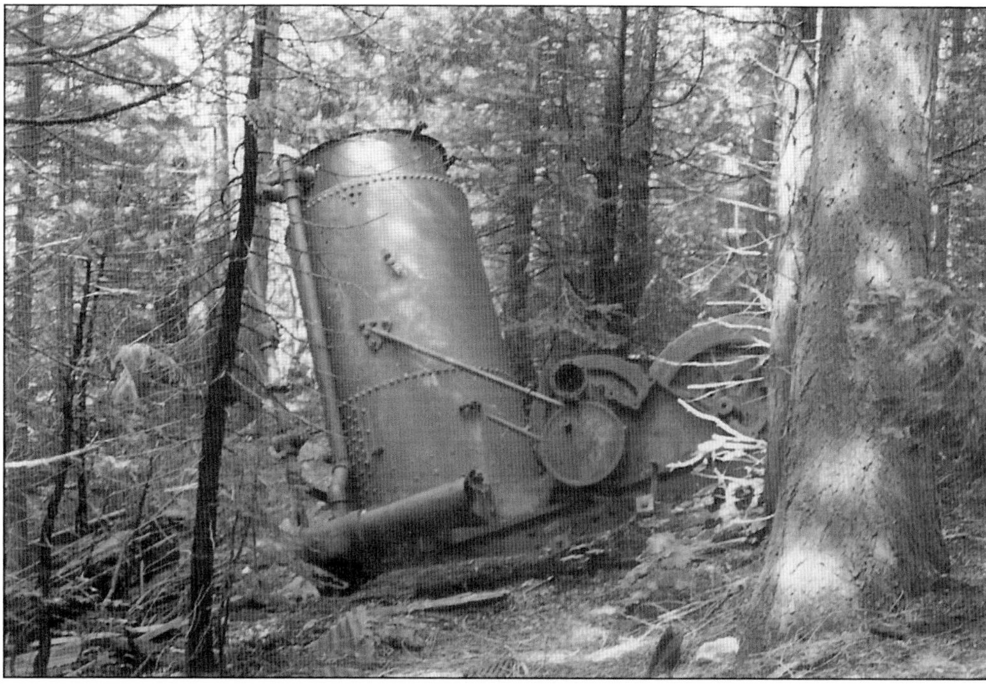

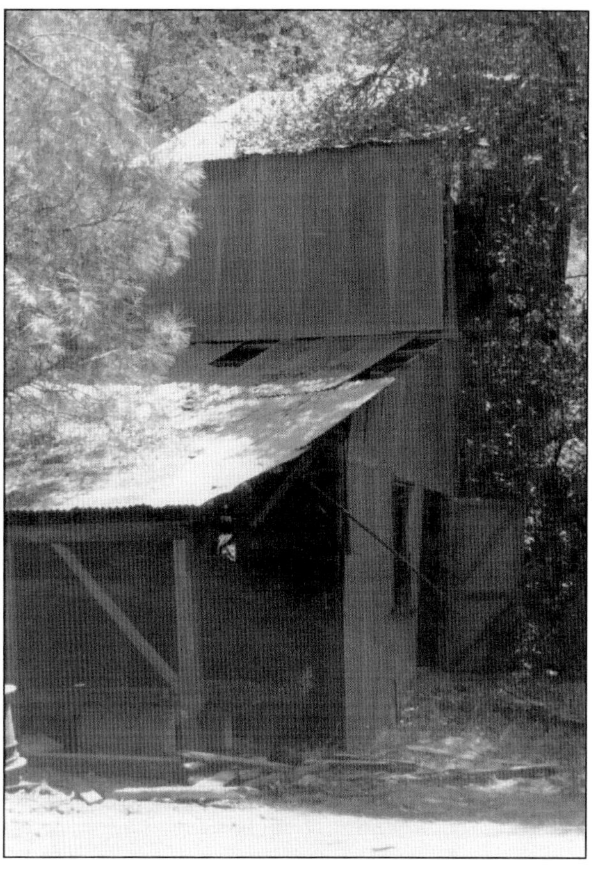

A heavily rusted steam donkey disintegrates in the forest just off the North Fork of the Tuolumne River in this c. 1975 photograph. A popular hiking trail that begins on Buchanan Mine Road goes along the pathway of the main line of the West Side railway, and artifacts such as these are not too difficult for hikers to find.

This aluminum-sided and wood-framed building houses the remains of the Mine Stamp Mill from the Lady Washington Mine. A working model of this mill is in the Tuolumne City Museum.

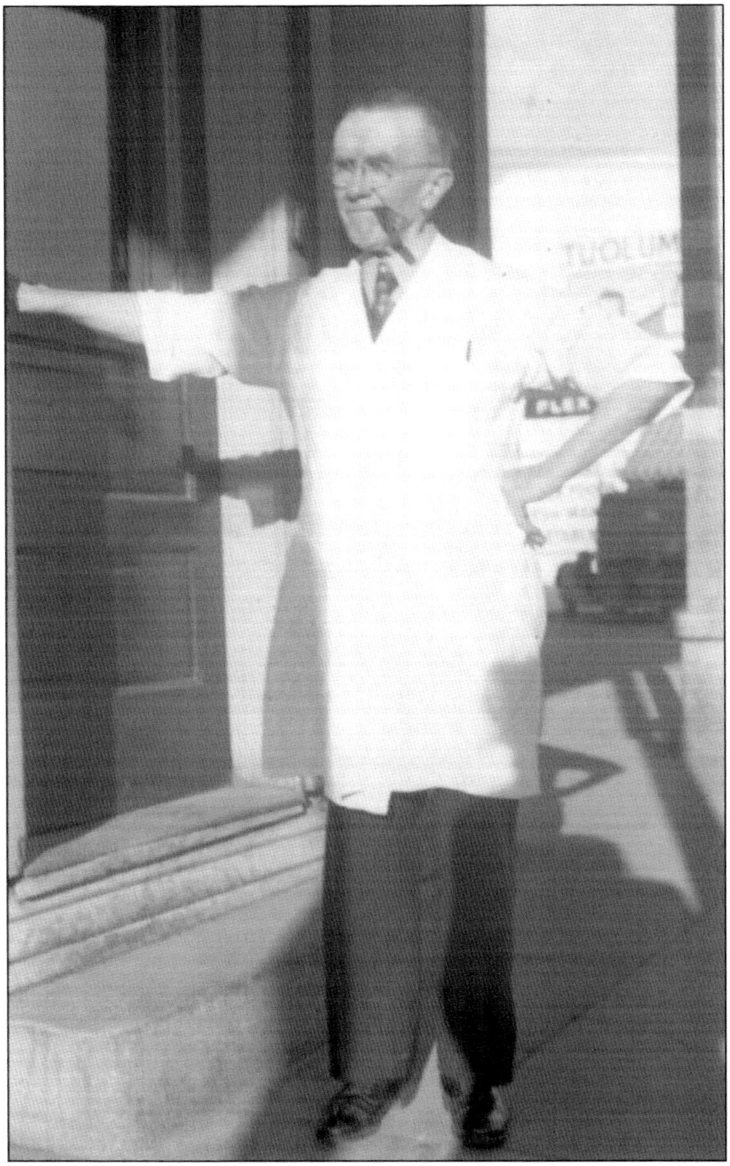

Known simply as Johnny the Barber, Johannes "Johnny" Wittorf was by far the most popular barber in Tuolumne's golden age and one of the more well-known citizens. Wittorf, who was of German descent, arrived in town while it was still known as Carters when he was just 20 years old. He initially worked as an apprentice with fellow German Henry Scheer, who operated the Wittorf and Scheer: Tonsorial Artists shop; people from all over the county would travel to his shop to get a well-done and cheap haircut. Wittorf was also known for his generosity because he always left large tips at the various businesses around town and wanted to share his considerable estate with his fellow Americans, whom he viewed as integral parts of his achievement of the American Dream. Upon his death on November 4, 1959, he devoted all of his wealth (he had no relatives) to local churches and a large portion of his stocks to Summerville Elementary. The stocks were profitable enough to provide the school with a new library and new books annually; as a thank you, each year on Memorial Day a group of students makes the short trip to his grave at Carters Cemetery (his is the only marker with a barber pole) and decorates his grave with flowers.

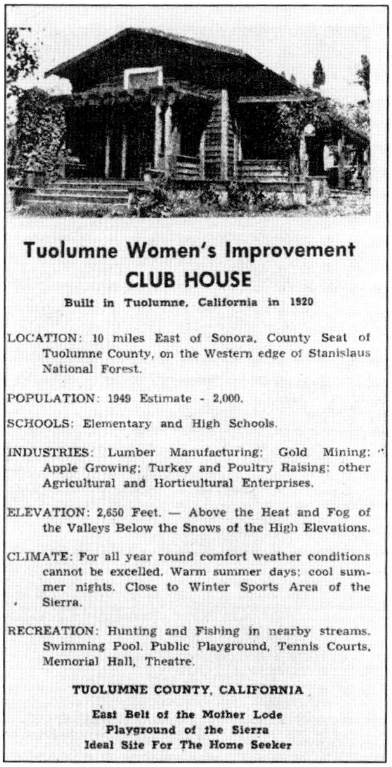
Tuolumne Women's Improvement
CLUB HOUSE
Built in Tuolumne, California in 1920

LOCATION: 10 miles East of Sonora, County Seat of Tuolumne County, on the Western edge of Stanislaus National Forest.

POPULATION: 1949 Estimate - 2,000.

SCHOOLS: Elementary and High Schools.

INDUSTRIES: Lumber Manufacturing; Gold Mining; Apple Growing; Turkey and Poultry Raising; other Agricultural and Horticultural Enterprises.

ELEVATION: 2,650 Feet. — Above the Heat and Fog of the Valleys Below the Snows of the High Elevations.

CLIMATE: For all year round comfort weather conditions cannot be excelled. Warm summer days; cool summer nights. Close to Winter Sports Area of the Sierra.

RECREATION: Hunting and Fishing in nearby streams. Swimming Pool. Public Playground, Tennis Courts, Memorial Hall, Theatre.

TUOLUMNE COUNTY, CALIFORNIA

East Belt of the Mother Lode
Playground of the Sierra
Ideal Site For The Home Seeker

This flyer advertising the Tuolumne Women's Improvement Club House is more of a plug for Tuolumne than the club. It was built in 1921 on land donated by the West Side Lumber Company and WSLC vice president George Johnson. A classic Craftsman-style building, it served not only as the women's club meeting spot, but also as the local library and a site for birthday parties, wedding and baby showers, dance classes, Scout meetings, and other small community events for the next 45 years. As membership in the Women's Improvement Club aged and waned, the building fell into disrepair (seen below) and was finally closed in the mid-1970s, as it was deemed unsafe to occupy.

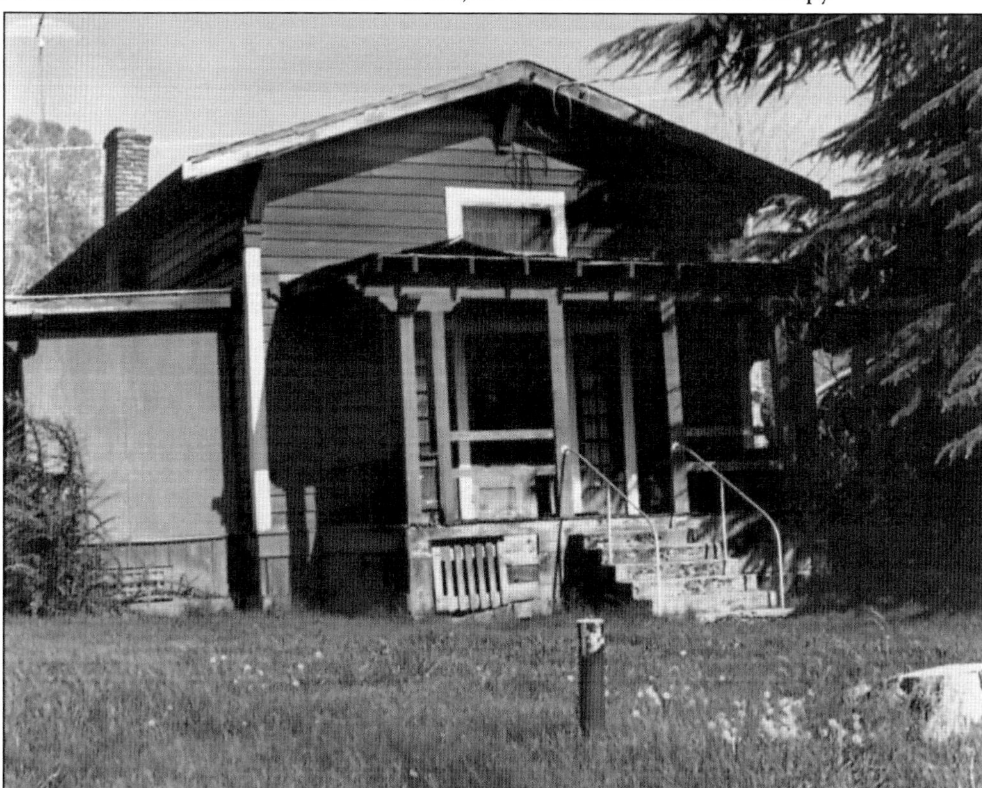

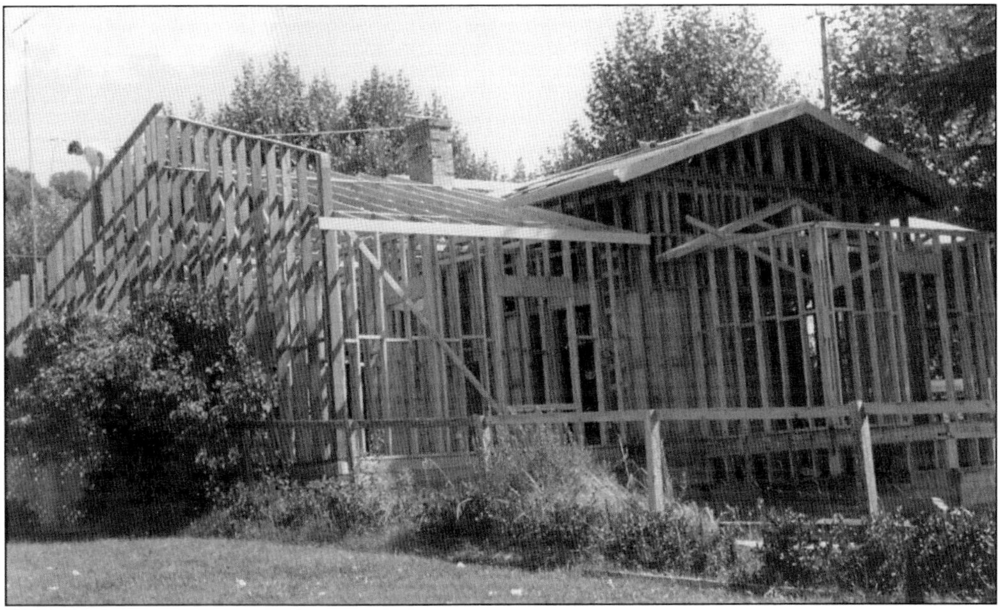

The Tuolumne Women's Improvement Club donated the deed to its cabin to the newly formed Tuolumne Memorial City Museum in 1981. The central location and corner lot proved to be a great home for the museum, and in 1982, a construction project began to restore and completely renovate the clubhouse, which was deeded to the museum.

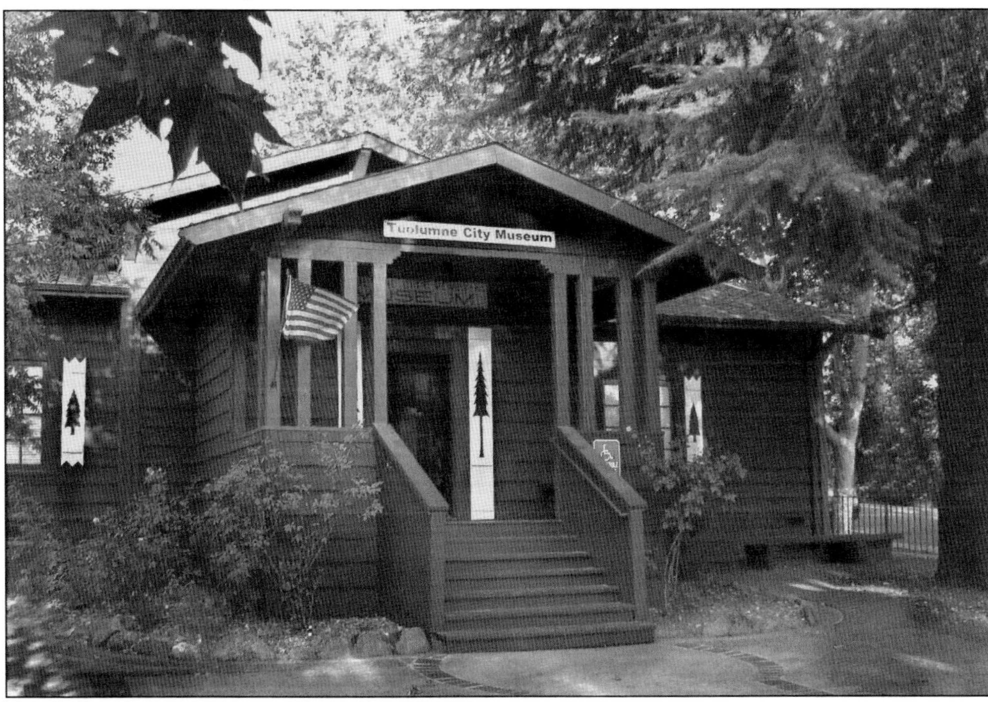

By Christmas 1984, the brand-new Tuolumne Memorial City Museum was open for business. Although Don Grover (architect), John Feriani (contractor), and Eve Pecchenino (interior designer) were key in finalizing the project, it could not have been completed without the help of numerous volunteers from throughout the town.

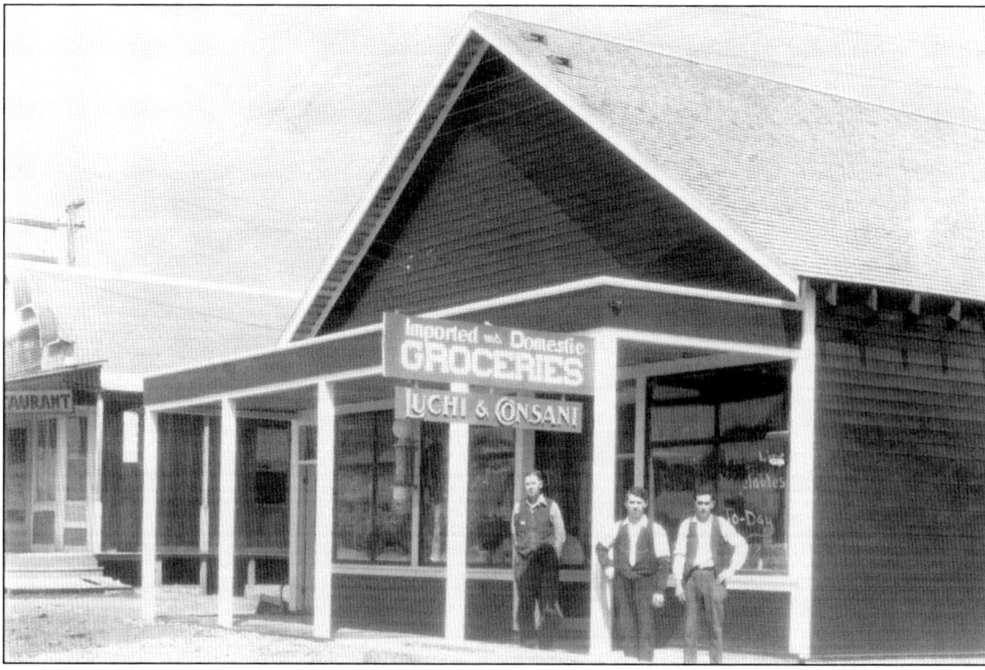

Tuolumne has always had a strong contingent of Italian-American immigrant families who traveled west in hopes of finding the American Dream. Here, the Luchi & Consani grocery store stands on the corner of Carter Street and Chestnut Avenue. This building was lost in the fire of 1918.

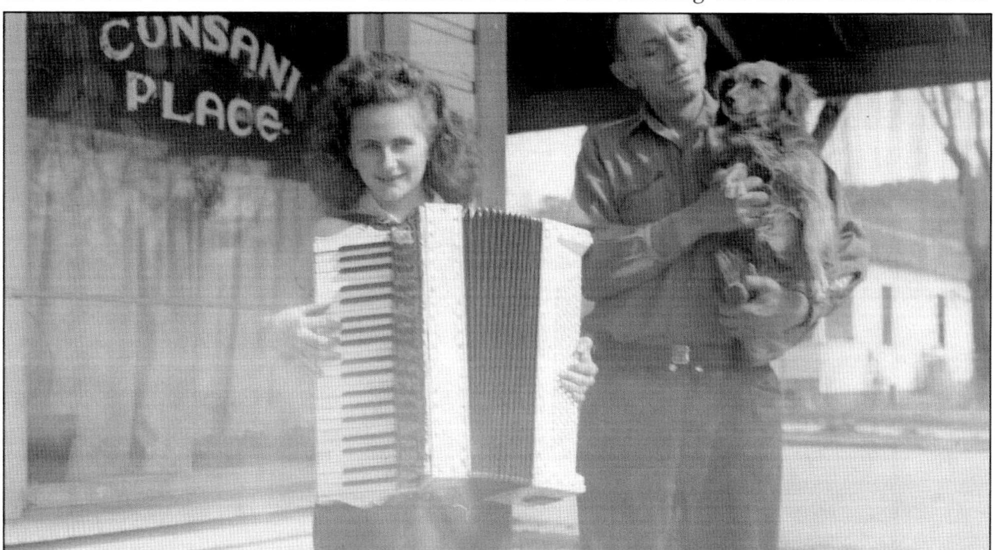

The Consanis eventually rebuilt, however, and their family's descendents continue to live in Tuolumne. No longer aligned with Luchi, Consani Place was a restaurant that served Italian food, which was very popular with the mill workers. Here, Junie Consani and her father, Tony, are shown in front of the new restaurant around 1950. The restaurant was in the downstairs portion of a two-story building on the corner. Perhaps Tuolumne's most unique home is the Consani house on Carter Street, which was built by Consani himself and features all hand-laid stonework as facing.

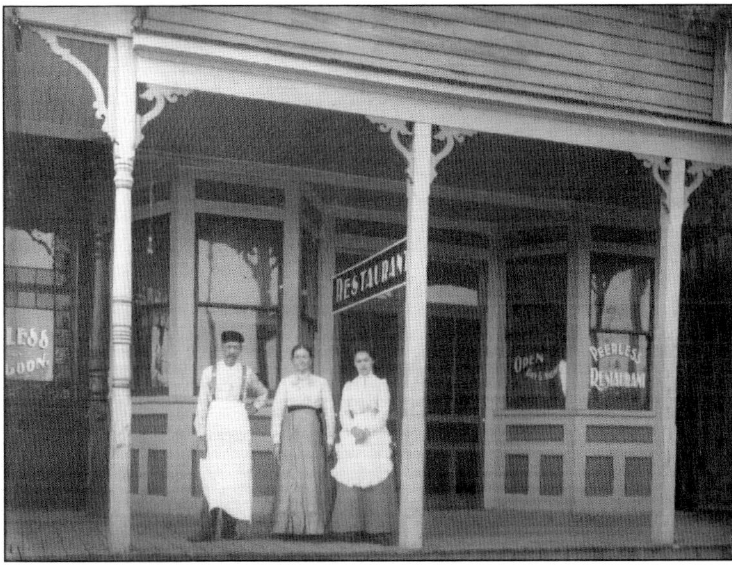

Restaurants were one industry that survived fires, economic downturns, and just about everything else that Tuolumne dealt with throughout the years. In this c. 1920 photograph, employees stand in front of the Peerless Restaurant and Saloon on Chestnut Avenue.

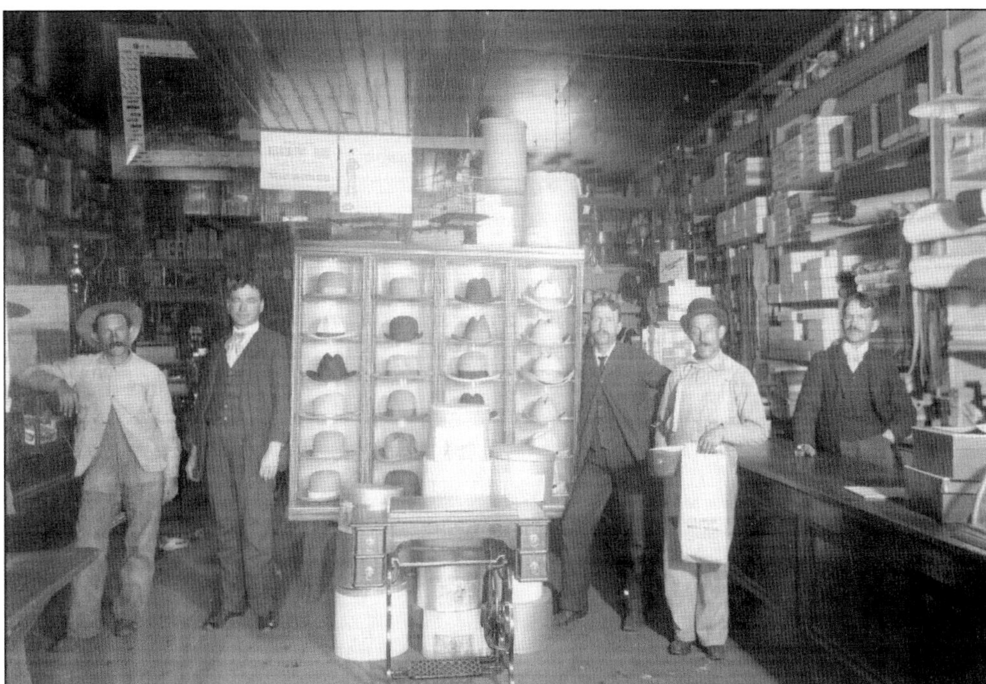

Hat shops, on the other hand, were not quite as popular. This 1890s photograph shows some unidentified gentlemen standing beside the latest fashions in men's head wear in the interior of Carter's store in Old Town (Carters). General merchandise shops were popular in Tuolumne's early days as one-stop shops for miners and lumberjacks.

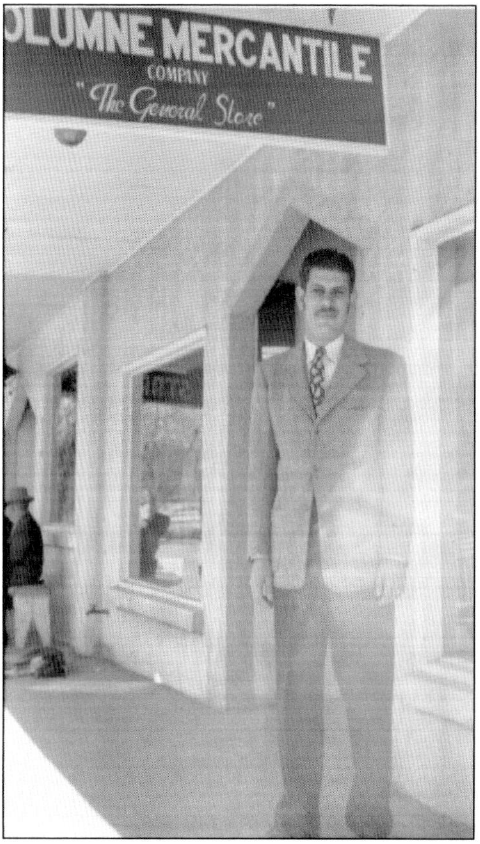

The Tuolumne Mercantile Company, located on Bay Street across from Memorial Park, was a clothing and general merchandise shop. Various wares, including groceries, were available for purchase. Pictured here is the owner, a Mr. Weinberger. During Tuolumne's heyday, several outlets offered groceries and dry goods, but that number slowly dwindled to the only one that now remains, the Tuolumne Market, which is situated in the town square off Tuolumne Road.

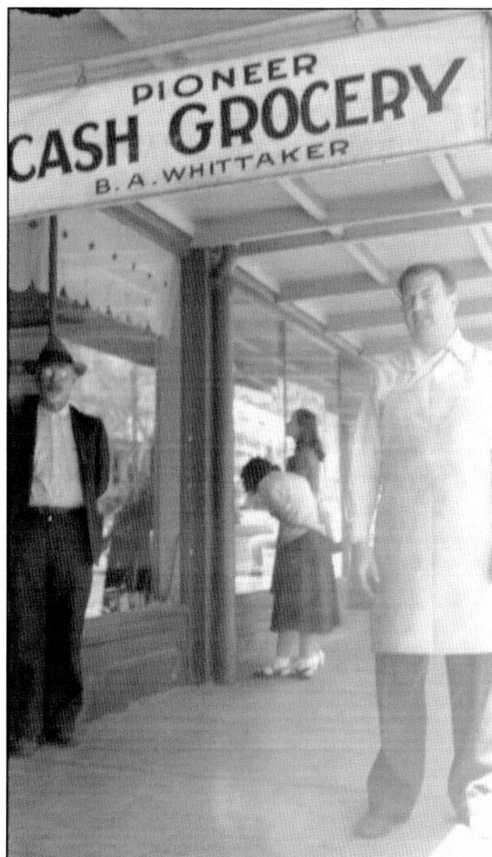

The Pioneer Cash Grocery, operated by Barney A. Whittaker (at right), was another grocery store located in the West Side building on Main Street, next to Max Raff's Clothing Store. Hank James is the man in the hat on the left. The decline in Tuolumne and the closing of shops such as the Pioneer Cash Grocery and Tuolumne Mercantile Company went hand-in-hand with the decline and eventual closing of the West Side mill, located in the main West Side building. The store featured old oiled floors, bulk foods sold in barrels and boxes, and a wood-burning stove for heat.

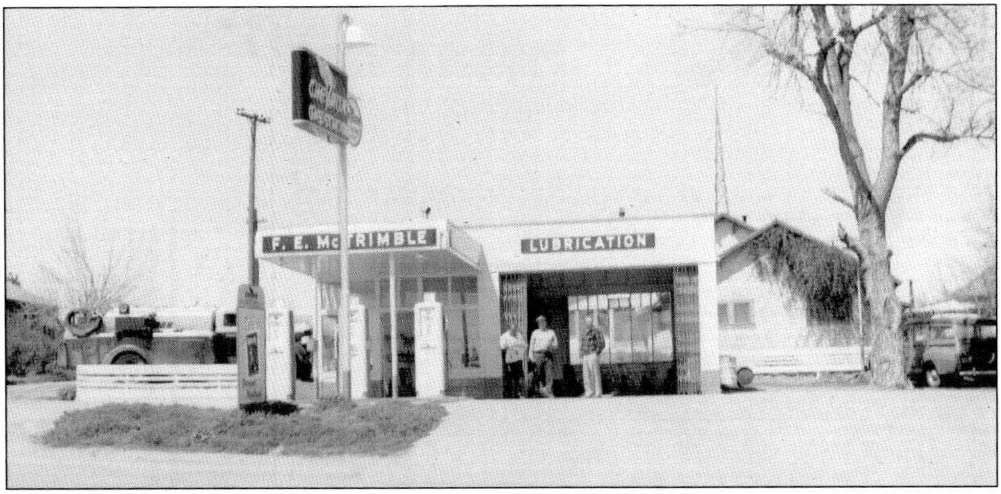

During Tuolumne's boom in the 1950s, there were plenty of automobiles cruising around town and room for several gas stations and full-service garages. Here, the F.E. McTrimble Chevron station sits at the corner of Carter Street and Tuolumne Road, just across the street from the historical marker denoting the geographic center of the East Belt Gold Rush. McTrimble's station operated from the 1940s through the gas shortage of the early 1970s. Gas was only about 25¢ at the time this photograph was taken. This station, along with all the others from this era, is closed—the only gas station left in town is the recently completed Bear Creek Station on the Black Oak Casino compound.

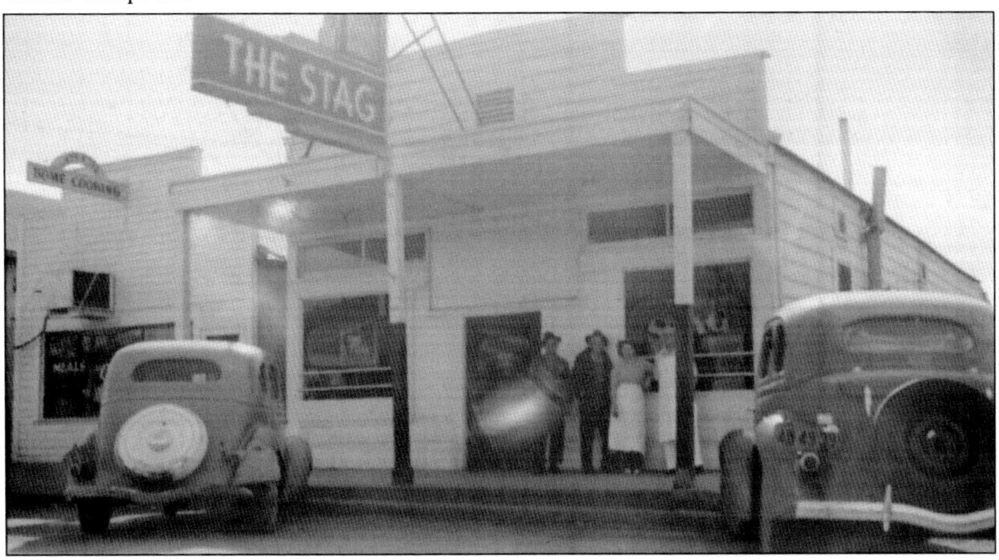

The Stag and Hi-Lead were two separate cafés operating side by side (separated by a vacant lot formerly occupied by the original Firemen's Opera House) on Chestnut Street. Following the lifting of Prohibition, if an establishment served liquor, it was also required to serve food, so all of Tuolumne's bars featured some kind of food service. Usually, they hired a cook to come in and cook a hot lunch and dinner, which mill workers always enjoyed. In some cases, the cook was the owner/operator or the wife of the bar owner. Some bars became better known for their food and were frequented by families at dinnertime, as well as by bar patrons. It was the advent of television, in addition to the closing of the mill, which spelled the end of popularity for these establishments.

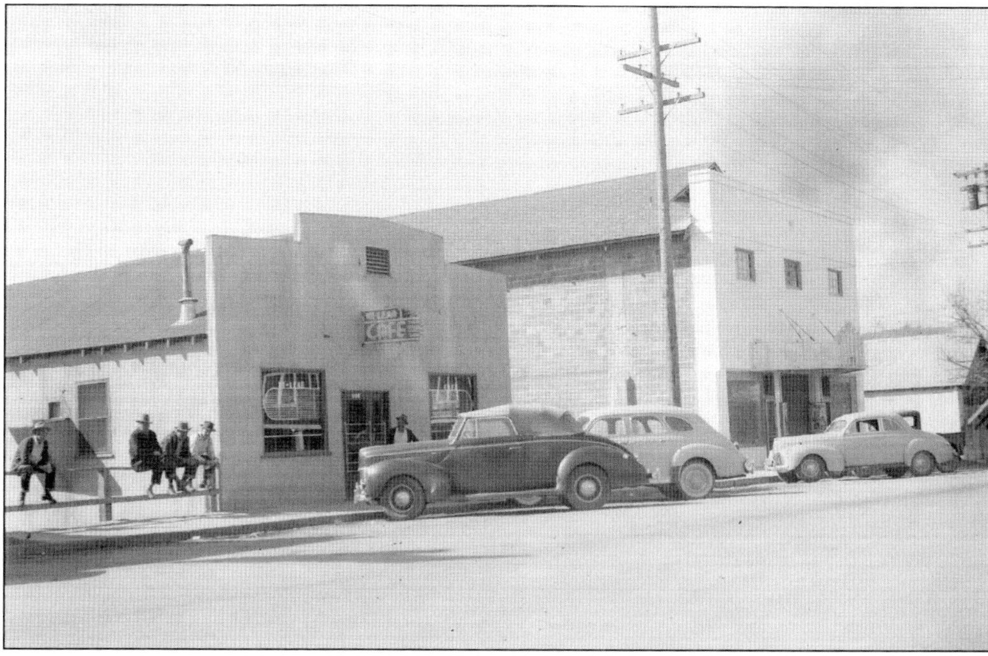

Another shot of The Stag from the 1940s shows the adjacent Fireman's Theatre. Across Main Street, behind the theater, is the West Side main office building after it was relocated to Main Street after burning down. As of this writing, all three of these buildings are vacant.

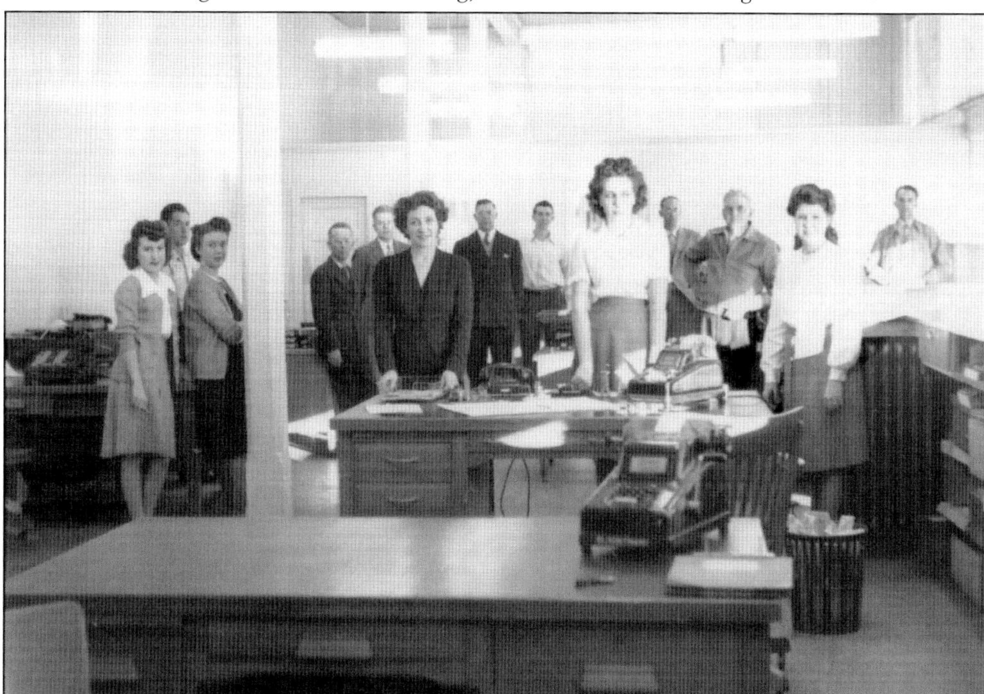

Going into its final decade, the West Side office building was still a busy place, as West Side Lumber Company was still the town's biggest employer. Several of the office workers inside the Main Street building posed for this picture around 1955.

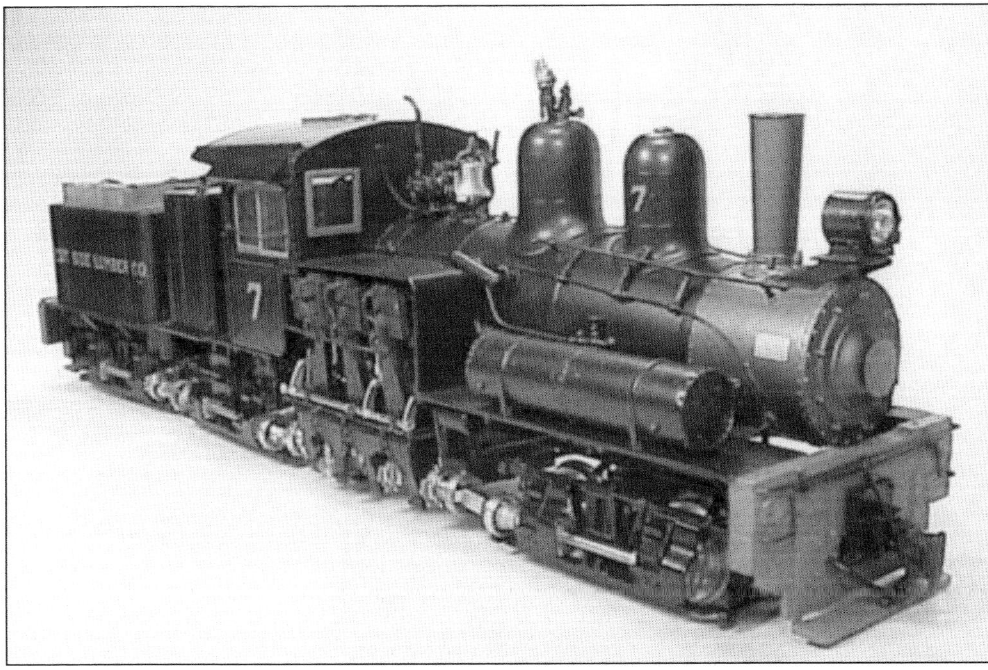

A model-train-sized replica of the West Side Lumber Company No. 7 locomotive made a great toy for a young boy or even the adult hobbyist. Due to the narrow-gauge railroad employed by West Side, these locomotives—both the full- and model-sized variations—are in high demand and extremely popular with rail enthusiasts, even decades after their peak operation.

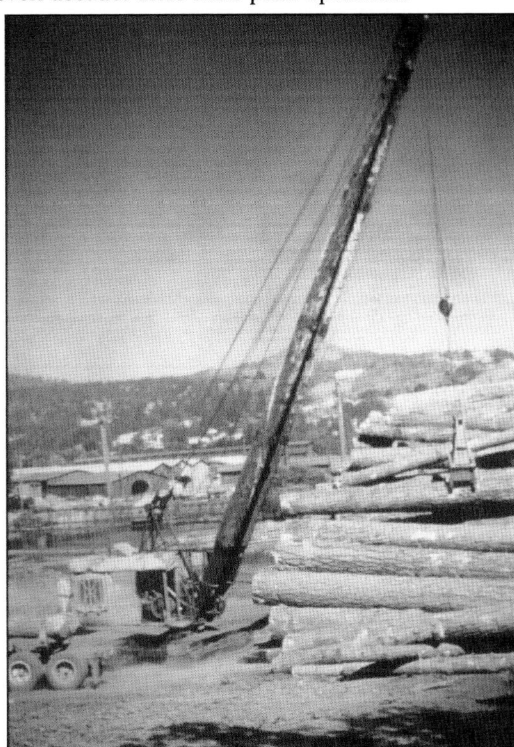

In this c. 1955 photograph, a large crane stacks towering logs in the West Side Lumber Company compound. Technology rapidly changed the way West Side and the timber industry in general operated, reducing the labor force dramatically by speeding up jobs that used to take hours with several men and steam donkeys.

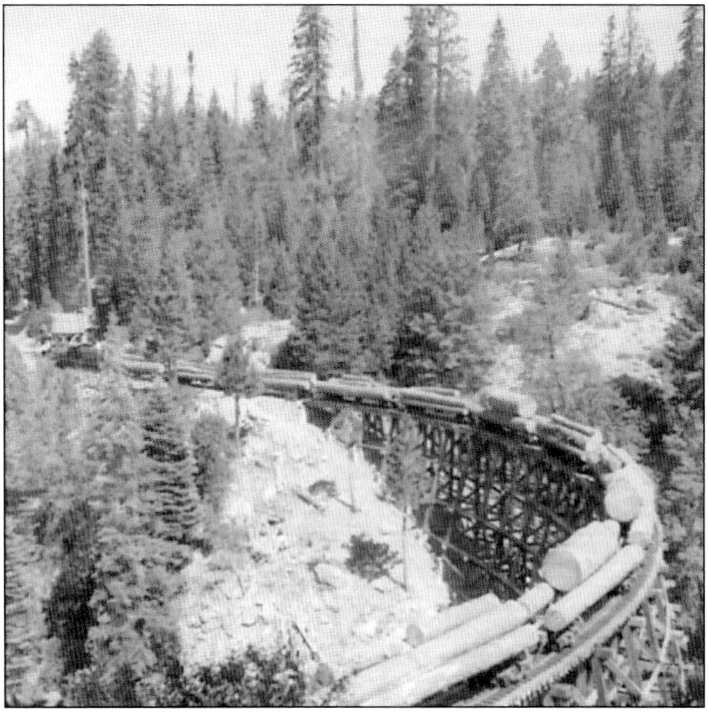

This c. 1950 image is one of the last photographs of a West Side locomotive making its way across the treacherous-looking Bourland Trestle. The small shack at left, just off the tracks, housed a full-time bridge spotter who ensured that no coal embers from the train's engine would start a fire that could destroy the trestle in no time.

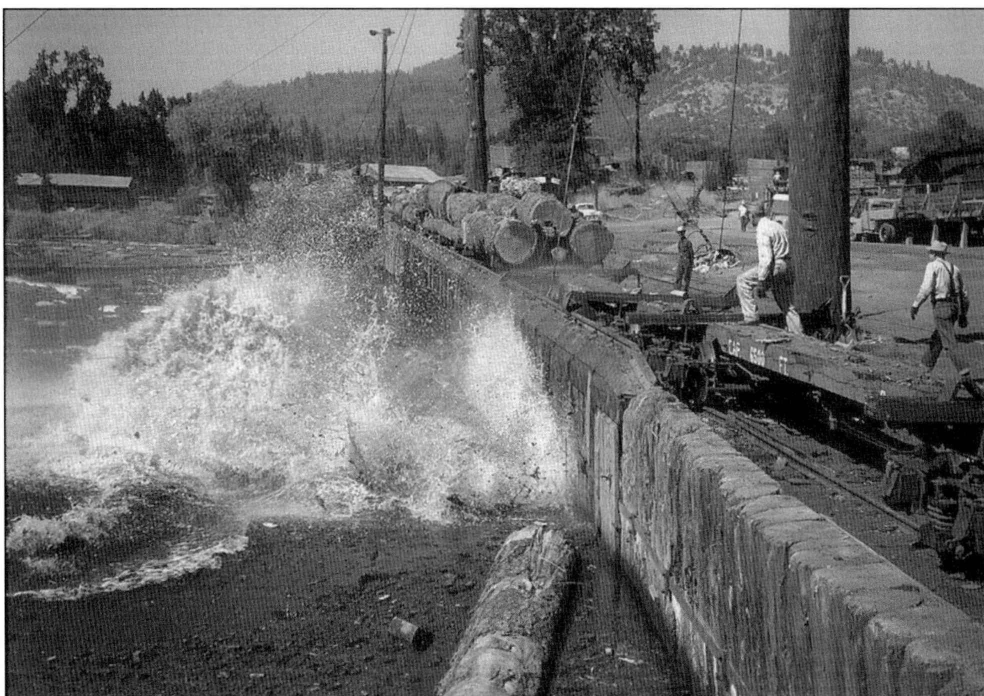

This fantastic 1950s photograph shows just how the lumberjacks at the yard deposited timber in the millpond. The track ran right along the edge of the dam that created the pond, and all workers had to do was unharness the load and use a hoist to drop the logs into the body of water below, where they would stay safe for up to six months.

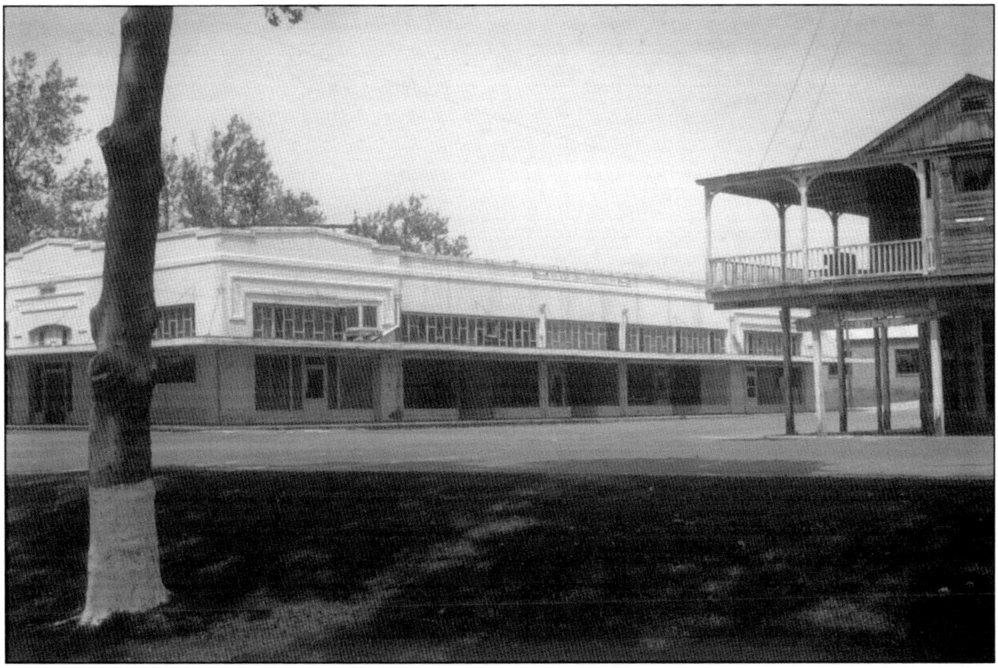

Taken looking northwest from the Tuolumne Memorial Park, this c. 1965 photograph shows the already defunct and deserted West Side Lumber Company building along Main Street; the building has changed little besides deterioration. The Tuolumne Fire Department is located at the north end of this building, just out of view. The sycamore trees with white trunks are the same ones that were planted after the devastating 1918 fire, marking its boundaries. The trees were purchased by Caroline "Carrie" Canfield Thorsen, one of the founders of the Women's Improvement Club.

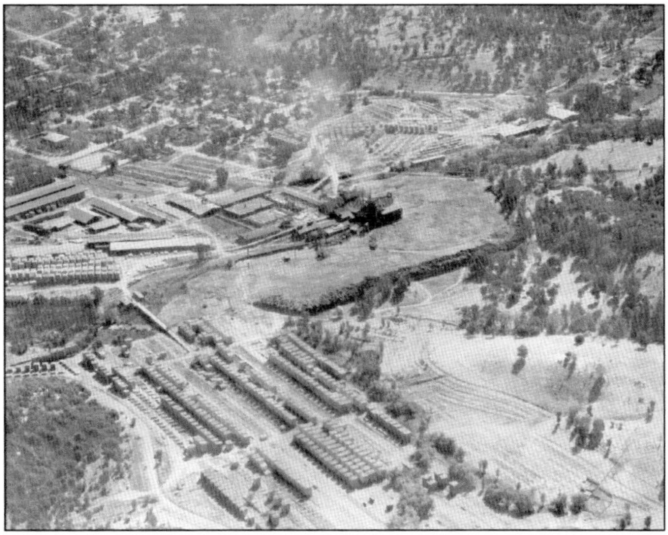

This aerial view of the West Side Lumber Company's holdings is a great way to close discussion of the company that—more than any other organization, group, or movement—shaped Tuolumne. The office building is the large structure along the left side, with Main Street running diagonally across the upper right of the image. This was West Side at its busiest, just years before its closure. The amount of board feet of timber in this frame is hard to quantify.

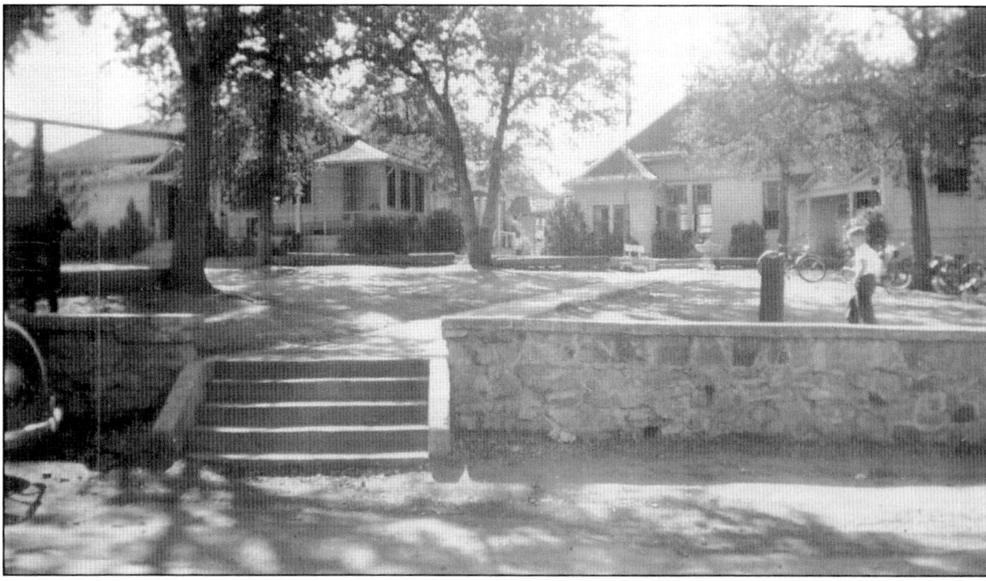

Though modest in its beginnings, the Summerville Elementary School grew into one of the larger grammar schools in Tuolumne County (after Sonora and Twain Harte). This 1940s photograph shows the common lawn where children enjoyed recess.

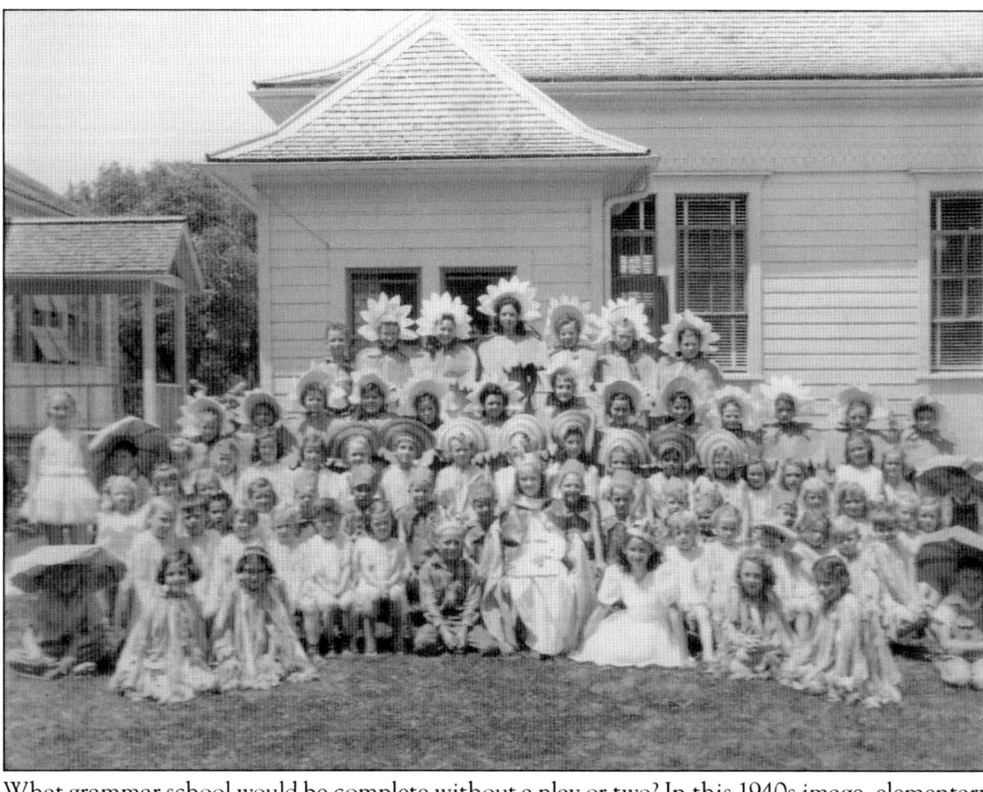

What grammar school would be complete without a play or two? In this 1940s image, elementary school students pose for a picture in front of the main building to show off their costumes for a spring play.

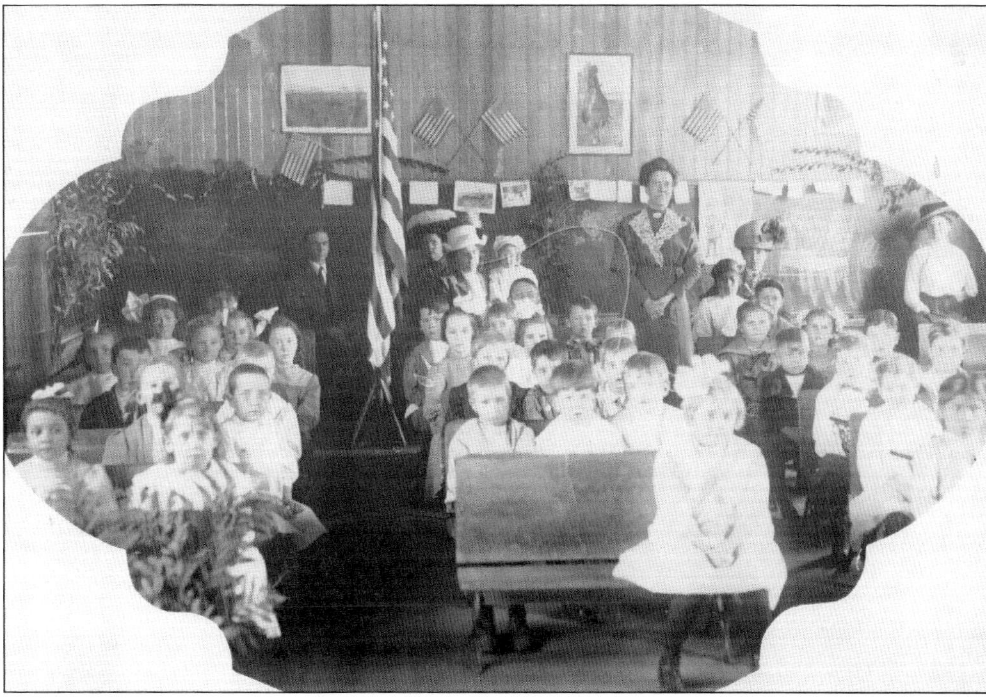

Although this c. 1915 image was captured from inside the same building shown in the previous two pictures, the interior was drastically different. Several wings were eventually added onto this original structure, and modern desks replaced the benches. Summerville Elementary has been in operation for over 140 years.

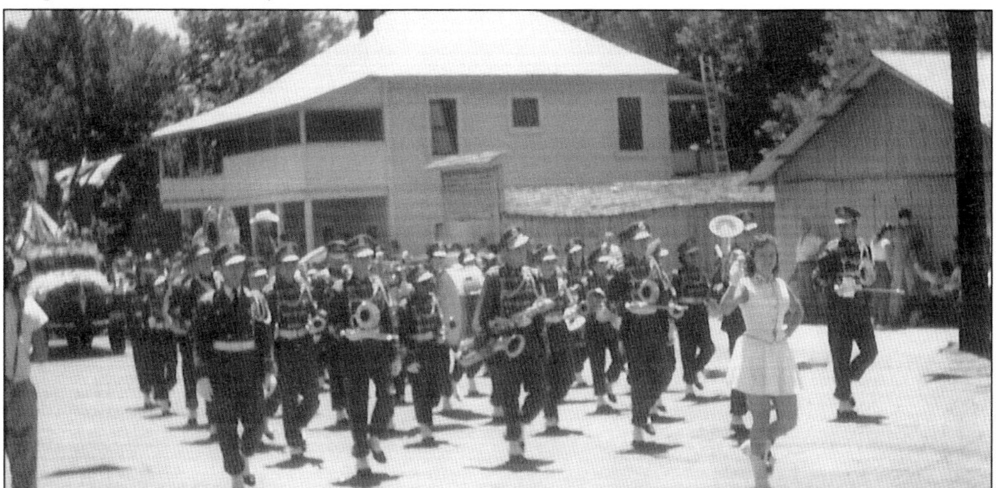

The bands for both Summerville Elementary and Summerville High Schools have always played an important part in town parades, such as this Lumber Jubilee parade. Earlier days saw the Marshall Band or Tuolumne Brass Band take up marching duties, but during the golden age, that role often fell to the eager and willing Beavers and Bears from Summerville Elementary and Summerville High, respectively. This c. 1958 photograph shows the Summerville High School Band being led by drum majorette Darlene Nelson and band teacher Bill Crawford (on the left, without an instrument).

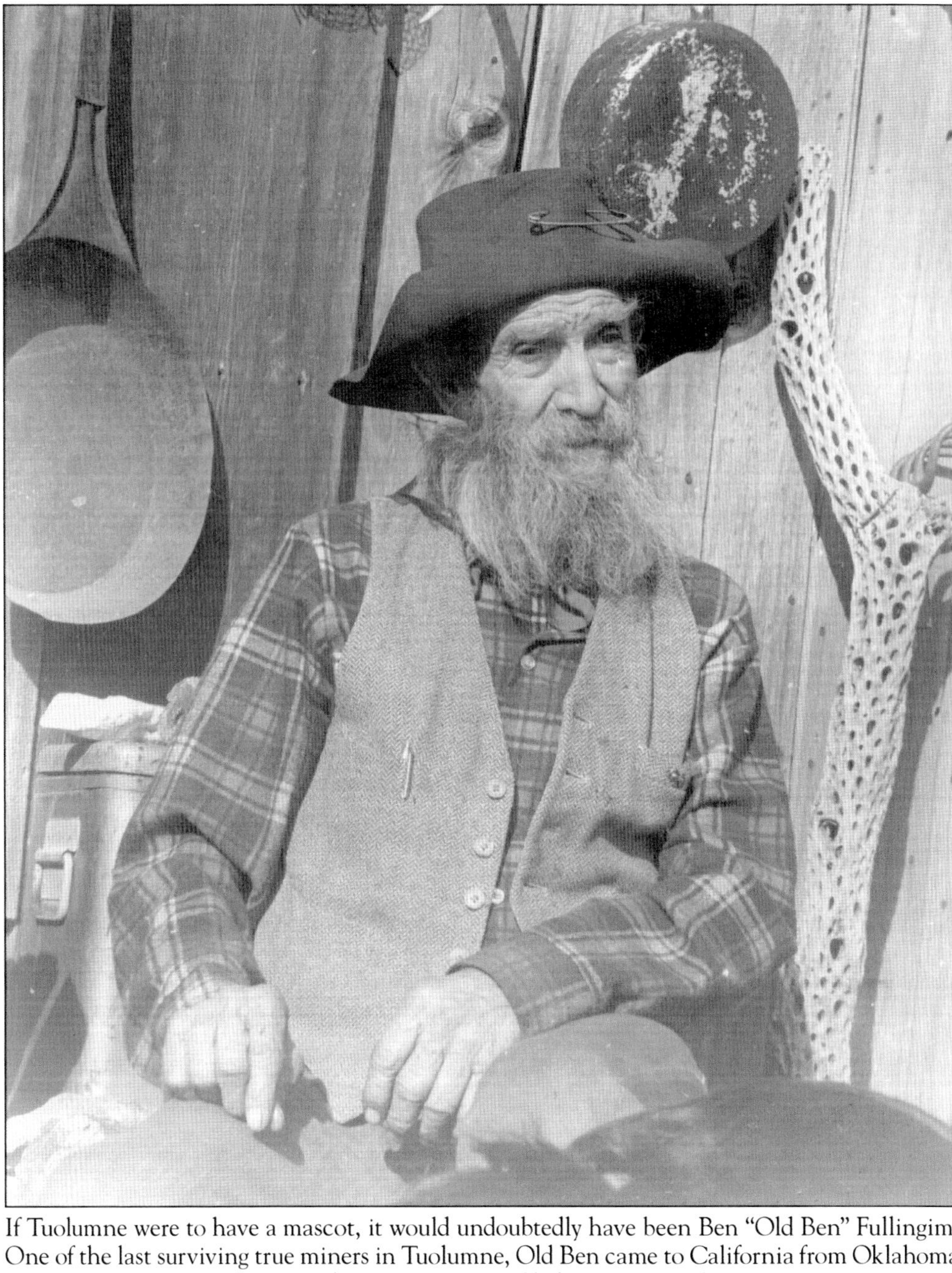

If Tuolumne were to have a mascot, it would undoubtedly have been Ben "Old Ben" Fullingim. One of the last surviving true miners in Tuolumne, Old Ben came to California from Oklahoma in 1948 and was soon mining in the mountains. He filed two 20-acre claims near Mt. Eaton, and under mining law, if he could produce gold and make $100 a year in improvements, the land was his. Over the years, he built several small cabins, a workshop, and a mill and gradually began to allow Boy Scouts and other youngsters camp out on his claim and get a dose of nature.

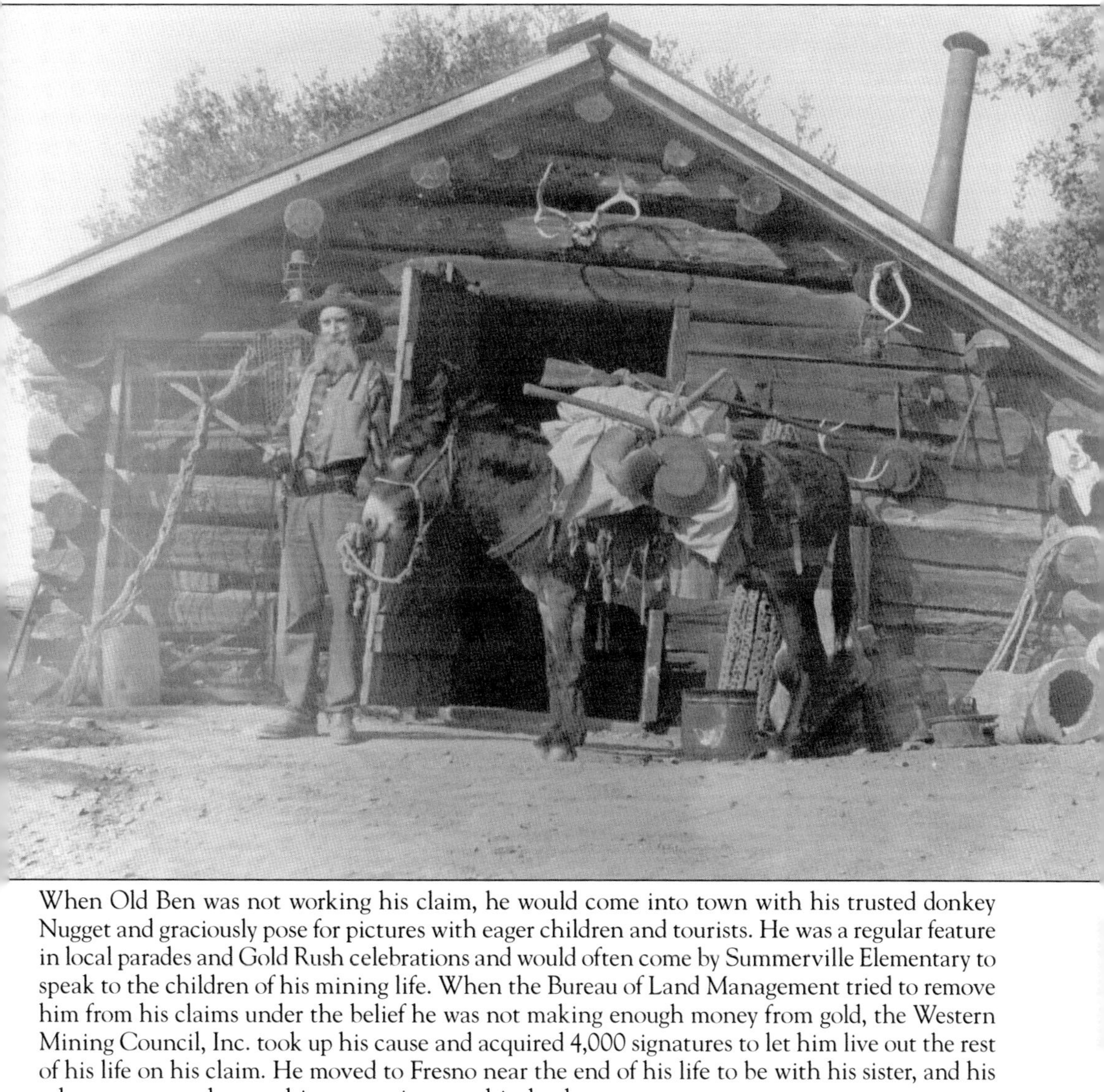

When Old Ben was not working his claim, he would come into town with his trusted donkey Nugget and graciously pose for pictures with eager children and tourists. He was a regular feature in local parades and Gold Rush celebrations and would often come by Summerville Elementary to speak to the children of his mining life. When the Bureau of Land Management tried to remove him from his claims under the belief he was not making enough money from gold, the Western Mining Council, Inc. took up his cause and acquired 4,000 signatures to let him live out the rest of his life on his claim. He moved to Fresno near the end of his life to be with his sister, and his ashes were spread across his mountain upon his death.

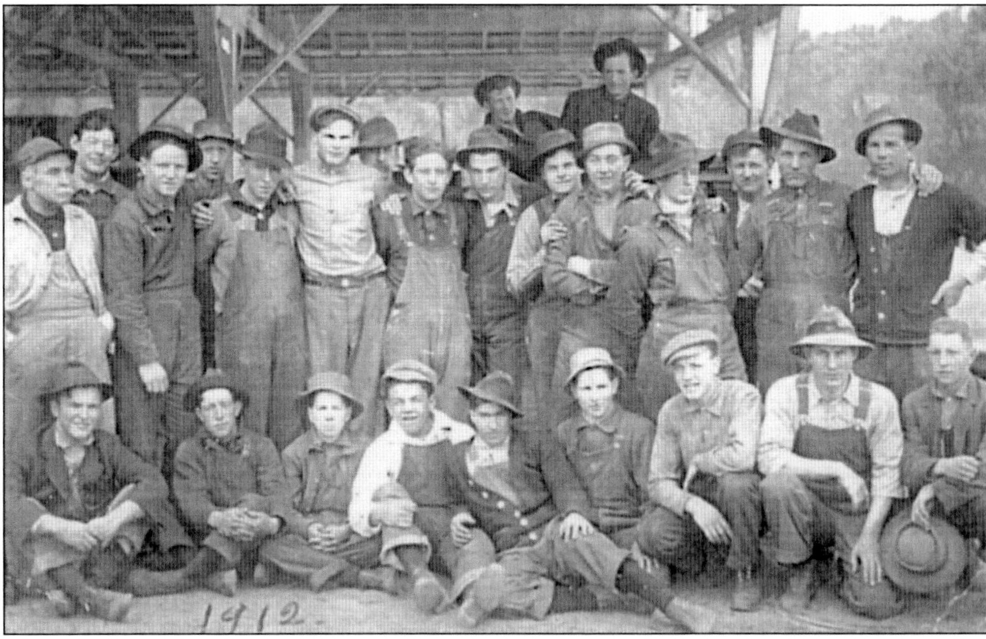

A good portion of the West Side Lumber Company's boards and planks initially went toward furnishing produce boxes for several exclusive fruit and vegetable growers in the nearby Central Valley. Appropriately enough, the area near the south side of West Side's compound, where these boxes were furnished, was known as the Box Factory, and this 1912 photograph shows the entire Box Factory crew. The road at the southern end of town is still called Box Factory Road. Sixth from the left in the first row sits a young Ed Sullivan, the long oiler featured earlier in the book.

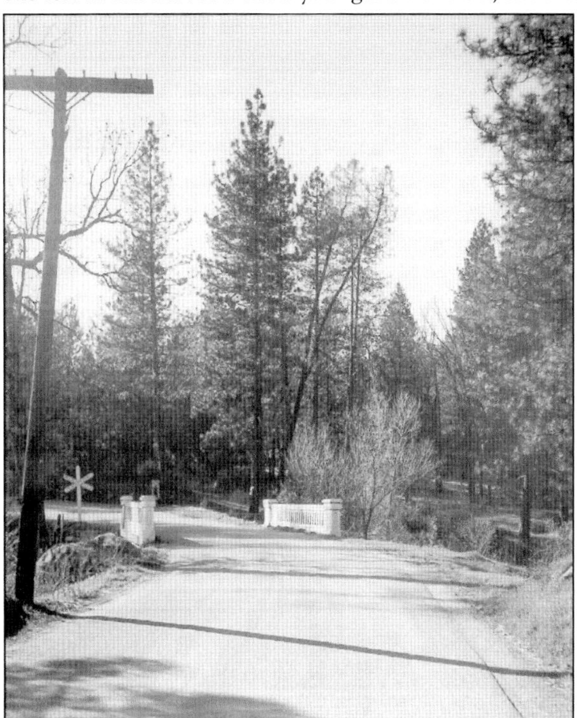

This c. 1940 picture from the other end of town shows the bridge heading to Sonora along Tuolumne Road that crosses Turnback Creek. The railroad crossing sign was still active but without an actual signal.

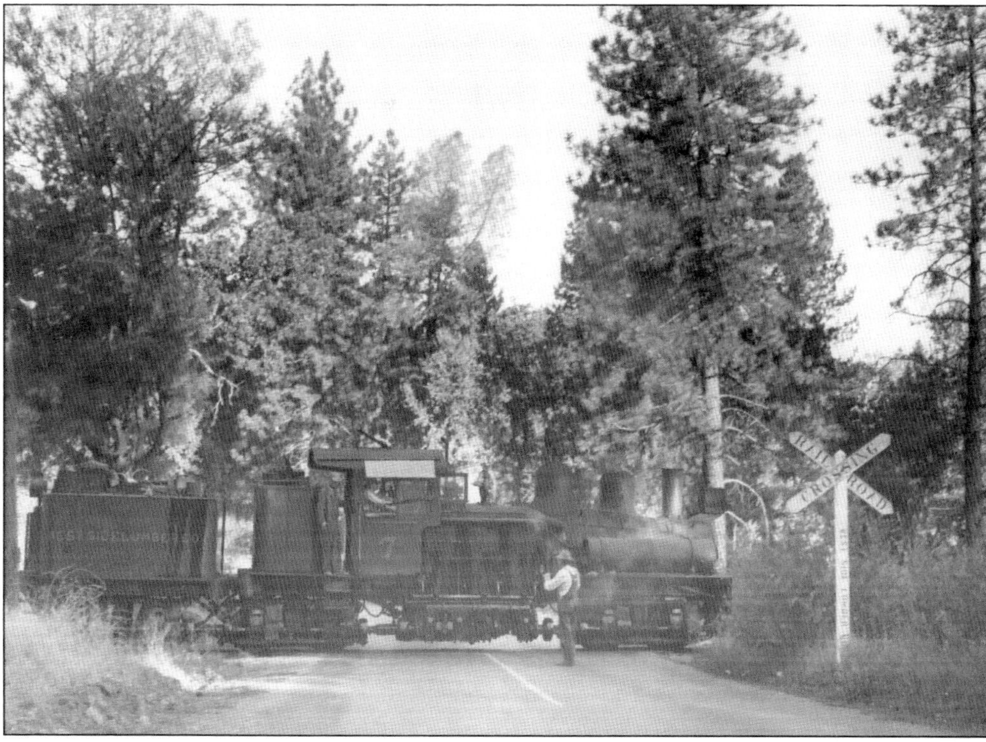

Engineers would often step out of the locomotive and manually direct traffic, as seen in this photograph taken along Tuolumne Road (heading into town from Sonora), showing the West Side Engine No. 7 as it returns to town. The train tracks are still visible today but are no longer in use.

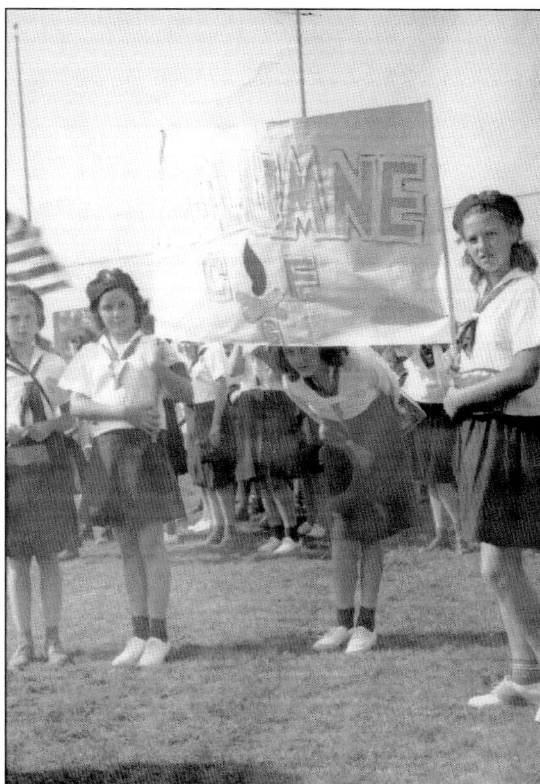

In areas like Tuolumne, children are encouraged to embrace the outdoors, and no organization embodied that more than the Camp Fire Girls of America. The Tuolumne chapter, pictured here around 1950, was one of several local contingents of the nationwide organization (now known as Camp Fire USA) that began in 1910. Members gained environmental and camping education and performed confidence-building group exercises. The Tuolumne chapter was founded by Marie Rozier, featured earlier in this book.

Bibliography

Hix, Brenda, Erline Heldstab, Dorothy Tate, et al. *Tuolumne Sesquicentennial—Celebrating 150 Years of Community, 1854-2004*. Tuolumne, CA: Tuolumne Sesquicentennial Committee, 2004.

Kauppi, Art, Lynne Jerome, Rick Jerome et al. *Discovering the West Side Lumber Company Trail—A Guide to the First Six Miles of the Trail Flume to River Bridge*. Tuolumne, CA: Tuolumne City Memorial Museum, 2008.

Jerome, Rick, Lynne Jerome, Patricia Gurney, et al. *Gold Mining in Tuolumne's East Belt*. Tuolumne, CA: Tuolumne City Memorial Museum, 2005.

Thornton, Mark V., Charla Meacham Francis, Anne Bloomfield, et al. *Tuolumne Community Cultural Resources Survey*. Sonora, CA: Tuolumne County Historic Preservation Review Commission, 2002.

ABOUT THE TUOLUMNE CITY MEMORIAL MUSEUM

In the early 20th century, a group of historically minded women set the wheels in motion for the founding of the Tuolumne City Memorial Museum, which provided all of the pictures and knowledge contained herein, making this book possible. They created an organization known as the Tuolumne Women's Improvement Club with the purpose of (as might be divined from its title) cleaning up and improving the town.

During that time, since the mining boom was still in full swing, many miners who moved away would leave their pack donkeys behind. While children loved them, the creatures wreaked havoc on local crops, gardens, and the newly planted trees shading homes along the city streets. While the Women's Improvement Club successfully corralled the burros and diminished their numbers, strays could still be found roaming the fields in and around town until the 1950s.

In 1920, the women built a clubhouse for their regular meetings; it also served as the town's library and de facto community center. In February 1948, two members of the Improvement Club—Patsy McMahon and Marie Rozier—began collecting pictures and artifacts of Tuolumne Township. Since both hailed from original Tuolumne pioneer families, they wanted to begin restoring and documenting the history of the town they so dearly loved.

The museum had several homes, beginning in the old Tuolumne Telephone Company building at the corner of Pine Street and Chestnut Avenue. By 1950, a larger building was necessary, and the two women sought help from the Tuolumne City Progressive Association, which agreed to sponsor the Tuolumne City Memorial Museum. With the leadership of Ernest Muller Sr., a log cabin was built in Tuolumne Park to house the museum, which opened on February 28, 1951.

By 1970, because of the deterioration of the cabin, all the articles were moved into the new Tuolumne Telephone Company warehouse courtesy of John Wise. By 1974, Hugh and Dorothy Kellogg were instrumental in relocating the museum to the West Side Lumber Company building on Main Street. When the West Side Park needed the space, everything was packed up again and stored in various club members' homes to wait for a permanent museum.

The Tuolumne City Memorial Museum was formed in 1976 and incorporated in 1978. Finally, in May 1981, the Tuolumne Women's Improvement Club gift-deeded its property at the corner of Carter and Bay Streets to the museum. On April 12, 1982, the go-ahead was given to reconstruct the building with Don Grover as the architect and John Feriani as the contractor and with the help of many volunteers. The overall planning for the inside, including rooms and displays, was organized with the leadership of Eve Pecchenino. By Christmas of 1984, with two wings added, a celebration was held for the museum—the dreams of McMahon and Rozier (who was there for the opening) came true.

Discover Thousands of Local History Books Featuring Millions of Vintage Images

Arcadia Publishing, the leading local history publisher in the United States, is committed to making history accessible and meaningful through publishing books that celebrate and preserve the heritage of America's people and places.

Find more books like this at
www.arcadiapublishing.com

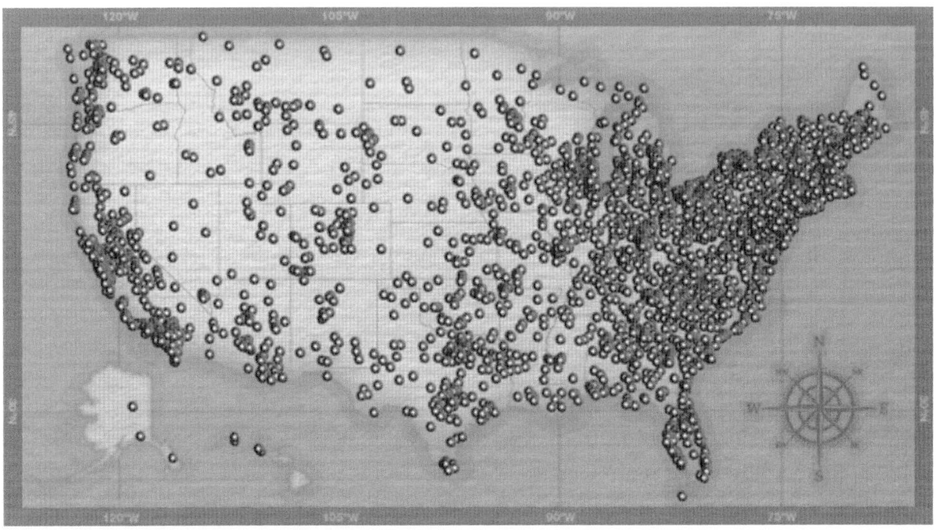

Search for your hometown history, your old stomping grounds, and even your favorite sports team.

Consistent with our mission to preserve history on a local level, this book was printed in South Carolina on American-made paper and manufactured entirely in the United States. Products carrying the accredited Forest Stewardship Council (FSC) label are printed on 100 percent FSC-certified paper.

MADE IN THE USA